History in the World

Questions about the relationship between historical research and contemporary social and practical problems have posed a challenge to generations of historians, as well as to philosophers and theorists of history. In recent years, views regarding the isolation of academic history from real-world issues and affairs have come under increasing criticism. The contributions to this volume all focus on history's role in the world today and on the possibilities for, and limits to, engagement resulting from disciplinary practices and conventions. The authors undertake their assessment of history's relevance in different ways, combining case studies of political clashes, public debates, and practices of commemoration with sophisticated theoretical discussions of identity construction, the material manifestations of power, and the relationship between historicizing and expectations concerning future actions. These studies highlight the difficulty of distinguishing between history and politics, and between disciplinary accounts and activism, and contribute significantly towards an improved understanding of our relationship with the past.

This book was originally published as a special issue of *Rethinking History.*

Kalle Pihlainen is Senior Research Fellow at the School of Humanities at Tallinn University, Estonia, and Adjunct Professor of Philosophy and Cultural Theory at Åbo Akademi University, Finland. His research focuses on the theory and philosophy of history as well as on literary and historical culture.

This fascinating collection looks at the relationship between investigations into the past and contemporary political agendas from a variety of different perspectives that all highlight the complexity of that relationship between 'history' and 'politics'. Whilst scholars still all-too-often resort to an alleged professionalism as protection against history politics, the contributors to this volume remind readers that all history-writing is situated in political contexts.

– Stefan Berger

This book features a new generation of historical theorists who tackle the question of history's social function through both case studies and debates about the need for history in conceiving the future. The collection highlights the inseparability of history and political engagement and sheds light on the specific mechanisms historians use to endow their narratives with political relevance.

– Ewa Domańska

History in the World

Edited by
Kalle Pihlainen

LONDON AND NEW YORK

First published 2018 by Routledge

2 Park Square, Milton Park, Abingdon, Oxfordshire OX14 4RN
52 Vanderbilt Avenue, New York, NY 10017

Routledge is an imprint of the Taylor & Francis Group, an informa business

First issued in paperback 2019

British Library Cataloguing in Publication Data
A catalogue record for this book is available from the British Library

ISBN 13: 978-0-415-78863-2 (hbk)
ISBN 13: 978-0-367-23387-7 (pbk)

Typeset in Minion Pro
by RefineCatch Limited, Bungay, Suffolk

Publisher's Note
The publisher accepts responsibility for any inconsistencies that may have
arisen during the conversion of this book from journal articles to book chapters,
namely the possible inclusion of journal terminology.

Disclaimer
Every effort has been made to contact copyright holders for their permission to
reprint material in this book. The publishers would be grateful to hear from any
copyright holder who is not here acknowledged and will undertake to rectify
any errors or omissions in future editions of this book.

Contents

Citation Information   vii
Notes on Contributors   ix

Introduction: Historians and 'the current situation'   1
Kalle Pihlainen

1. The republic of historians: historians as nation-builders in Estonia
   (late 1980s–early 1990s)   12
   Marek Tamm

2. The 'age of commemoration' as a narrative construct: a critique of the
   discourse on the contemporary crisis of memory in France   30
   Kenan Van De Mieroop

3. Thinking the past politically: Palestine, power and pedagogy   50
   Claire Norton and Mark Donnelly

4. The ideal of objectivity and the public role of the historian: some
   lessons from the *Historikerstreit* and the History Wars   75
   Anton Froeyman

5. Calliope's ascent: defragmenting philosophy of history by rhetoric   93
   Rik Peters

6. We are history: the outlines of a quasi-substantive philosophy
   of history   117
   Zoltán Boldizsár Simon

7. History, power and visual communication artefacts   138
   Katherine Hepworth

Index   161

Citation Information

The chapters in this book were originally published in *Rethinking History*, volume 20, issue 2 (June 2016). When citing this material, please use the original page numbering for each article, as follows:

Introduction
Historians and 'the current situation'
Kalle Pihlainen
Rethinking History, volume 20, issue 2 (June 2016), pp. 143–153

Chapter 1
The republic of historians: historians as nation-builders in Estonia (late 1980s–early 1990s)
Marek Tamm
Rethinking History, volume 20, issue 2 (June 2016), pp. 154–171

Chapter 2
The 'age of commemoration' as a narrative construct: a critique of the discourse on the contemporary crisis of memory in France
Kenan Van De Mieroop
Rethinking History, volume 20, issue 2 (June 2016), pp. 172–191

Chapter 3
Thinking the past politically: Palestine, power and pedagogy
Claire Norton and Mark Donnelly
Rethinking History, volume 20, issue 2 (June 2016), pp. 192–216

Chapter 4
The ideal of objectivity and the public role of the historian: some lessons from the Historikerstreit *and the History Wars*
Anton Froeyman
Rethinking History, volume 20, issue 2 (June 2016), pp. 217–234

Chapter 5

Calliope's ascent: defragmenting philosophy of history by rhetoric
Rik Peters
Rethinking History, volume 20, issue 2 (June 2016), pp. 235–258

Chapter 6

We are history: the outlines of a quasi-substantive philosophy of history
Zoltán Boldizsár Simon
Rethinking History, volume 20, issue 2 (June 2016), pp. 259–279

Chapter 7

History, power and visual communication artefacts
Katherine Hepworth
Rethinking History, volume 20, issue 2 (June 2016), pp. 280–302

For any permission-related enquiries please visit:
http://www.tandfonline.com/page/help/permissions

Notes on Contributors

Mark Donnelly is a Senior Lecturer in History at St Mary's University, UK. He is also Director of the MA in Public History.

Anton Froeyman is a Post-Doctoral Researcher at the Centre for Logic and Philosophy of Science at Ghent University, Belgium.

Katherine Hepworth is an Assistant Professor of Visual Journalism at the University of Nevada, Reno, USA. Her current research interests lie in adapting her 'Discursive Method', a relativist historical method, to assess modern-day visual communication effectiveness.

Claire Norton is a Senior Lecturer in History at St Mary's University, UK. She teaches and writes about the cultural politics of historicisation and Islamic history.

Rik Peters is Associate Professor at the University of Groningen, The Netherlands, where he lectures in Theory of History, Rhetoric, and Learning Histories and Organizations.

Kalle Pihlainen is Senior Research Fellow at the School of Humanities at Tallinn University, Estonia, and Adjunct Professor of Philosophy and Cultural Theory at Åbo Akademi University, Finland. His research focuses on the theory and philosophy of history as well as literary and historical culture, with particular emphasis on the ethics and politics of historical representation, embodiment and existential phenomenology.

Zoltán Boldizsár Simon is a Doctoral Research Associate at the Bielefeld Graduate School in History and Sociology, at the University of Bielefeld, Germany. His essays can be read in *History and Theory*, *European Review of History*, the *Journal of the Philosophy of History* and *Rethinking History*.

Marek Tamm is Professor of Cultural History and Senior Researcher in Medieval Studies at the School of Humanities at Tallinn University, Estonia. His primary research fields are the cultural history of medieval Europe, the theory and history of historiography, and cultural memory studies.

Kenan Van De Mieroop has recently completed his PhD at Ghent University in Belgium and now teaches at the history department there. He is a founding member of the International Network for Theory of History.

Historians and 'the current situation'

Kalle Pihlainen

Åbo Akademi University, Finland

This issue of *Rethinking History*, like the forthcoming one, 'Futures for the past' (20:3), has been a long time in the making. Originally, the idea was to bring together a selection of authors who had participated in the inaugural conference of the International Network for Theory of History (INTH), held in Ghent in the summer of 2013. Both issues were to be devoted to a further exploration of the main topic of that conference, namely, 'The future of the theory and philosophy of history'. Plans have, as plans do, mutated along the way, however. The foci envisioned for these two special issues soon diverged, with the idea that one would be called 'Historians as engaged intellectuals' and the other 'The future of historical theory'. But then, changes again: as the articles came in, it became clearer and clearer that these were, in fact, themes that are far harder to separate than I had expected, especially in the current climate in talk about history and its nature and role.

Without actually attempting to make firm pronouncements about anything as nebulous as 'the current situation', or even 'our' current situation, it seems clear that historians as well as theorists of history have recently been increasingly interested in the relation of academic history to contemporary experience – and, some of them, in historians' responsibilities regarding social and practical problems. Hence it also seems safe to say that the future for thinking about history will continue to involve the question of the historian's social and political role. Crucially, however, interest is not focused on a politics of history alone – or indeed even primarily. (Notwithstanding, of course, the fact that everything is about politics *too*, in the sense employed here.) While the questions of the purpose of historical research and writing remain significant, there is now also a strong sense of the inevitable presence of 'history' in all things human, a sentiment that has, I would say, not yet been as explicitly articulated in the recent debates on the public role or public relevance of history. (For relatively recent views, see the forum on 'The Public Role of History' in the October 2005 issue of *History and Theory* and the essays collected from *Historically Speaking* in Yerxa 2009.)

Even though history as a discipline is obviously a historical phenomenon – and, as such, has always been in the service of specific interests – it seems that there is again more talk about historians as existentially *historically* positioned and aware, as if their investment in academic history is always necessarily part and parcel of all personal experiences. For adherents of this point of view, there is some inescapable connection that historians (and perhaps people in general) have with the historical past, the past beyond their subjective experience, which is present in their daily lives. Particularly in this context, it is at times hard to see exactly what 'history' and 'historicity' are being used to signify, and collective rethinking of the employment of those terms is needed.

At least in the immediate vicinity of such more experiential and practically formed climes, three broad but reasonably distinct alternatives present themselves for approaching the question of historians' responsibilities – and thus the question of the nature of history as a discipline too: the first, and for me personally the most obvious, would be to continue to focus on the construction of meaning in historical discourse and hence also on the ideological and political consequences of doing history. In such blunt form at least, this approach may be out of sync with current sensibilities in the field, however. The second alternative is to think history in the very broad strokes already described above. Although such an all-encompassing 'historical' viewpoint still permits discussion of what historians should do on a number of practical levels (of epistemology, sensibilities or character, for example), it does not to me seem the most productive for tackling the theme of historians as engaged intellectuals that has informed this present special issue. The impact of history is automatically spread to society at large and any responsibilities here are primarily to the past and to some innate or 'natural' way of relating to it. The third alternative might be best evoked with Stanley Fish's characteristically catchy and pragmatic appeal to academics to *Save the World on Your Own Time* (2008); for history, this would effectively mean shoring up the integrity of *historical* knowledge and separating it from more general talk about the significance of the past. Much like the more romantic option of viewing history as self-evident (and consequently of historical knowledge as self-regulating, by one means or another), also this alternative could be seen to let historians off the hook with respect to social responsibility, leaving it to disciplinary consensus and 'methods'.

Whichever view of history and relating to the past one opts for, 'taking a stand' appears, at present, a fashionable thing for historians and theorists to be doing. Perhaps surprisingly, given its evident affinities with the last of these alternatives, Michael Oakeshott's idea of 'the practical past' – brought to centre stage in theory of history by Hayden White during the last decade – is being used to articulate large swathes of the debate. Even the interest in some more general historicalness and 'historicity' *within the discipline* is now collecting under the umbrella of this term. Responding to this trend, several of the articles in this issue – and even more in the forthcoming one – position themselves with regard to the feasibility of the separation between the practical past and what is often viewed as its detached other, 'the historical past'. For that reason too, and not only to remember Ghent in 2013, I am pleased that this set of essays will appear in time for the second conference of the INTH. The theme of this second network conference – to be held in Ouro Preto, Brazil, this August – is 'The practical past: On the advantages and disadvantages of history for life'.

Of my many attempts to think up a title for this special issue that would embrace all these various aspects of historians' ties to present-day challenges and experience, 'History in the world' finally felt most appropriate. So much so, in fact, that I could not then let go of it despite having already used it for an essay of my own before. As in that essay, which tackled the question of history's social and political engagement by investigating the relation between historians and readers in Hayden White's work, the most important consideration for using this formulation here is to highlight the simultaneous obviousness and contradictions of thinking history as 'in the world'. The title was originally inspired by Ronald Aronson's classic 1980 book on Sartre, *Jean-Paul Sartre: Philosophy in the World*. In this formula, *engagement* and the social responsibility of the philosopher-intellectual are foregrounded without implying that these can somehow be separated from personal, experiential conditions. Other reasons for choosing the 'history in the world' rubric are hopefully equally evident. Foremost, it seems effective for incorporating the (at least so often intuitively assumed) link between the past, present and future, as well as related ideas about the significance of the past 'in itself'. While I personally take issue with ideas of any 'natural' historicity, and particularly with any ethical or political conclusions that might be drawn thereof, that dimension is not excluded by the formulation either. Thus it can readily suggest more involved descriptions of the dynamics between stories, language and lived experience in 'our' engagements with the past too, whether those be 'historical' or 'practical'. Finally, it continues to invite discussion of new and experimental forms and sites for history.

Against this admittedly broad background, then, the articles in this issue tackle more focused instances of 'history in the world'. The first of the articles, 'The republic of historians' by Marek Tamm, presents the case of historians' involvement in the construction of the Estonian state in the 1980s and 1990s. The Estonian case is particularly relevant here because of the concentration of historians who assumed an active role in politics. While this overlap between historical and political thinking is interesting in and of itself, Tamm's examination further gives the impression of historical arguments having been used effectively for a 'progressive' politics – something that theoretical approaches to historians' political engagement do not always present as the most obvious outcome. In his exploration, Tamm has deliberately avoided elaborate theorizations of the case, instead using the rich empirical material to show readers how particular discourses were constructed and how the past was used in quite different ways.

3

By investigating the legacy of Pierre Nora's idea of the 'age of commemoration', Kenan Van De Mieroop's article foregrounds and questions the neutrality so easily ascribed to history as a discipline. In 'The "age of commemoration" as a narrative construct', Van De Mieroop illuminates the dynamics by which alternative voices become suppressed through appeals to history – even history in the present. In his analysis, dissenting opinions are incorporated into the over-arching narrative of the crisis of French identity, and history and historians somehow continue to be viewed as immune to the dangerous presentism that memory discourses are, instead, claimed to involve. The social role of historians here has not been small: as a consequence of the focus on the contest between history and memory, many pressing issues relating to – as Tony Judt (1998, 10) had it – the country's 'intolerable burden of competing pasts' have been side-lined.

In their article, 'Thinking the past politically', Claire Norton and Mark Donnelly tackle the issue of historians' responsibilities head-on in the context of the Israeli-Palestinian conflict. For Norton and Donnelly, historical practices are unavoidably political and the discipline continues to serve and reinforce agendas of nation-states. The construction of collective identities and the sanctioning of actions in the present are thus an integral part of the historian's work. And this work is carried out by connecting the present to the past and to the future through diverse disciplinary practices – foremost, perhaps, epistemology, methodology and conventional forms. The article aims to counter the privileged standing of history by offering up alternative political and artistic framings that lead audiences to reconsider traditional practices and to question the logics of history as they have come to know it.

In an equally engaged manner, Anton Froeyman studies historians' roles in the *Historikerstreit* and the Australian 'History Wars' in terms of, as his title puts it, 'The ideal of objectivity and the public role of the historian'. Froeyman's take is that, in both of these cases, views of historians as objective significantly interfered with their public engagement. This interference did not play out as one might expect, however: According to Froeyman's analysis, the ideal of objectivity and the related emphasis on facts and scholarly competence was present in the rhetoric used to undermine opposing views but failed to temper the historians' own moral and political arguments. As Froeyman points out, the fact that so many of the underlying commitments remain unpronounced, as tacit assumptions of the historians' 'creed', is a significant factor in making possible the kinds of confusions and acting at cross-purposes that he unearths here.

In 'Calliope's ascent', Rik Peters finds the solution to the question of history's practical relevance in reconnecting historical knowledge with action. Here, separation between history and any practical past is not an option. Instead, his article focuses on outlining the connections between narration, experience and action, in order to show how history inevitably functions as a form of practical knowledge. Importantly, this is not a simple pragmatic matter of how history can be used, but a redescription of our understandings of history, returning to the sensibilities of 'classic' and, arguably, 'historicist' philosophers of history. For Peters, meaningful contextualization and understanding the emotional connections forged through language between the participants of a communication offer the means to 'cure' history of its current shortcomings. In this conceptualization, historians are necessarily engaged because their work inscribes them into history and points toward the future.

Like Peters, Zoltán Boldizsár Simon takes on the question of how conceiving of the past unavoidably connects to orientations in the present and hence also to visions of the future. Simon's approach is very different, however. His focus is not on continuities and 'historical' understanding but on the identity dynamics of dissociating with the past as it is represented by historical knowledge. That version of the past only defines what 'we' no longer can be, and the ethical impetus for change comes from the future. Whether intentionally or not, his essay title accepts Sir Bob Geldof's recent challenge to intellectuals as reflected in name of the essay collection *You're History!* (Brown and Kelly 2005), affirming that, indeed, 'We are history' – but with a twist. For Simon, history as a public endeavour only makes sense once we readmit the idea of history as a course of events to our thinking, yet without reanimating classic philosophy of history positions.

The final article here, 'History, power and visual communication artefacts' by Katherine Hepworth, rounds off the issue most appropriately. I am happy to have been able to poach her article from among the regular contributions to the journal. Her investigation of the complexity of the conditions of knowledge production and communication promises to offer improved tools to historians' for 'reading' the past. Even though the article does not engage directly with the social role of history, it sheds much-needed light on how practices of power persist in material culture and hence infiltrate historians' work. Hepworth provides convincing examples of how 'history' can not only be thought of as 'in the world', but to thoroughly permeate it. In making clearer the means by which the past exerts its influence through cultural artefacts, her analysis thus also aids in understanding why the past is so often and easily spoken of as still being 'present' to us. With an opening up to this kind of thinking, perhaps history and historians can finally begin to take on board other similar approaches – actor-network theory, for instance.

Before handing over to the authors, I want to revisit some related debates and discuss basic principles. Over the last decade or so, it has become something of a mantra to say that theory of history has over-indulged on the problematics of the linguistic turn. According to this storyline, it is time to leave behind the long-prominent focus on language and 'narrativism'. A problem with popular receptions of the 'narrativist' debate, however, is that it has insistently been misunderstood in terms of its scope. And most of the objections to it have been based on this misunderstanding. Those on the 'narrativist' side have, in fact, and when one goes back and reads these theorists rather than historians' interpretations of them, never offered a theory of history (in the sense of the discipline) or of some kind of History, but only a theory of history *writing* (again, the need to find some shared understanding concerning the most basic vocabulary). When one reads the debates with that point in mind, it seems impossible to miss the qualification that narrative or constructivist theorists of history only talk about what can be characterized as the representational aspect or 'the writing phase' of the historian's work, never really about their investigations of the past, 'the research phase'. (For an explicit discussion of this, see White 2014; also see, for example, Jenkins 2009.)

One thing that this differentiation between the research and writing 'phases' (which is only a heuristic distinction, to be sure) should make immediately clear is that what we tend to often think and talk about as 'theory of history' is a theory of representational problematics, somewhat tailored to the specific questions that history writing faces, *but in reality only quite minimally*. The other thing that this realization highlights is that historical methodology offers almost nothing to this representational side of the practice. Indeed, there is instead a very strong contradiction between the aims and intentions involved, and there is also baggage attached in the form of commitments to rather different ideologies: the practice of history is constituted quite conservatively, often simply as an undisclosed reflection of bourgeois values and etiquette, whereas the philosophical problematics of representation are significantly attached to various 'radical' and 'oppositional' positions.

The way that this contradiction between the academic and the engaged roles of the historian plays out in contemporary expectations has been provocatively noted by Howard Zinn (2006, 72), who writes: 'We're historians; we're supposed to be here to talk about history and present our papers and leave matters of life and death to politicians … we no longer have a citizen among us. Somebody who will go beyond our professional prison and take part in the combat for social justice'. In this same 'into the world' register, we may also recall Tony Judt's reminders regarding the responsibility of scholars to assume the roles of citizen and engaged intellectual. For Judt, according to one oft-quoted claim, 'the disposition to disagree, to reject and to dissent – however irritating it may be when taken to extremes – is the very lifeblood of an open society. We need people who make a virtue of opposing mainstream opinion. A democracy of permanent consensus will not long remain a democracy' (Judt 2010, 155; see also Judt 1998. Viewed in this context, Zoltán Boldizsár Simon's idea of the 'apophatic' past assumes a greater urgency too).

This general notion of the historian-citizen who participates in 'the combat for social justice' serves well to frame the idea of *historians* 'in the world' here. What position a historian takes on a particular issue is not, however, determined either by their being intellectuals or historians. Examples of conservative as well as radical historians abound. But accepting the charge to dissent changes the situation. Such dissent and 'disobedience' (see Jenkins 2009), the 'virtue of opposing mainstream opinion', offers more prescriptive force for determining historians' values. Nevertheless, because of the nature of history as a discipline there *are* complications to which historians are especially vulnerable. (See especially the article by Claire Norton and Mark Donnelly in this issue for their analysis but also regarding the work of Martin Davies on this matter.) As a case in point, although *The History Manifesto* by Jo Guldi and David Armitage (2014) has recently made a big splash for its advocacy of history's 'speaking truth to power' in 'big' and improved ways, it seems blind to some of the core problems that theorists of history have already been grappling with over the last half-century. (A number of the authors in this issue, as well as in the coming one, refer to *The History Manifesto*, yet it appears to divide opinion among them too.) To me, there is no arguing either with the social diagnosis that Guldi and Armitage offer, or indeed their basic premise that historians could and even should be more involved with public concerns; the means that they end up recommending seem, nevertheless, to lead to quite conventional and problematic history. (For other recent work on the idea of historians as socially engaged and/or dissenting, see, for example, Berger 2016 and Dorfman 2016).

None of this is intended to say that historians cannot engage with socially significant questions in productive ways as public intellectuals. (The articles here give numerous examples of historians doing precisely that.) They may often be unable to do this in their professional capacity, however, since in the case of *history* 'in the world' – of historians acting as historians as opposed to acting as citizens – the discipline and the various attachments to intuitions about the meaningfulness of the past interfere. The hard question thus is: Can history as historians tend to do it, following some 'historical methodology' (even one augmented by something like 'big data', for instance), accommodate political engagement? More specifically, can the discipline offer opportunities for engaged or radical histories?

In a brief but memorable celebration of radical history in a theme issue of the similarly entitled journal, historian Ellen DuBois, like other contributors to the volume, placed that term firmly in the context of the political commitments of the 1960s, identifying it with a 'passion for social change' (DuBois 2001, 91). But, for her, radical history is not only about the engaged nature of intellectual activity. It does something more: 'what distinguishes "radical history" for me from other sorts of subversive intellectual and academic postures is the degree to which it incorporates a commitment to remain active and engaged in *historical* change in the present' (DuBois, 2001, 92, emphasis added). Something particular appears to result from being a historian, then. According to Dubois: 'The great gift of our profession, if we choose to take it, is having the long view, knowing that "it" has happened before, will happen again, and is always different'. From this at once engaged but also 'historically' committed perspective, and acknowledging the acceptability or even demand for alternative points of view and the espousal of contradiction and disagreement within the historical profession today, she ends by proclaiming: 'radical history rules!' (DuBois, 2001, 92)

While it seems that even mainstream academic history has indeed come a long way since the struggles of the 1960s to include oppositional viewpoints and to recognize the complexities of truthful representation, the historian's dual commitment continues to hold a tension. On the one hand, the kind of presentism advocated in all these calls is admittedly often today seen as a desideratum for history. Think also Dominick LaCapra, Hayden White and Keith Jenkins, for instance, but also of the way that attention to historians' practical and contemporary perspective has spread to quite standard rhetoric concerning history – a cynic might say that mounting pressure on scholars in the humanities to justify the value of their work has something to do with this overall emphasis. On the other hand, however, there still exists the lingering and disciplinarily ingrained belief that the investigation of past reality can effectively control ideological abuse. There is something in the specifically 'historical' nature of knowledge, of change, and so on, that is supposed to keep us on the right path. Again, a cynic might suggest that this is the only available route to sufficiently pragmatic justifications of historians' work in a consumption-oriented culture. It offers quick and easy appeal. What is history for, after all, if not to teach lessons and to show us some truth about being human? Or to curb excesses that result from too short a perspective on things. And so on. Taking this route now also offers a quick and easy way to history's (continued) domestication, however.

The mutual hostility that the different attachments construct between 'proper' history on one side and 'activism' and 'politics' (or even 'revisionism' or 'propaganda') on the other gives the impression that the creation of a theoretically and formally sensitive and simultaneously historically accurate and disciplinarily acceptable work of history is extremely difficult. Yet why wouldn't a conventional but sufficiently 'reflexive' historian be capable of history in an engaged or radical register too (regardless of the specific take on the nature of history that they have)? One way of explaining this is indeed to say that they will feel the need to be well-mannered and tame. They are, to echo Zinn, simply 'supposed to be here to talk about history and present their papers'. And when they venture beyond their 'professional prison' (or safe-house, depending on how one views it), they risk being left outside the practice proper – consider, for example, the view that many historians promote of Zinn as 'shaky' on the history-front. (Although perhaps the risk is not always so great; Anton Froeyman's article in this issue goes a long way toward reminding how far respected historians can stray from their professional role without it causing problems.) Another way of explaining things lies in digging into the automatic disciplinary assumption that if historians simply take care of history, history will take care of itself. But even that formulation of 'historical' responsibility can be thought of differently: 'To sustain a commitment to the "time before now" … suggests that we must continually develop our relationship with it and that part of that process of commitment is to dissent from orthodoxies. All historians have, in effect, a duty of discontent'. (Jenkins, Morgan & Munslow 2007, 1)

One argument deserving to be made is that we don't have the same kind of radically disobedient or oppositional histories as we have literatures, for example, as a consequence of the nature of the theory (or more precisely non-theory) concerning the research 'phase' and historian's professional expertise. If the theory and method of historical research are a reflection of the ideals that influenced history's formation as an academic genre – and what else would they be? – then it is no wonder that oppositional efforts *within* history are so easily incorporated into a disciplined, polite and non-contrarian discourse. In this setting, it appears to be fine to debate the facts but not the values that those facts are used to justify (or which the facts are simply presented as 'in themselves' legitimating). But what sense does that make in any world beyond polite and proper dinner conversation? Why so much fuss about arguing over individual facts – the establishment of which should, after all, be par for the course for the discipline – rather than the ideologies informing the work?

What all these various problems suggest is that to follow any 'post-narrativist' storyline successfully, and, perhaps more importantly, to build any kind of sensible theory of the cognitive and research practices of history, we still need proper analyses of the contents and formation of historians' expertise as well as practice-based studies of what historians do. Even then, this would in no way alter the problematics outlined by the 'discursive' or 'narrativist' side. It might, however, make the complexity of the theoretical issues more evident to a broader range of historians. One central difficulty has long involved intuitions about 'reality' and its accessibility. Core understandings regarding the figuring of facts and the creation of 'fictions' by historians, the argument regarding there being no entailment from individual facts to values, or the inevitability of our 'discursive condition' (as Elizabeth Deeds Ermarth has so aptly labelled the situation), all continue to be regularly countered by furious pointings at something concrete. Yet the fundamentals of social construction should be especially clear to historians – and the finger-stabbing could thus be far more nuanced.

With sensitive readings of the philosophical problematics on both sides of the debate, it will hopefully be possible to find more common ground. The common intuitive experience of some 'entailment' from, or 'meaning' in, concrete reality could then be rehabilitated to more theoretical talk about history too, as long as it is first sufficiently clear that we are only ever operating with socially constructed reality, both as we encounter it 'now', 'immediately' and as it extends into the present from the past. On this level, there is no denying that the discursive networks we are all embedded in have at least some hold in the ways they mediate experience as well as in the ways they extend into our present from the past in terms of the commitments they involve us in *vis-à-vis* 'the current situation'. Yet none of this is to claim that these engagements cannot still be rejected (there is no entailment, after all), but only to point out that any acceptance or rejection takes place in relation to endless discourses, practices and objects, and hence needs to expressly negotiate them. There is never a way of ignoring our (socially and discursively constructed) realities and the web of valuations that we always already find ourselves in. Indeed, the notion of 'figuration' alone, as introduced into the debates by Hayden White, captures this dynamic clearly enough, despite the various critiques of 'narrativism' as some absurd textualism.

After taking into account all these qualifications, there is then nothing very wrong with thinking that the concrete too is 'present' and 'accessible' through the discursive reality that we are thrown into, which constitutes us, and which we in turn reconstitute. (This process has long since been wonderfully elaborated by Jean-Paul Sartre in terms of a continuing dynamics of an internalization and externalization of meanings and valuations, for example.) From a pragmatic point of view, one compromise can simply be to take these influences and this reality seriously in terms of at least a 'call' to a certain type of action, if never a straightforward entailment. Crucially, the role of 'past-talk' in this nexus of meanings is quite different to what it is if we think we are attending to questions of truth and reference. As in the argument for there being no entailment from 'brute' facts to values, focus needs to be on the level at which meaning is constituted. At the same time, this meaning constitution should not – especially from a politically concerned point of view or in a discussion of engaged intellectuals – be conceived of as radically subjective but as part of projects of communication. The most interesting challenges for historians are thus not primarily epistemological or disciplinary ones. Whether facts are 'true' or 'false' or values or beliefs are 'right' or 'wrong' is not the problem. The question is how we deal with them.

Disclosure statement

No potential conflict of interest was reported by the author.

References

Berger, Stefan, ed. 2016. *Historians as Engaged Intellectuals*. New York: Berghahn Books.

Brown, Michelle P., and Richard Kelly, eds. 2005. *You're History! How People Make the Difference*. With a foreword by Bob Geldof. London: Bloomsbury.

Dorfman, Ben, ed. 2016. *Dissent Refracted: Historical Images of Dissent*. Bern: Peter Lang.

DuBois, Ellen Carol. 2001. "Long Live Radical History!" *Radical History Review* 79: 91–92.

Guldi, Jo, and David Armitage. 2014. *The History Manifesto*. Cambridge: Cambridge University Press.

Jenkins, Keith, Sue Morgan, and Alun Munslow. 2007. "Introduction: On fidelity and diversity." In *Manifestos for History*, edited and introduced by Keith Jenkins, Sue Morgan, and Alun Munslow, 1–10. London: Routledge.

Jenkins, Keith. 2009. *At the Limits of History: Essays on Theory and Practice*. London: Routledge.

Judt, Tony. 1998. *The Burden of Responsibility: Blum, Camus, Aron, and the French Twentieth Century*. Chicago, IL: University of Chicago Press.

Judt, Tony. 2010. *Ill Fares the Land: A Treatise on Our Present Discontents*. London: Penguin Press.

White, Hayden. 2014. "On the research and the writing phase of the historian's work." *Historein* 14: 71–74.

Yerxa, Donald A., ed. 2009. *Recent Themes on Historians and the Public: Historians in Conversation*. Columbia, SC: University of South Carolina Press.

Zinn, Howard. 2006. *Original Zinn: Conversations on History and Politics*, with David Barsamian. Foreword by Arundhati Roy. New York: HarperCollins.

The republic of historians: historians as nation-builders in Estonia (late 1980s–early 1990s)

Marek Tamm

School of Humanities, Tallinn University, Tallinn, Estonia

ABSTRACT

The restoration of the Estonian Republic in late 1980s and early 1990s can be described as the construction of 'the Republic of Historians'. A great many founders and leaders of the newly independent republic had received their education from the Department of History at the University of Tartu, and first gained their public renown as leaders of the national heritage movement and publicists on historical issues. The whole of the period, often called the 'new era of awakening', was characterized by an ideology of restoration, worked out by politically minded historians and historically minded political dissidents. In essence, all the political steps taken were motivated by a desire to return to pre-war laws, traditions, and institutions – to rehabilitate and restitute everything that had been destroyed or condemned to oblivion in the Soviet period. The major role of historical arguments and restoration ideology in the Estonian independence movement was not without several important sociopolitical consequences, especially in the realm of citizenship and property policy, which departed from a strict idea of legal continuity.

Introduction

On 20 August 1991, as the Estonian Parliament declared that after a half century of Soviet annexation Estonia no longer formed part of the Soviet Union and was once again an independent state, an interesting fact began to emerge – namely, that the leadership of the restored republic consisted, for the most part, of historians. The then prime minister, one of the figureheads of the Estonian independence movement Edgar Savisaar (b. 1950), had studied history at the University of Tartu. The same was true of the opposition leaders – right-wing party leaders Mart Laar (b. in 1960), soon to become the next prime minister, and Tunne Kelam (b. in 1936), vice speaker of the next parliament. The foreign minister, a year later the first President Elect of the restored Republic, Lennart Meri (1929–2006), had likewise graduated from the University of Tartu with a degree in history. Numerous other historians are to be found both in the government formed by Mart Laar in 1992 (including the expatriate Estonian professor of history at Kiel University, Hain Rebas, as minister of defence, and Chairman of the Estonian National Heritage Society, Trivimi Velliste, as minister of foreign affairs,[1]) and in the next parliament (Küllo Arjakas, Rein Helme, Mart Nutt, Lauri Vahtre, and others). Transitional Estonia thus offers a superb example of the importance of 'engaged historians' in public life, and the Estonian 'Republic of Historians', as one might call it (Tamm 2008, 505), deserves a closer look in the present special issue. I will focus primarily on the question, why did the restoration of the Republic of Estonia take the form of a Republic of Historians, or, put differently, how can the major role assumed by historians in restoring independence and leading the state be explained? In order to answer this question we must, however, also examine the importance of historical arguments and role models in the Estonian politics of the late 1980s and the first half of 1990s.[2]

'A new era of awakening': heritage protection and nation building

The fountains of the Estonian independence movement spring from two currents that gradually assumed an increasingly articulate shape in the 1980s: the protection of the environment and the protection of national heritage. These two popular movements, initially lacking any clear political ambitions but encouraged by the perestroika, prepared the ground for an extensive mobilisation of Estonian society. Although the importance of environmental protection for the awakening nation's political awareness must not be underestimated, particularly with respect to the so-called Phosphorite War that broke out in 1987 to 1988 and involved public resistance to the Soviet Union's central authorities' plan of opening phosphorite mines in north-east Estonia (see Kaski 1997; Auer 1998; Aare 1999; Liikanen 2001, for a wider perspective, see Galbreath 2010), it must be admitted that the impact of the national heritage movement was longer lived and more significant. The national heritage movement was the first true mass movement in Soviet Estonia, supplying the framework for formulating a political programme for the restoration of independence and providing the foremost political platform for the historians willing to contribute to the restoration of independence and to leading the country.

The roots of the Estonian national heritage movement go back to the second half of the 1970s, when several informal societies aimed at systematising and popularising the Estonian national heritage sprang up in Tallinn and in the university town Tartu (Tamm, J. 2012). Although these societies may seem apolitical at first glance, their activities relating to the systematisation of national heritage – emphasising as they did the value of national history and cultural milieu – clearly had political significance in a totalitarian society. As the political conditions eased up in 1986, the movement became better articulated, the work carried out by separate heritage clubs began to be coordinated, and formal policies were adopted for creating a common organisation – The Estonian Heritage Society. The first joint meeting of 12 heritage clubs, with their total of a few hundred members, was held on 18 October 1986. Less than a year later, the number of clubs had risen to 31 and that of members approached one thousand; and by the end of 1988, there were 185 clubs with about 6000 members (Laar 1998, 397).

The Estonian Heritage Society was officially founded on 12 December 1987, when the statute of the Society was adopted and a chairman, board and council were elected. There are good grounds for regarding the Society as the first nationwide democratic mass organisation in Estonia during the Soviet period. The Society's main objective is formulated in point six of the new statute: 'The Estonian National Heritage Society seeks to maintain the continuity of culture, to preserve and reinforce the nation's historical memory, and maintain a living environment humane and amenable to a culture that agrees with the historically evolved values of the people.' ('Eesti Muinsuskaitse Seltsi põhikiri', 1988). While the wording in the statute is understandably restrained, the speeches made at the inaugural meeting were far more vigorous. Sulev Vahtre, professor of Estonian history at the University of Tartu and former teacher of many of the future politicians, declared from the podium: 'For more than forty years, Estonian history has not been taught in Estonian schools, or it has been taught very little, very deficiently.' He added: 'We ought to try and find practical ways for diminishing the damage done over decades. What we need is to offer a full account of Estonian history as a whole. (…) The final objective is to become true masters of our past.' (Kask and Tiivel 1988, 281). The final objective, as formulated by Vahtre, epitomised well the main pathos of the national heritage movement: to restore the Estonians' control over 'their past' or, as phrased by Mart Laar, the future prime minister, 'to restore to the people their expropriated history' (Laar 1988b, 11).

Yet, at that same inaugural meeting, even more radical speeches were made, with the more audacious among them expanding the concept of 'heritage' to the nation as a whole. Thus one of the delegates, Helmut Elstrok, insisted that 'the number one heritage must be the land and people of Estonia, together with everything created by the people' (Kask and Tiivel 1988, 280). If the memoirs of Mart Laar, written almost thirty years later, are to be believed, the leader of the heritage movement, Trivimi Velliste, declared that the main objective of the Society was the restoration of the Republic of Estonia as 'the greatest heritage' already in October 1986, at the first meeting of the heritage clubs (Laar 2015, 18). In a similar vein, Sulev Vahtre also identified Estonia as 'the greatest historical and cultural monument to be protected by the national heritage movement' in his speech at the national heritage days' meeting held in Tartu on 14 April 1988 (Laar et al. 1996b, 424).[3] These declarations vividly demonstrate how the heritage movement rapidly became politicised and began to set up the objective of independent statehood.

In February 1988, the newly founded Estonian Heritage Society published its first call for collecting historical traditions entitled 'Is It a New Era of Awakening?' This phrase, 'a new era of awakening', quickly became the most popular name for the period as a whole and is repeated in the recent general academic overview of Estonian history (Vahtre 2005, 376–379). The 'Era of Awakening' is a historical term referring to the process that took place in the second half of the nineteenth century, which gave rise to the evolution of Estonian national self-consciousness and the gradual emergence of a national intelligentsia (see Raun 2003; Jansen 2004). The call by the Heritage Society opens with a quotation from one of the leaders of the nineteenth-century national awakening, Jakob Hurt (1839–1907), and observes that Hurt's words about the great changes of the mid-nineteenth century are still relevant today; that, once again, an 'awakening mentality' is discernible. The anonymous authors of the call (there is reason to believe that the leading author was Mart Laar) answer the question posed by the title in the affirmative, 'because the present age has a familiar air for the historians'. They add: 'However, the spirit of the Era of Awakening holds obligations for us, too. First and foremost, it obliges us to be worthy of our forebears, to celebrate and honor this age not only with monuments and acclamations, but also to live up to it, spiritually.' They then go on to point out that the central watchwords of the new era are 'history' and 'memory': 'It is the struggle for our history, our memory, that seems to emerge as one of the most resonating ideas of the "new era of awakening".' (Eesti Muinsuskaitse Selts 1988, 257–258)

It is not in February 1988 that the 'new era of awakening' was born as a general name for the period, however; to the best of our evidence, that phrase was first launched by Rein Veidemann, literary critic and editor-in-chief of the cultural magazine *Vikerkaar*, in his article 'In the Era of Re-Awakening', published in the daily paper *Edasi* on 16 January 1987. Admittedly, Veidemann is still rather restrained in drawing parallels, and uses the phrase in quite a figurative manner:

> Of course, in Estonia 'awakening' itself is surrounded by a definite tradition (the national awakening of the last century), however, this should not prevent us from terming the present era in the same way, since in a deeper sense its content is one and the same, namely the people's (and every single individual's) realization of themselves, their coming to a consciousness that they are masters of their own destiny to the extent that it is really and truly possible to have a say in important matters of societal development. (Veidemann 1987)

Despite this initial restraint, the new name spread like wildfire and can be encountered in numerous contemporary speeches and articles; among others, Mart Laar observes in April 1987: 'Recently there has been very much talk about the "new era of awakening". It indeed seems that there is a great surge of interest in the past of our land and people, including in the age of the national movement and the ideals that inspired it.' (Laar 1987, 553) The 'new era of awakening' is thus semantically a very loaded concept: on the one hand, it refers to a strong idea of continuity, to a notion that the struggle that had started in the mid-nineteenth century was being continued at the end of the twentieth; on the other hand, however, it perpetuates the old romantic notion of an eternal, although perhaps dormant nation, just waiting to awaken from its slumber.

One of the more popular initiatives of the Heritage Society, the collecting of oral histories bears testimony to a quite conscious emulation of the nine-teenth-century age of awakening. In early 1988, the council of the Society convened and decided to initiate, from February 22 on, a nationwide campaign to collect 'historical memories'. The date was not chosen casually: exactly 100 years earlier, Jakob Hurt had published an appeal inviting all Estonians to record oral traditions and send their records to him. Hurt's appeal proved very popular, it launched the first nationwide collecting campaign and yielded almost 115,000 pages of folklore of all genres (Viidalepp 1980; Laar 1995, 144–176). The Heritage Society's initiative followed the example set by Hurt while linking the recording of historical memories to the pathos of 'giving history back to the people':

> By writing down one's own or one's ancestors' memories, everyone can participate in giving our history back to our people. Because it is of these individual desti-nies that the great mosaic – the history of Estonia – is made up of. And even if we sometimes, perhaps, dislike that history, it is still our own, and by remaining ignorant of it we ourselves cleave asunder the roots that attach us to our native soil. (Laar 2012, 252)

A few months later, one of the main initiators of the undertaking, Mart Laar, commented on the aims of the initiative: 'The aim is to obtain truthful facts about the history of Estonia, to preserve memories of the past for future gen-erations, to safeguard and protect our historical memory.' (Laar 1988a, 76) The collecting campaign proved a success, with thousands of people contributing, and according to the organisers it yielded within a few years more than 100,000 pages of all sorts of historical materials, now held in the archives of the Estonian Literary Museum in Tartu (Laar 2012, 255).

'The return of the repressed': national trauma work

While the heritage movement at first aimed primarily at preserving material patrimony, the second half of the 1980s saw an increasing tendency towards recording traumatic experiences of recent history. The 'Questionnaire of

Historical Tradition', drawn up by the Heritage Society in 1989 and intended as an aid in the campaign for collecting oral histories pays great attention to everything that had occurred during and after World War II (*Ajaloopärimuse küsimustik* 1989, 4–6). At the same time, more and more memories and analyses of the traumatic aspects of the past were featured in the press: repressions, deportations, guerilla warfare, the tragic fate of the political elite, and so on (see Anepaio 2002). A few years earlier, traumatic, and formerly taboo, historical themes had begun to surface in fiction – including plays performed very successfully on numerous stages. I have previously described the intense contemplation of past sufferings that is characteristic to those years as 'the return of the repressed' (Tamm 2013, 653) because that was then all the experiences and traumas repressed by half a century of Soviet power, all of a sudden, came to the surface.

In November 1988, as Mart Laar drew up the first interim review of the Heritage Society's campaign for collecting historical memories, he entitled the resulting article 'The Time of Horrors', focusing on the repressions of the 1940s. The tone of the piece is set by the opening sentences:

> Many phenomena and periods (the War of Independence, the huge significance of the Republic of Estonia to our nation's survival, etc.) are beginning to find their appropriate place in our nation's historical consciousness. Yet this largely remains information acquired, as it were, on the emotional level; frequently people are unable to give these facts any specific content or meaning. And what is worst: it seems to me that we are still unable of realising the extent and horror of the sufferings that have befallen our people. We must finally come to grips with the fact that there is practically no family in Estonia that has not had to see some of its members deported to Siberia, killed, repressed, or flee into exile. (Laar 1988a, 76)

Laar's article attracted an unexpected amount of attention and even lent a hint of martyr's glory to his activities because, a few months later, the prosecutor's office of the Estonian Soviet Socialist Republic (SSR) decided to open a criminal case against him, accusing him of presenting and publicly disseminating historical falsehoods. The decision was met with sharp criticism, with both historians and jurists vocally opposing it (e.g. Lindmäe and Sootak 1989). According to Laar, the decision was motivated by the hope that he would choose to remain in exile (the proceedings were announced while he was abroad); instead, he decided to return home and present evidence to support his claims (Laar 2012, 254). A year later, after rapid changes in the political situation, the prosecutor's office quietly dropped the allegations.

The outpouring of memories, analyses, and artistic expressions of the repressions culminated in March 1989, on the 40th anniversary of the great deportation of Estonians to Siberia in 1949. That tragic anniversary was commemorated with various mass ceremonies, extensive media coverage, and the rehabilitative joint 'Address to the Inhabitants of Estonia' by the then institutions of power ('Pöördumine …' 1989). On March 25 of the same year, the Memento Union, an organisation uniting and representing the victims of repression, was founded and tasked itself with protecting the legal and social interests of the repressed, as well as recording and perpetuating their memory. Some months earlier, on 7 December 1988, the Supreme Soviet of the Estonian SSR had passed a law 'On the Extrajudicial Mass Repressions in Soviet Estonia During the 1940s and 1950s', which declared, among other things, that 'the extra-judicial mass repressions carried out in Soviet Estonia in the 1940s and 1950s must be completely and unconditionally condemned and denounced as unlawful acts and crimes against humanity' (Tamm 2013, 653). To put it briefly, in the Estonia of the late 1980s, history became both a stock of positive models and an object of trauma work; the past at once inspired and frightened, but left no-one indifferent.

The restoration of Estonia's independence by restoring historical truth

It was not only in the framework of the heritage movement that history became the battleground for political struggles, historical arguments also played a major role in the early stages of the political independence movement in Soviet Estonia. Dissident activities had had relatively little influence and only a limited number of participants; if they gained wider resonance in 1987, it was primarily through interest in historical topics. On 15 August 1987, a small number of former political prisoners founded the first political association in the Soviet Estonia, The Estonian Group on Publication of the Molotov-Ribbentrop Pact (MRP-AEG). The main aim of the group was to make public the contents, and effect on the Baltics, of that shady agreement that Hitler and Stalin made in 1939. The first public event of the MRP-AEG was held in Tallinn on the anniversary of the pact, 23 August 1987. Even though authorities pressured a move away from the main square of the Old Town into a neighbouring park, the meeting drew unexpectedly large crowds and is considered to have been the opening signal of the Estonian independence movement (Niitsoo 1997, 157; Niitsoo 2002, 10–16; Tannberg 2007; Graf 2008, 216–224). The meeting was opened by a lengthy speech by the main organiser, Tiit Madisson, which constituted primarily a history lecture on the pact between Hitler and Stalin and on Stalinist repressions in Estonia. The speech ended with a call for publicising 'the true history':

> We must honestly make public the history of our nation. In the process, many things will have to be reassessed. All the crimes against humanity must be decisively condemned. The Stalinist executioners, many of whom are currently drawing personal pensions, must be taken to justice. Only then can we be sure that all this will not play itself out, once again. (Pärnaste and Niitsoo, 1998, 13)

Energised by the unexpected success of this meeting, the MRP-AEG decided to target another important historical date, namely February 2 (1920), when Soviet Russia and Estonia signed a peace treaty by which Russia officially recognised Estonia's independence. The public meeting, held in Tartu on 2 February 1988, took place under the control of the security forces and under otherwise complicated circumstances (several organisers were arrested before the event and the crowds that turned up for the meeting were scattered with the help of militia units and dogs); nevertheless, it had broad resonance and communicated a new actuality to the Tartu Peace Treaty (Pärnaste and Niitsoo, 1998, 232–262; Niitsoo 2002, 25–31). Following up on this success, the next anniversary targeted was the 70th jubilee of the Republic of Estonia, on February 24 – one of the greatest historical taboos under the Soviet regime. The ruling regime went to great lengths in order to prevent the activities of MRP-AEG ahead of that anniversary, both by isolating the organisers and through a vigorous media campaign. In the media, the chairman of the Presidium of the Supreme Soviet of the Estonian SSR, Arnold Rüütel – later the president of Estonia – weighed in, recognising the people's growing appetite for history in the first part of his speech, while warning against the abuse of that interest in the second:

> It is quite another matter when interest in history is used in a way that can only be described as an incentive for exacerbating topical problems, so as to oppose our society's course towards renewal; as nothing but an irresponsible attitude towards the issues related to our own, as well as all other Soviet nations', future and destiny. ('Eesti NSV Ülemnõukogu …', 405–406)

Nevertheless, on 24 February 1988, the MRP-AEG succeeded in bringing an estimated 20,000–30,000 people into the streets of Tallinn, who moved around the town in a procession, listening to spontaneous speeches here and there (Niitsoo 2002, 31–38). The MRP-AEG continued its actions aimed at actualising various historical events in the days to come, commemorating, for instance, the anniversary of the 1949 great deportation of Estonians to Siberia on 25 March 1988.

The activities of the MRP-AEG were not, however, very long-lived – the group soon merged into a new political party that was being created. That party, initiated mainly by former dissidents and political prisoners and called The Estonian National Independence Party, was officially established in August 1988, although preparations for it had begun already at the beginning of the year. It was the first non-communist party in Soviet Estonia. Although the party at first lacked a programme, this was substituted for by a declaration adopted at the inaugural meeting, which formulated the final aim of the party as 'the restoration of Estonian nation-state independence and sovereignty' (Pärnaste 1988). It is worth noting, however, that this important document also envisaged the restoration of Estonian statehood through a restoration of historical justice, as the opening chapter of the declaration emphasises the importance for Estonia of 'a restoration of historical truth' (see Pettai 2004, 60–61). In an interview given a few months later Tunne Kelam, a leading author of the declaration and one of the new party's leaders, stressed how the political changes of recent times had materialised thanks to a new understanding of history:

> In the events of the last two years a very important role has been played by the making public of Estonian history. I believe that this has changed in people's

(especially young people's) consciousness their understanding of our actual situation. We became conscious of the 1940 occupation, of the fact that the official hierarchy is illegal, that in 1940 a special kind of *coup d'état* took place in Estonia (…). (Kelam 1989, 646)

Historians in power: the triumph of restorationism

By the end of the 1980s, Estonian society was clearly on its way to regain independence, with the growing conviction that the aim was not to create a new independent state but to restore the old pre-war Republic of Estonia, based on the idea of legal continuity. In other words, the predominant ideology tended to be one of legal restorationism, worked out by politically minded historians and historically minded political dissidents. In essence, all the political steps taken over the next few years were motivated by a desire to return to pre-war laws, traditions, and institutions, to rehabilitate and restitute everything that had been destroyed or condemned to oblivion during the Soviet period (see Lagerspetz 1999; Aleksahhina 2006; Pettai 2004, 2007, 2010). The restorationist ideology took on very specific and diverse forms. One of the earliest examples was the restoration of the War of Independence memorials, in the course of which more than 100 monuments were reconstructed or built up anew (Strauss 2002, 307–308; Tamm, J. 2012, 57–59). In parallel, most of the pre-war names of places, streets and institutions as well as the pre-war calendar of holidays were reinstated at the end of the 1980s. The reburial of several politicians of pre-war Estonia into their native soil drew great public attention, most significant of these surely being the search for the grave of the first President of the Republic, Konstantin Päts (1874–1956), in the village of Burashevo near Moscow in 1988–1989, and the bringing of his remains back to Estonia in October 1990 (Lõugas 1991). The spirit of restoration was also expressed in the historiography of the transitional period, both in history teaching (Ahonen 2001) and in academic studies (Kivimäe 1999; Kivimäe and Kivimäe 2002), but most clearly perhaps in the short popular overview of Estonian history, entitled 'The Story of Home' (*Kodu lugu*), written by Mart Laar, Lauri Vahtre and Heiki Valk and published in two slim volumes in 1989 (see Kaljundi 2009). The book happily captures the historical credo of the time: 'By clinging to their past, the Estonians in fact constructed for themselves a path into the future.' (Laar et al. 1989, 66) Even a quarter of a century later, Mart Laar still recalls the struggles of the late 1980s in the same register: 'The past had again become real and was creating the future.' (Laar 2015, 20) Meike Wulf and Pertti Grönholm succinctly summarise the attitude of the Estonian historians of that period: 'they turned to the past to find guidance for the present and the future' (Wulf and Grönholm 2010, 372).

However, restoration ideology was not the only political choice on offer at the end of the 1980s, since a new political association, the Popular Front established on Edgar Savisaar's initiative in October 1988 and quickly evolving into a great mass organisation, preferred the political strategy of creating an independent state on the basis of the Estonian SSR (Eestimaa Rahvarinne 1989, 16). Trivimi Velliste, head of the National Heritage Society, has very clearly formulated the dilemma faced at that time: 'By the beginning of 1989 the idea of independence was widespread in Estonia. (...) But now the entire question became: independence, yes, but of what kind, on what basis, to what degree?' (Laar et al. 1996a, 325) Although the leader of the Popular Front, Edgar Savisaar, was also a historian by education, historical arguments had no great role to play in the rhetorics of this movement, created in support of perestroika and dedicated to first obtaining economic independence and then gradually founding a new independent state, with citizenship based not only on continuity with that of the pre-war Republic of Estonia, but on residence in the territory of Estonia (see Veskimäe 2008). Regardless of the great support for the Popular Front, the restorationist ideas of the opposite camp finally came out on top.

The interesting thing to note about this debate – a debate that, unfortunately, is too complex to be discussed in full here – is the way in which historical models were employed to legitimate differences over current political issues. Thus, for example, Mart Laar, who, as a historian, paid particular attention to how and why the Estonian national movement split up, frequently likened the twentieth-century standoff between the Heritage Society and the Popular Front to the nineteenth-century conflict between the nationally minded and uncompromising followers of Jakob Hurt and those of Carl Robert Jakobson (1841–1882), who appealed to the support of the Russian Tsar and represented what could be called *Realpolitik* (Laar 1989, 943). 'Probably the dilemma of Jakobson and (...) Hurt (...) has worked its way into the present, too,' he observes in 1988 (Laar 1988c, 678).

On 24 February 1989, the Estonian National Independence Party and the Estonian Heritage Society launched an appeal for creating committees of the citizens of the Republic of Estonia, with the aim of registering legitimate Estonian citizens and convoking an Estonian Congress to represent their will and restore the Republic of Estonia on the basis of legal continuity (Pärnaste 2000). The process of politically implementing restorationist ideology was thus officially launched. From this modest start, the formation of committees and registration of citizens surged massively during the spring, and by mid-July 1989 71 citizens' committees had been founded and almost 150,000 Estonian citizens and applicants for citizenship had been registered; three months later, the latter number had risen to 314,521. In only a few months the restorationist ideology had been introduced so successfully that the masses embraced it; to the extent that, when the elections for the Estonian Congress were held in February 1990, more than 520,000 registered citizens, or the majority of Estonians, went to the ballot boxes (Vahtre 2005, 385). Although the Estonian Congress was acting in a legal vacuum, since according to the constitution, the Supreme Soviet of the Estonian SSR (whose new composition had been elected in March 1990) was still the only legitimate parliament, subsequent events confirmed that ideologically, the doctrine of legal continuity advocated by the Congress had prevailed over the conception of creating a new state preferred by the Popular Front and the Supreme Soviet. The beginning of a coup in Moscow on 19 August 1991, created a singular historical opportunity for Estonia to regain national independence. The Estonian Congress managed to persuade the Supreme Soviet to declare independence based on legal continuity, and thus, on 20 August 1991, the Supreme Soviet declared Estonia's independence restored de facto. Historical thinking had prevailed over pragmatic thinking. When the new parliament convened a few months later and the president was elected, it became clear that all the key offices of the restored state, beginning with prime minister Mart Laar and president Lennart Meri, were held by historians and former leaders of the Heritage Society.

Conclusion: a Proustian project and its consequences

Well-known Estonian novelist Tõnu Õnnepalu has asserted aptly that:

> In the year 1991, we decisively set out on a road leading into the past; from then on, everything happened under the label of restoration, of restitution. Parishes, schools, monuments, street names, property, money. The new was only allowed to be the old regained; the Republic of Estonia became a truly Proustian project: a journey into time regained. (Õnnepalu 2011)

The struggle for the 'restoration of true history' was integral to the Estonian struggle for independence; at the end of the 1980s and the beginning of the 1990s, history spoke not only about the past, but 'became an argument in regaining national independence' (Kõresaar 2005, 20). Recalling recently the activities of the Estonian Heritage Society, Mart Laar considered them very successful because 'not only had national memory and the bond between various periods been restored, not only had the Estonian people regained its history, it had also regained its statehood' (Laar 2012, 255). It must be admitted that never before had history and historians played so material a role in shaping Estonia's political destiny.[4]

The Estonian independence movement as a whole proceeded very much under the guidance of historians, a great deal of the political activism was carried by a desire to reinterpret Estonian history. In the spirit of the times, historian Ea Jansen wrote as early as February 1988 that:

> At present, a shortage of history, indeed a hunger for history is emerging in the Estonian, and all Soviet, public sphere, related not just to immediate political projections, the so-called blank spots in treatments of recent past. A general deep (re) interpretation of historical processes has become acutely topical, in order to find an answer to the question: who are we, where have we come from? (Jansen 1988)

A popular figure of speech during that period was, as Jansen points out, one of 'filling in the blank spots' of history – something that was seen as the main task of historians. Strictly speaking, however, history during the transitional period was decidedly not about simply introducing previously unknown or forbidden historical episodes and personalities to the general public, but also about shaping a new politics of history and memory. As sociologist Mikko Lagerspetz has rightly pointed out:

> The new historical awareness of the late 1980s did not merely bring forth a filling up of the blank spots, the revelation of historical facts hitherto unknown by the public at large. What took place was not only a *reconstruction* of the historical memory: it was also a process of *construction*. Not only were new facts presented to the public, but also what was previously known came to be interpreted in a new way. (Lagerspetz 1995, 279)

History became the influential 'science of legitimation' (Schöttler 1997) in transitional Estonia, helping to gain, justify and preserve power in a new social situation. Needless to say, the major role of historical arguments and of restorationist ideology in the Estonian independence movement was not without several important sociopolitical consequences that have continued to shape Estonian society up to the present day (see Pettai 2007). To name only a few of the most important realms that were affected: the restoration doctrine shaped Estonia's very strict citizenship policy, automatically depriving nearly a third of the society – the immigrants of the Soviet period and their descendants – of citizenship. The restoration doctrine is also behind Estonia's property policy, which departed from a strict idea of legal succession and dictated that Soviet-nationalised property be returned to its former owners. This decision basically annulled half a century of property use and forced many people to move out of their homes in return for compensation. In 'the Republic of Historians', the principle of historical justice overruled that of social justice. The historians' influence began to wane in Estonia only after 1994, when Mart Laar's government fell and the prospect of joining the European Union and NATO shifted attention from the past to questions of the future.

Of course Estonia was not the only country that began, after the collapse of the Soviet Union, to construct its new identity with historians at the steering wheel and taking its cue from historical continuity. As Stefan Berger has rightly stated, while mapping the return of national histories in post-Cold-War Europe: 'For the new states in post-Communist Eastern Europe, it was important to construct continuities which demonstrated the historicity of their nation states. History everywhere became intensely politicised.' (Berger and Conrad 2015, 329; see also Berger 2015; Kopeček 2008) Thus, we find many historians at the core of the Solidarność movement in Poland, many of whom later became renowned politicians (see Górny 2007). Historians and historical arguments similarly played an important role in post-Communist Hungary where 'centre right-wing governments have persistently promoted nationalist history, whenever they have been in power since the 1990s' (Berger and Conrad 2015, 327; see also Ivanišević et al. 2002; Trencsényi and Apor 2007). Nor should we underestimate the importance of dissident historians in the independence movement of Czechoslovakia, where the politics of human rights were smoothly entwined into the construction of a new canon of national history (Kopeček 2012, 2013).

Looking at Estonia's closer neighbours, Latvia and Lithuania, it can be said that 'setting straight' historical injustice and filling in 'the blank spots' of the past formed an inseparable part of the process of regaining independence. Similarly to Estonia, but unlike Lithuania, Latvia also engaged very strongly in restoration politics and re-established the state following the principles of legal continuity (see Onken 2003; Budryte 2005; Pettai and Pettai 2015). Yet in none of the above-mentioned states did historians gain similar positions to those they held in Estonia, nor did historical examples and arguments acquire such great political weight. Estonia's peculiar position as a 'Republic of Historians' will certainly be worth a more thoroughgoing comparative analysis in the future.

Notes

1. Velliste in fact had graduated from the university as English philologist, but gained his public renown and political capital in the 1980s as the leader of the national heritage movement and a publicist on historical issues.
2. In recent years, Estonian history and memory politics have attracted the attention of several scholars but research has mainly centred on the developments of the 2000s (e.g. Onken 2007; Brüggemann and Kasekamp 2008, 2009; Wulf 2010; Smith 2011; Tamm 2013; Selg and Ruutsoo 2014) and the transition period of the 1980s to 1990s has largely lain fallow; among the few attempts made are Lagerspetz 1995; Ruutsoo 1995; Hackmann 2003.
3. Sulev Vahtre (1926–2007) offers a perfect example of an academically committed historian and long-time university professor, who did not think it too much to contribute actively to the restoration of the Republic of Estonia and thereby to the building of the new Republic of Historians. In an interview from 1996, he recalled how his social engagement began, considering the speech made at the Tartu Heritage Days of 1988 to be the starting point: 'But as to the delivery, I considered myself quite successful. From then on, I had more and more invitations to speak: the openings of all those War of Independence memorials, and very often just invitations to speak about Estonian history. It was a kind of popular university, sometimes I even had to speak just in the street, every now and then somebody would ask, hey, historian, tell me how this or that actually happened? So I felt like a travelling preacher that year. It was rather strenuous, but also very uplifting! It was a very fine time!' (Laar et al. 1996b, 316).
4. Aadu Must (2010, 81) has made a very similar point: 'Historians played a disproportionately significant role among the leaders of the movement to re-establish independence, and in parliament.' It is true that historians also played an important role in the foundation of the Republic of Estonia at the beginning of the twentieth century, yet this is not comparable to their importance in the restoration of the republic. It is worth noting that in 1994, Sulev Vahtre dedicated a whole article to the political role of historians over the 'critical years' of Estonian history, 1918/1919 and 1987/1989 (Vahtre 1994). More recently, Jörg Hackmann has also analysed historians' political activity in Estonian history,

focusing on the roles of Hans Kruus (1891–1976) and Mart Laar (Hackmann 2005; see also Hackmann 2010).

Acknowledgments

I am grateful to Kalle Pihlainen for the invitation to contribute to this special issue and for his editorial work as well as to Antoon De Baets for his perceptive criticism.

Disclosure statement

No potential conflict of interest was reported by the author.

Funding

This work was supported financially by the Estonian Research Council [grant number IUT3–2], [IUT18–8].

References

Aare, J. 1999. *Fosforiidisõda 1971–1989* [The Phosphorite War, 1971–1989]. Tallinn: Kirilille Kirjastus.

Ahonen, S. 2001. "Politics of Identity through History Curriculum: Narratives of the Past for Social Exclusion – or Inclusion?" *Journal of Curriculum Studies* 33 (2): 179–194.

Ajaloopärimuse küsimustik [Questionnaire of Historical Tradition]. 1989. Tallinn: Eesti Muinsuskaitse Seltsi Ajalootoimkond.

Aleksahhina, M. 2006. "Historical Discourse in the Legitimation of Estonian Politics: Principle of Restitution." *Human Affairs* 6 (1): 66–82.

Anepaio, T. 2002. "Reception of the Topic of Repressions in the Estonian Society." *Pro Ethnologia* 14: 47–65.

Auer, M. R. 1998. "Environmentalism and Estonia's Independence Movement." *Nationalities Papers* 26: 659–676.

Berger, S. 2015. "The Return of National History." In *The Impact of History? Histories at the Beginning of the Twenty-first Century*, edited by P. R. Pinto and B. Taithe, 82–94. New York: Routledge.

Berger, S., and C. Conrad. 2015. *The Past as History: National Identity and Historical Consciousness in Modern Europe*. Basingstoke: Palgrave Macmillan.

Brüggemann, K., and A. Kasekamp. 2008. "The Politics of History and the "War of Monuments" in Estonia." *Nationalities Papers* 36 (3): 425–448.

Brüggemann, K., and A. Kasekamp. 2009. "Identity Politics and Contested Histories in Divided Societies: The Case of Estonian War Monuments." In *Identity and Foreign Policy: Baltic-Russian Relations in the Context of European Integration*, edited by E. Berg and P. Ehin, 51–64. Farnham: Ashgate.

Budryte, D. 2005. *Taming Nationalism? Political Community Building in the Post-Soviet Baltic States*. Aldershot: Ashgate.

Eesti Muinsuskaitse Selts [Estonian Heritage Society]. 1988. "Kas uus ärkamisaeg?" [Is It a New Era of Awakening?] *Looming* 2: 257–258.

"Eesti Muinsuskaitse Seltsi põhikiri." [The Satute of the Estonian National Heritage Society] 1988. *Sirp ja Vasar*, March 18.

Eestimaa Rahvarinne. 1989. *Eestimaa Rahvarinde valimisplatvorm* [The Election Platform of the Estonian Popular Front]. Tallinn: Eestimaa Rahvarinne.

Galbreath, D. J., ed. 2010. *Contemporary Environmentalism in the Baltic States: From Phosphate Springs to 'Nordstream'*. New York: Routledge.

Górny, M. 2007. "From Splendid Past into the Unknown Future: Historical Studies in Poland after 1989." In *Narratives Unbound. Historical Studies in Post-Communist Eastern Europe*, edited by S. Antohi, B. Trencsényi, and P. Apor, 101–172. Budapest: CEU Press.

Graf, M. 2008. *Kalevipoja kojutulek* [The Return of the Son of Kalev]. Tallinn: Argo.

Hackmann, J. 2003. "Past Politics in North-Eastern Europe: The Role of History in Post-Cold War Identity Politics." In *Post-Cold War Identity Politics. Northern and Baltic Experiences*, edited by M. Lehti and D. J. Smith, 78–100. London: Franc Cass.

Hackmann, J.. 2005. "'Historians as Nation-Builders': Historiographie und Nation in Estland von Hans Kruus bis Mart Laar." ['Historians as Nation-Builders': History Writing and Nation in Estonia from Hans Kruus to Mart Laar] In *Beruf und Berufung. Geschichtswissenschaft und Nationsbildung in Ostmittel- und Südosteuropa im 19. und 20. Jahrhundert* [Profession and Vocation. History Writing and Nation Building in Central and Southeastern Europe in the 19th and 20th Centuries], edited by M. Krzoska and H.-C. Maner, 125–142. Münster: Lit.

Hackmann, J. 2010. "Narrating the Building of a Small Nation: Divergence and Convergence in the Historiography of Estonian 'National Awakening', 1868–2005." In *Nationalizing the Past: Historians as Nation Builders in Modern Europe*, edited by S. Berger and C. Lorenz, 170–191. Basingstoke: Palgrave Macmillan.

Ivanišević, A., A. Kappeler, W. Lukan, and A. Suppan, eds. 2002. *Klio ohne Fesseln? Historiographie im östlichen Europa nach dem Zusammenbruch des Kommunismus* [Clio without Shackles? History Writing in Eastern Europe after the Collapse of Communism]. Vienna: Peter Lang.

Jansen, E. 1988. "Mõtteid rahvuskultuuri ajaloo uurimisest." [Some Thoughts about the Historical Research into the National Culture] *Sirp ja Vasar*, February 12.

Jansen, E. 2004. "The National Awakening of the Estonian Nation." In *Estonia: Identity and Independence*, edited by J.-J. Subrenat, 83–105. Amsterdam: Rodopi.

Kaljundi, L. 2009. "'Ein sicherer Halt': Zum Verhältnis von Geschichte und Analogieprinzip in 'Kodu Lugu.'" ['A Safe Hold': On the Relationship between History and the Principle of Analogy in 'Kodu Lugu'] *Forschungen zur baltischen Geschichte* 4: 238–248.

Kask, P., and T. Tiivel. 1988. "Uus ärkamisaeg. Eesti Muinsuskaitse Seltsi asutamiselt." [A New Era of Awakening. From the Founding Meeting of the Estonian Heritage Society] *Looming* 2: 278–281.

Kaski, A. 1997. "The Phosphorite War: The Role of Environmental Protest in the Estonian Independence Movement of the 1980s." *Idäntutkimus* 4: 21–38.

Kelam, T. 1989. "Eesti Vabariik kui reaalsus. Intervjuu Toomas Haugile [The Republic of Estonia as Reality. Interview to Toomas Haug]." *Looming* 5: 646–653.

Kivimäe, J. 1999. "Re-writing Estonian History?" In *National History and Identity*, edited by M. Branch, 205–212. Helsinki: Finnish Literature Society.

Kivimäe, S., and J. Kivimäe. 2002. "Geschichtsschreibung und Geshichtsforschung in Estland 1988–2001." [History Writing and Historical Research on Estonia, 1988–2001] *Österreichische Osthefte* 44 (1/2): 159–170.

Kopeček, M., ed. 2008. *Past in the Making. Historical Revisionism in Central Europe after 1989*. Budapest: CEU Press.

Kopeček, M. 2012. "Human Rights facing a National Past. Dissident 'Civic Patriotism' and the Return of History in East Central Europe 1968–1989." *Geschichte und Gesellschaft* 38 (4): 573–602.

Kopeček, M. 2013. "Von der Geschichtspolitik zur Erinnerung als politischer Sprache: Der tschechische Umgang mit der kommunistischen Vergangenheit nach 1989." [From the History Politics to the Memory as a Political Language: Czech Coming to Terms with the Communist Past after 1989] In *Geschichtspolitik in Europa seit 1989. Deutschland, Frankreich und Polen im internationalen Vergleich* [History Politics in Europe since 1989. Germany, France and Poland in International Comparison], edited by E. François, K. Kończal, R. Traba, and S. Troebst, 356–395. Göttingen: Wallstein.

Kõresaar, E. 2005. *Elu ideoloogiad. Kollektiivne mälu ja autobiograafiline minevikutõlgendus eestlaste elulugudes* [Ideologies of Life: Collective Memory and Autobiographical Meaning-Making of the Past in Estonian Life Stories]. Tartu: Eesti Rahva Muuseum.

Laar, M. 1987. "Ärkamisajast nii ja teisiti." [Different Looks at the Era of Awaking] *Looming* 4: 553–555.

Laar, M. 1988a. "Õuduste aeg." [The Time of Horrors] *Vikerkaar* 11: 76–78.

Laar, M. 1988b. "Veidi meie ajaloolisest mälust." [A Little Bit about Our Historical Memory] *Kultuur ja Elu* 4: 11–13.

Laar, M. 1988c. "Mõtteid Eesti Vabariigist." [Some Thoughts about the Republic of Estonia] *Looming* 5: 677–678.

Laar, M. 1989. "Jakob Hurt ja meie." [Jakob Hurt and Us] *Looming* 7: 942–947.

Laar, M. 1995. *Raamat Jakob Hurdast* [A Book about Jakob Hurt]. Tartu: Ilmamaa.

Laar, M. 1998. "Mait Rauna romaani ajalooline taust." [The Historical Background of the Novel by Mait Raun] In *Wake up. Naiivseid mälestusi ajaloost 1987–1988* [Wake Up. Naive Memories on History, 1987–1988], edited by M. Raun, 392–406. Tallinn: SE&JS.

Laar, M. 2012. "Eesti Muinsuskaitse Seltsi ajalootoimkonnast." [On the History Commission of the Estonian Heritage Society] In *Eesti Muinsuskaitse Selts 25* [Estonian Heritage Society 25], edited by J. Tamm, 250–255. Tallinn: Eesti Muinsuskaitse Selts.

Laar, M. 2015. *Pööre. Mälestusi I* [Turn. Memories I]. Tallinn: Read OÜ.

Laar, M., L. Vahtre, and H. Valk. 1989. *Kodu lugu II* [The Story of Home II]. Tallinn: Perioodika.

Laar, M., U. Ott, and S. Endre. 1996a. *Teine Eesti. Eesti iseseisvuse taassünd 1986–1992* [The Second Estonia. The Rebirth of Estonian Independence, 1986–1992]. Tallinn: SE&JS.

Laar, M., U. Ott, and S. Endre. 1996b. *Eeslava. Eesti iseseisvuse taassünd 1986–1991: intervjuud, dokumendid, kõned, artiklid* [A Proscenium. Rebirth of Estonian Independence, 1986–1992]. Tallinn: SE&JS.

Lagerspetz, M. 1995. "Reconstructing Historical Memory: The Change in Estonian Historical Discourse in the Late 1980s." In *Uurimusi keelest, kirjandusest ja kultuurist* [Studies into Language, Literature and Culture], edited by M. Lotman and T. Viik, 269–286. Tallinn: Eesti Humanitaarinstitut.

Lagerspetz, M. 1999. "Postsocialism as a Return: Notes on a Discursive Strategy." *East European Politics and Societies* 13 (2): 377–390.

Liikanen, I. 2001. "Environmental Campaigns and Political Mobilization in the Northwestern Border Areas of the Former Soviet Union." In *Cooperation, Environment, and Sustainability in Border Regions*, edited by Paul Ganster, 275–286. San Diego, CA: San Diego State University Press.

Lindmäe, H., and J. Sootak. 1989. "Eesti NSV Prokuratuuris on algatatud kriminaalasi." [Estonian SSR Prosecutor's Office Has Initiated a Criminal Case] *Edasi*, March 19.

Lõugas, V. 1991. "The Archaelogy of Terror. Archaelogical Excavations of Mass-murder Sites in the Soviet Union." *Fennoscandia archaeologica* 8: 80–84.

Must, A. 2010. "Estonia." In *Atlas of European Historiography: The Making of a Profession 1800–2005*, edited by I. Porciani and L. Raphael, 80–81. Basingstoke: Palgrave Macmillan.

Niitsoo, V. 1997. *Vastupanu 1955–1985* [Resistance, 1955–1985]. Tartu: Tartu Ülikooli Kirjastus.

Niitsoo, V. 2002. *Müürimurdjad: MRP-AEG ja ERSP lugu* [The Wall Breakers: The Story of MRP-AEG and ERSP]. Tallinn: Ortwil.

Onken, E.-C. 2003. *Demokratisierung der Geschichte in Lettland. Staatsbürgerliches Bewusstsein und Geschichtspolitik im Ersten Jahrzehnt der Unabhängigkeit* [Democratization of History in Latvia. Civic Consciousness and History Politics in the First Decade of Independence]. Hamburg: R. Krämer.

Onken, E.-C. 2007. "The Baltic states and Moscow's 9 May commemoration: Analysing memory politics in Europe." *Europe-Asia Studies* 59 (1): 23–46.

Õnnepalu, T. 2011. "1911". *Sirp*, August 5.

Pärnaste, E., ed. 1988. *Eesti Rahvusliku Sõltumatuse Partei loomine 1988* [The Creation of the Estonian National Independence Party in 1988]. Tallinn.

Pärnaste, E., ed. 2000. *Eesti Kongress: Siis ja praegu* [Estonian Congress: Then and Now]. Tallinn: Eesti Vabariigi Riigikantselei.

Pärnaste, E., and V. Niitsoo, eds. 1998. *Kogumik "MRP-AEG Infobülletään. 1987–1988"* [Collection of 'The Information Bulletin of MRP-AEG, 1987–1988']. Tallinn: SE & JS.

Pettai, E.-C., and V. Pettai. 2015. *Transitional and Retrospective Justice in the Baltic States*. Cambridge: Cambridge University Press.

Pettai, V. 2004. "Framing the Past as Future: The Power of Legal Restorationism in Estonia." PhD diss., Columbia University. https://www.academia.edu/3413597/PhD_Dissertation_Columbia_2004_Framing_the_Past_as_Future_The_Power_of_Legal_Restorationism_in_Estonia

Pettai, V. 2007. "The Construction of State Identity and its Legacies: Legal Restorationism in Estonia." *Ab Imperio* 3: 403–426.

Pettai, V. 2010. "State Identity in Estonia During the 1990s: Inheriting and Inventing." In *Inheriting the 1990s: The Baltic Countries*, edited by B. Metuzāle-Kangere, 153–174. Uppsala: Uppsala University.

"Pöördumine Eestimaa elanike poole." [Address to the Inhabitants of Estonia] 1989. *Rahva Hääl*, June 14.

Raun, T. U. 2003. "Nineteenth- and Early Twentieth-century Estonian Nationalism Revisited." *Nations and Nationalism* 9 (1): 129–147.

Ruutsoo, R. 1995. "The Perception of Historical Identity and the Restoration of Estonian National Independence." *Nationalities Papers* 23 (1): 167–179.

Schöttler, P., ed. 1997. *Geschichtsschreibung als Legitimationswissenschaft 1918–1945* [History Writing as Science of Legitimation, 1918–1945]. Frankfurt am Main: Suhrkamp.

Selg, P., and R. Ruutsoo. 2014. "Teleological Historical Narrative as a Strategy for Constructing Political Antagonism: The Example of the Narrative of Estonia's Regaining of Independence." *Semiotica* 202: 365–393.

Smith, D. J. 2011. "'You've got to know History!' Remembering and Forgetting the Past in the Present-Day Baltic." In *Forgotten Pages of the Baltic History: Diversity and Inclusion*, edited by M. Housden and D. J. Smith, 281–300. Amsterdam: Rodopi.

Strauss, M., ed. 2002. *Vabadussõja mälestusmärgid I* [The Memorials of the War of Independence I]. Keila: M. Strauss.

Tamm, J. 2012. "Kuidas asutati Eesti Muinsuskaitse Selts." [How the Estonian Heritage Society was Founded] In *Eesti Muinsuskaitse Selts 25* [The Estonian Heritage Society 25], edited by J. Tamm, 12–25. Tallinn: Eesti Muinsuskaitse Selts.

Tamm, M. 2008. "History as Cultural Memory: Mnemohistory and the Construction of the Estonian Nation." *Journal of Baltic Studies* 39 (4): 499–516.

Tamm, M. 2012. "Conflicting Communities of Memory: War Monuments and Monument Wars in Contemporary Estonia." In *Nation-Building in the Context of Post-Communist Transformation and Globalization*, edited by R. Vetik, 43–72. Frankfurt-am-Main: Peter Lang.

Tamm, M. 2013. "In Search of Lost Time: Memory Politics in Estonia, 1991–2011." *Nationalities Papers* 41 (4): 651–674.

Tannberg, T., ed. 2007. *Hirvepark 1987: 20 aastat kodanikualgatusest, mis muutis Eesti lähiajalugu* [Hirve Park 1987: Twenty Years from a Civic Initiative that Changed the Estonian Recent History]. Tallinn: Kultuuriselts Hirvepark.

Trencsényi, B., and P. Apor. 2007. "Fine-Tuning the Polyphonic Past: Hungarian Historical Writing in the 1990s." In *Narratives Unbound. Historical Studies in Post-Communist Eastern Europe*, edited by S. Antohi, B. Trencsényi, and P. Apor, 1–100. Budapest: CEU Press.

Vahtre, S. 1994. "Die Geschichtskunde und die Historiker in Estland in den kritischen Jahren 1918/1919 und 1987/1989." [Historical Science and the Historians in Estonia in the Critical Years 1918/1919 and 1987/1989] *Journal of Baltic Studies* 25 (2): 147–152.

Vahtre, S., ed. 2005. *Eesti ajalugu VI: Vabadussõjast taasiseseisvumiseni* [Estonian History VI: From the War of Independence to the Restoration of the Independence]. Tartu: Ilmamaa.

Veidemann, R. 1987. "Taasärkamisajal." [In the Era of Re-Awakening] *Edasi*, January 16.

Veskimäe, A., ed. 2008. *Rahvarinne 1988: Kakskümmend aastat hiljem* [Popular Front 1988: Twenty Years Later]. Tallinn: Tallinna Linnavalitsus.

Viidalepp, R. 1980. "Jakob Hurda üleskutse 'Paar palvid.'" [Jakob Hurt's Call 'Two Requests'] *Keel ja Kirjandus* 5: 282–290.

Wulf, M. 2010. "Politics of History in Estonia: Changing Memory Regimes 1987–2009." In *History of Communism in Europe*. Vol. 1: "Politics of Memory in Post-Communist Europe." edited by M. Neamtu, 245–267. Bucharest: Zeta Books.

Wulf, M., and P. Grönholm. 2010. "Generating Meaning Across Generations: The Role of Historians in the Codification of History in Soviet and Post-Soviet Estonia." *Journal of Baltic Studies* 41 (3): 351–382.

The 'age of commemoration' as a narrative construct: a critique of the discourse on the contemporary crisis of memory in France

Kenan Van De Mieroop

History Department, Ghent University, Ghent, Belgium

ABSTRACT

Pierre Nora's account of the 'age of commemoration' has been extremely influential in shaping the way that memory is understood in France as well as in other countries. But what those who adopt Nora's historical account of the rise of memory often overlook, is that the story of the 'age of commemoration' is a narrative construct. This article argues that Nora's historical explanation of the rise of memory constitutes memory as an historical object, and explains it through emplotment. Nora has constructed a story of crisis in which individual memories stand as 'symptoms' of, and reactions to, the 'acceleration of history'. The significance of memory is supposed to lie in what it tells us about the times in which 'we' live. Memory is thus construed as a panicked reaction to historical changes, and the manifestation of an existential crisis in France. Nora's account of memory is widely referred to in academic as well as public discussions on the memories of minority groups in France. These memory movements are viewed in the historical context of the 'age of commemoration'. But this historicization functions to circumscribe their meaning: emplotted into the story of the 'age of commemoration' minority memories are rendered as symptoms of a macrocosmic malaise. The content of their discourse is thereby marginalized, ignored or deemed insignificant.

> The influence of memory is so strong today that the commemorative bulimia of this epoch has absorbed even the attempt to master the phenomenon. (Nora 1997, 4687)

Have the tumultuous and dramatic changes that occurred during the twentieth century provoked a shift away from historical discourse? This is certainly a common claim in recent scholarship. For some, this shift constitutes nothing less than a serious challenge to what Ricoeur (2009, 351) has called history's 'hegemony in the space of retrospection.' Or as Assman (2010, 39) has put it: 'The historian has lost his monopoly over defining and presenting the past. What is called the "memory boom" is the immediate effect of the loss of the historian's singular unrivalled authority.' The claim that history is being challenged seems to be a popular idea, even if scholars are divided on the question of whether this turn away from history is good news or bad and whether the demise of history is inevitable or if it is in need of rehabilitation or, rather, reinvention.

It is ironic that this account of the rise of memory and decline of history is itself an historical one. A series of historical events and developments are said to have provoked the growth in memory. Scholarly studies of memory have often sought to explain recent mnemonic phenomena within the historical context of the late twentieth century. In a reference to Nietzsche's critique of history, Andreas Huyssen has, for example, remarked that 'our age' is characterized by a 'hypertrophy of memory' and a 'crisis of history.' For Huyssen, the rise of memory needs to be explained 'historically,' as a response to the traumas of the twentieth century, the Holocaust, Stalinism, decolonization, and so on, and the rapid pace of change in society in general (Huyssen 2003, 11). The combined effect of these being that 'at the end of the millennium the coordinates of space and time structuring our lives are increasingly subjected to new kinds of pressures.' In order to gain 'continuity' in this troubling time, many have turned to memory. Thus, for Huyssen, memory's rise is a response to historical conditions:

> My hypothesis is that, in this prominence of academic mnemo-history as well, memory and musealization together are called upon to provide a bulwark against obsolescence and disappearance to counter our deep anxiety about the speed of change and the ever-shrinking horizons of time and space. (Huyssen 2003, 23)

Variations of this account are found in numerous works on memory studies, but also in history and political science (Garapon 2008; Klein 2000; Matsuda 1996; Olick, Vinitzky-Seroussi, and Levy 2011, 3; Torpey 2006).

Nowhere are such arguments about the rise of memory and the concomitant decline of history as widespread as in France, however, where memory is currently the subject of much suspicion. In scholarship and popular discourse it has become commonplace to say that memory culture has taken on 'excessive' proportions. This excess is almost always understood in historical terms, as a characteristic of the 'age' in which 'we' are said to be living. Pierre Nora has dubbed the current epoch the 'age of commemoration,' and his periodization of the present has proven popular, both inside and outside academia. For Nora, and for many influenced by his writing, memory is the 'symptom' of the tumultuous age in which 'we' are living: it is a reaction to a late-twentieth-century temporal 'acceleration' (Nora 1984). France, according to Nora, is the first country to have 'suffered' what has now become a 'global phenomenon':

the emergence of a 'memory wave' that is sweeping up the entire epoch in its powerful currents (Nora 2011a, 13).

Nora's account of memory has been extremely influential. Michael Rothberg has claimed that it would be 'impossible to overstate the influence' of Nora's work, both in the French context and beyond. Rothberg explains that 'although emerging from a commitment to the exceptionality of France's relation to its national past, the approach pioneered in [the three volumes of] *Les lieux de mémoire* has proven highly exportable as a model for the consideration of diverse memory cultures' (2010, 3). The story of the 'memory boom' or the 'age of commemoration' has certainly been widely adopted. It has become an influential grand narrative. But it has rarely been subjected to the same scrutiny as have other grand narratives. This represents yet another irony because 'incredulity to meta-narratives narratives' (Lyotard 1979, 7) is itself often cited as one of the main historical events that has triggered the turn to memory in the first place – a postmodern loss of faith in *grands récits* has apparently driven us to memory as *petits récits*.

My intention in this article, therefore, is to use a narratological approach to analyze the historical narrative of the late-twentieth-century rise of memory and, taking inspiration from Hayden White, to show the extent to which this discourse on memory has constituted the very object that it 'pretends only to describe realistically and analyze objectively' (White 1978, 2). Such a critique is warranted because, as I intend to argue, the 'age of commemoration' is, manifestly, a narrative construct: it is a story about the existential crisis of a central subject, namely the French nation. In this representation, a diversity of phenomena are figured as 'memory' and, through the metaphor of the 'symptom', are made to stand as visible evidence of the 'age of commemoration'. Memory is given a place in this account as, at once, the cause, the effect and the manifestation of a macrocosmic malaise.

I will argue that this historical account of memory has facilitated a particular interpretation of the relationship between memory, history and French society. After reviewing some of the most common criticisms of memory in France, I claim that 'memory' and 'history' have been loaded with supplementary socio-political meanings. Through a series of dubious associations history is rendered equivalent with the French Republic while memory becomes synonymous with what the French call 'communities'. In part as a consequence of this alignment, both the virtues of history and the French Republic, and the vices of memory and *communautarisme*, are greatly exaggerated. Memory/*communautarisme* is characterized as divisive, identity-obsessed and irrational, while history/the French Republic is viewed as universal, inclusive and rational. The rise of memory is then described as an 'obsession', a 'mania' or a 'pathology' that has overcome the body that is France. But, I argue, many of these characterizations of memory depend on what we could call – again echoing White – a particular 'historical encodation' of observable phenomena.

When memory is contextualized in the 'age of commemoration', it is explained by emplotment.

A close reading of the account of the 'age of commemoration' demonstrates that this *historical* narrative exhibits many of the same characteristics for which memory is criticized. The dichotomy that has been created between memory and history collapses in on itself. The historical account is highly concerned with French identity. It is Franco-centric even though it presents itself as a universally relevant periodization, and it is nostalgic in its yearning for a return to an older France. Moreover, this narrative's claim to universality and its much-vaunted inclusiveness are also problematic because, while it is true that this historical narrative does include the discourse of memory groups, this inclusion functions to circumscribe their meaning: no matter what the content of the discourse of those groups deemed to engage in memory may be, they are said to signify a crisis of French identity. To view mnemonic phenomena in the context of the 'age of commemoration' is to submit said phenomena to a specific emplotment of a story about a national existential crisis.

1. The age of commemoration as a narrative construct

The story of the 'age of commemoration' can be briefly summarized: several 'shocking' events that occurred in post-Second World War Europe and in particular in France, combined with technological, economic and social changes to produce a rapid 'acceleration of history'. This acceleration of history in turn effected a generalized transformation in the consciousness of people, the result of which is the growth in memory and commemoration (Nora 1997, 4687, 2002, 27). Pierre Nora claims that the acceleration of history has created a feeling of 'uprootedness' (*déracinement*) as people in society have apparently lost all their traditional points of reference. In response to this feeling, people began to turn to memory in order to cling on to the past and to try to maintain a sense of stability and continuity in the midst of the upheaval. Nora describes memory as a therapy of sorts: it gives us stability and security by reinforcing group identity and constructing a line of continuity with the past. 'In the enormous slippage in which France is losing its footing today, the turn to memory reestablishes continuity' (Nora 1997, 4715).

Pierre Nora's account of memory is plainly a narrative representation that has been created through the emplotment of very specific events that occurred in France. Nora constructs the story of the 'age of commemoration' using a range of literary devices and his story about the rise of memory has a clear plot structure as well as a central subject that suffers a transformation in this plot. In what follows, I will point out some of the devices that Nora employs to figure forth a historical moment caught up in a crisis.

Nora first described this temporal acceleration in the introduction to the first volume of the *Lieux de Mémoire* trilogy and has continued to discuss it in his later writings. This trilogy is often referred to as one of the first important works on memory and is credited with being at the origin of the subsequent scholarly fascination with memory.[1] If we can indeed locate the origin of memory studies in the work of Nora, then it is interesting to observe that from the very first moment that memory was constituted as an object of academic inquiry it was also historicized: Nora's contributions to these volumes are replete with historical contextualizations of memory. It is significant that in the first paragraph of the first page of Volume One, Nora begins his account of memory by identifying the historical conditions that produced it, namely 'the acceleration of history', a phrase that Nora says is 'more than a metaphor' – it is a description of the really existing 'increasingly rapid slippage of the present into a historical past that is gone for good, a general perception that anything and everything may disappear …' (Nora 1989, 7). The paragraph ends with Nora's often cited and enigmatic phrase 'we speak so much of memory because there is so little of it left' (7).

Although Nora has often claimed that the rise of memory is a global phenomenon, his account of the 'age of commemoration' is as story that has a clearly identifiable central subject: France. It is France that suffers a change in state in this narrative. The series of 'shocks' that Nora claims provoked this temporal acceleration, which in turn set the stage for the sweeping of the 'wave of memory' across the world, are key events in the history of the French nation. For Nora, the origin of this new era can be traced to a precise moment in recent French history: the decade between 1970 and 1980, which was the decade that witnessed 'the most important national transformation since the revolutionary decade of 1789' (2011a, 13). What occurred during this pivotal decade was nothing less than the 'passage from one system of *identity* to another' (my emphasis). Certain political, economic and cultural developments combined to create this transformation. On the economic front in the 1970s, France was subjected to the global oil shock and the rapid rise of prices. Simultaneously, after two decades of growth, the economy began to slow. Meanwhile, by 1975, the French agricultural population had declined to 10% of what it had been before the war (2011a, 14). On the political front, Nora argues that the presidency of Valéry Giscard-d'Estaing marked a rupture with the Gaullist tradition and the embrace of a technocratic politics (15–16). The ideological struggles between Gaullism and Communism that had marked the previous period would decline over this decade. For Nora the publication of the French edition of Aleksandr Solzhenitsyn's *Gulag Archipelago* can be seen as symbolically marking the decline of communist ideology in France, a 'demarxisation' of the intelligentsia and even the abandonment of the goal of revolution (17). In his view, these 'civilizational' events combined with the rapid pace of technological change, with the decline of agricultural 'peasant' society and with globalization, to produce the 'acceleration of history' (Nora 1997, 4699–4715, 2011a, 14).

Thus the memory phenomenon is linked to a crisis of identity, and specifically, a crisis of French identity. The acceleration of history provoked an existential crisis in France. As Nora says quite explicitly 'This problematic rested on an analysis of the era: the advent of a historical sentiment of the present, the *painful passage from one model of the nation to another*, the metamorphosis of a history henceforth lived as memory' (2011a, 7–8, my emphasis). It is important to note, as I have done in this last passage, that this *historical* account is laden with affective language and that it is deeply interested and implicated in French identity. Noting this is important because, as I will argue later, it is inconsistent with views expressed by Nora and other French scholars concerning the distinction between memory and history. Identity and affect are most often associated with the former, while the latter is held to be universal and rational.

But Nora has recently revealed that it was not only French identity that was at stake in his account, but also his own identity as a Frenchman. In *Présent, nation, mémoire,* which was published decades after the first volume of *Les Lieux de Mémoire* as a sort of retrospective introduction, Nora explains that certain life experiences led him to his 'analysis of the epoch', to the conclusion that the current age is one of memory:

> As a citizen, each one of these national twists and turns confronted me, brutally and with permanence, like all others in my generation, with a certain 'idea of France', to the enigma of French identity. When I was not even 10 years old, there was the war and the stupefying spectacle of national meltdown, the humiliation of the foreign occupation. And since I was Jewish: [I experienced] exclusion, being hunted, the discovery of unexpected solidarities and betrayals, and the experience of seeking refuge with the 'maquis du Vercors'. An adventure inscribed in the flesh of memory that sufficed to make you different from all the other young French people of your age. Afterwards, there was the post-war period, the agonizing struggle between Gaullism and communism, the two marching wings that came out of the Resistance. It is, without a doubt, difficult for the young French of today to understand how both of these could be seductive and repulsive to a young intellectual in the 1950s and how each had a profound national legitimacy. Two plausible versions, both of which were entitled to incarnate France, the true France … We should consider that two generations of French were dramatically confronted with the national and patriotic ideal …. (2011a, 8–9)

The story of Nora's personal anxiety as a historian, faced with challenges to the nation, is interwoven into the story of the prologue to the memory wave – and one cannot tell them apart. But Nora does not expect us to read his account as a transference of a personal conundrum onto an entire generation of imagined contemporaries. Rather, his own experience is supposed to be a barometer for the collective experience of French society. Nora presents himself as a perspicacious observer of the 'times' who was able to discern the emerging crisis.

The 'age of commemoration' is fundamentally a story about a crisis, and it is the plot that conveys this sense of crisis. The emplotment of select events in French history in Nora's work takes the form of an incomplete story: the author offers an exposition and rising action, but he leaves the closing of the story in suspense. It is this incomplete plot, and the rising intensity towards an as-yet-unknown climax that conveys the sense of an 'explosion' of memory. The plot is propelled forward by the 'shocks' outlined above. With each passing decade the urgency of the 'memory boom' grows, new commemorations emerge, and the apex of the process seems more elusive. Nora is unable to predict where the 'avalanche' of memory will end. France, that 'nous' which is the main protagonist of the tale, cries out for a hero in increasing exasperation. The pressing question is whether France's saviour will take the form of a rejuvenated history or something else.

Meanwhile, in the years following the publication of *Les Lieux,* numerous new instances of 'memory' were identified by Nora – and described as yet another indication of the intensity of the temporal acceleration. In Nora's writing, the relationship between commemoration and temporal acceleration is circular since commemoration appears first as a result of the acceleration and later as a *symptom* through which that acceleration can be detected. Memory is the 'symptom' of the underlying malady that is imperceptible:

> All countries were brought, by the upheavals of the last century, to have an account to settle with their past. None is as uncomfortable as ours with its history, which is at once one of the most obvious *symptoms* and one of the most profound causes of the French malaise. No one has interiorized the memorial shock that has hit the entire world for the last thirty years more than the French who have had their historical *identity* shaken. (Nora 2006, 44)

Of course we cannot 'see' the 'age of commemoration', washing over us, we can only be told about it by Nora the author/narrator.[2] Only after knowing this story can we take commemorations as 'symptoms' of a macrocosmic malaise.

In short, for Nora, memory is to be understood historically, as a result of historical forces and as an answer to them. Memory is interesting, in his view, because of what it indicates about the time in which 'we' are living. What it reveals concerns 'our age', the presence of a crisis and the 'acceleration of history'. Discrete memories are said to be like 'symptoms' because they indicate the presence of an affliction.

2. 'Presentism' and the 'crisis' of history

Pierre Nora presents his account of the 'age of commemoration' as though it were a description of an objective, collective experience; a shared historical moment in which 'we' are all living. But this historical moment is actually a function of the narration of a selection of events, characters, and so on. Nora's periodization of memory, his historical account of the dawning of the 'age of commemoration', is what Frank Ankersmit would call a *narrative substance*.[3] The 'age of commemoration' names a narrative representation of a diversity of phenomena. It is a 'verbal fiction', as Hayden White has said of historical narratives (1978, 82).

Nevertheless, many have taken up Nora's account of the rise of memory in 'our age' as a periodization, and scholars have sought to explain discrete instances of 'memory' by placing them in the context of the 'memory wave'. Because it is understood as a periodization, the 'age of commemoration', is deemed to concern everything within a given chronological span, and this partly explains why, in France, the designation of a phenomenon as mnemonic or memorial has almost automatically come to imply historicizing it – that is to say, viewing it against the background of the 'age' that produced it.

But those who use Nora's periodization often seem to forget that the 'age of commemoration' is not an objective description of the signs of the times. Of course, the fact that the 'age of commemoration' is a narrative representation is not problematic in and of itself. But it should be noted that to insist on viewing memory in this particular frame, is really to insist on explaining memory by emplotment – to borrow a phrase form Hayden White. To view a given phenomenon in the historical context of the 'age of commemoration' is to emplot it within a story of the crisis of French identity. Problems arise when it is forgotten that because the 'age of commemoration' is a narrative entity, it ascribes a particular narrative meaning to what it emplots. A plot, as White and other narrative theorists of history explain, is not a neutral container: to emplot something in the narrative of the 'age of commemoration' is to give it a place in a syntagmatic arrangement in the story of a late twentieth-century existential crisis and thus to relate it to that crisis. It is therefore not surprising that when phenomena are viewed within the context of the 'age of commemoration', they are felt to indicate the presence of a crisis. Because it has become so common in France to see the issue of memory though this historical frame, each new mnemonic phenomenon is perceived as yet another example of the mounting 'memory wave', and thus as yet another indication of the crisis of identity that threatens France and even history itself.

Many scholars have adopted Nora's account of the rise of memory in 'our age'. For example, his history of memory lies at the heart of François Hartog's famous theory of 'presentism'. First published in 2003, Hartog's account often reads as a sweeping grand narrative in which a series of different regimes of historicity are delineated. A later edition of his book adds clarification and nuance to his project and sharpens his notions of 'regime of historicity' and 'presentism'.[4] 'Regimes of historicity' are not to be understood as historical epochs, but as akin to Weberian 'ideal types', tools that can help us to 'elucidate' the experiences of time in a given era and place (2012, 15). Hartog claims that his term 'regime of historicity' is only offering a method to understand, and to name, the way that the relationship between, past present and future has been 'articulated' in various times and places. Unlike Nora, Hartog readily admits that his regimes of historicity are 'constructed by the historian' and are not a 'given reality' (2012, 15). But Hartog's careful qualification of his own categories of analysis contrasts with his relatively uncritical adoption of Nora's historical account of memory. Moreover, his category of presentism has certainly been received as a description of the contemporary *Zeitgeist*.

Hartog brings his tools to an analysis of 'our contemporary age' and finds that 'we' are currently undergoing a 'crisis of time.' Again, memory appears as the harbinger of this crisis. This is not an accident: the contemporary age is already prefigured in Hartog's account as the 'age of commemoration'. Hartog's account of the current 'crisis of time' can be read as a reiteration of Nora's work. Hartog refers to Nora on numerous occasions throughout his books, even describing Nora's writing – and the 'acceleration of history' he 'diagnosed' (Hartog 2012, 170, 2013, 42) – as evidence of 'fault lines' in time (Hartog 2012, 21). Hartog also wholeheartedly adopts Nora's view that there has been an 'acceleration' of time in the last decades: whereas Nora's account of the age of memory begins with a series of 'shocks', Hartog speaks of *brèches*, or breaches, between the space of experience and the horizon of expectation, two categories that Hartog borrows from Reinhart Koselleck and which he believes can be used to detect changes in the ways in which humans experience time or, in his vocabulary, in 'regimes of historicity' (2012, 21). Hartog claims that these breaches point to a new regime of historicity that he calls presentism: and this presentism is defined by the exact same characteristics as Nora's 'age of commemoration', namely by the generalized feeling of uprootedness that goes along with this temporal acceleration, the decline of the idea of the future as a source of legitimacy, the abandonment of utopian ideologies, and, finally, a loss of faith in history itself. In Hartog's account, memory appears as the symptom through which the 'crisis of time' can be detected. In his own words, memory is 'at once an expression and a response to this rise of the present' (2013, 40).

In both Hartog's and Nora's accounts of memory therefore, commemorations are understood to be epiphenomenal of a greater historical shift. A relationship is constructed between the individual phenomenon labelled as 'memory' and the broader 'age' for which it stands. In the work of Nora and Hartog this is often achieved by employing the metaphor of the 'symptom': commemorations are said to be 'symptoms' which signify a specific relationship to time. This is not a personal relationship to time, but a generalized one shared by contemporaries; it is 'our present' that is at stake (Hartog 2012, 270–271).

In Hartog's account, the relationship between the symptom and presentism is also circular. Hartog begins by looking for symptoms of a crisis of time, and then concludes that the symptoms he has found indicate the presence of presentism, which is of course simply his name for the contemporary crisis of time. This is clearly visible at the beginning of *Régimes d'historicité*, where Hartog states that his method consists of looking at certain phenomena in the world around him and asking what regime of historicity is behind them:

> I approached these phenomena laterally, asking myself what temporali-
> ties ... arrange them. By which order of time are they supported? Which order

do they convey or are they symptoms of? Of what order, of what crisis of time are they indications? (2013, 18).

Since his analysis is intended to reveal a collective experience of time, shared by contemporaries, the unfolding of Hartog's story of the crisis of time is viewed from the perspective of prominent Frenchmen who were shrewd enough to have observed the emergence of a new era. Perceiving the plot through the eyes of a character lends the impression that a collectivity of French people have observed the arrival of the 'crisis of time', and that it is the generalized experience of a generation. Thus Nora appears in Hartog's account, as a prophet, able to stand above the melee and perceive the emergence of the presentist regime by 'registering' the acceleration of time – again, like a 'seismograph'.[5] In his later book *Croire en l'Histoire*, Hartog speaks through Nora:

> At the same moment, Pierre Nora diagnosed that the 'present has become the category of our self-comprehension.' The historian 'must explain the present to the present.' He who positions himself 'between the blind question and the enlightened response, between public pressure and the solitary patience of the *laboratory*, between those who feel and those who know.' That was indeed the approach of the author of *Les Lieux de Mémoire*. (2013, 42, my emphasis)

Though the masses of French may 'feel' the present time, as a professional historian Nora can 'know' it. The trick is, of course, to identify the symptoms, which Nora could do only after retreating to the 'laboratory'. Nora's work is presented as a scientific process: he read the signs of the times that were all around and then explained them to us.

What the average French man or woman might see as simple commemoration, is better understood as a visible manifestation of temporal acceleration, according to Nora and Hartog. By figuring memory as a symptom, these scholars are able to assert that the significance of memory lies in what it indicates about the current time. In the work of both authors, memory is evidence of the presence of a crisis: a crisis of history and time in the case of Hartog, and a crisis of history and of French identity in the case of Nora.

3. The memory malady

It appears that Pierre Nora's diagnosis of the signs of the times has been widely heeded: It is remarkable to note how common it has become to speak of memory using the language of pathology: Henry Rousso famously proclaimed that France was suffering from the Vichy 'syndrome' (Rousso 1994, 2007, 3), but more recently Ferenczi (2002) has asked *La France est-elle malade de sa mémoire?* – 'is France sick from its memory?' Dosse (2010) has said that France is suffering from a *commémorite aiguë* or an 'acute commemoritis'. Joel Candau labels the same phenomenon *mnémotropisme* (1998, 2). The emergence of commemoration onto the scene is described in Nora's earlier work as though it were a sort of 'obsession' (1997, 4687). The figural and metaphorical language of the 'explosion' or the 'wave' of memory construes a collectivity falling victim to a mnemonic pathology. At one point Nora goes as far as referring to the 'bulimia' of commemoration (4687).

As this striking language indicates, the rise of memory in France has been the source of much disquiet for many intellectuals. More than 10 years ago, Sarah Gensburger and Marie-Claire Lavabre remarked that 'the denunciation of the notion of the "duty of memory" has little by little become a veritable paradigm of reflection on memory' in France (2005, 1). Warnings about the dangers posed by memory gained momentum in the 1990s when the issue of France's Vichy period was brought to the forefront of public attention during the trials of Klaus Barbie, Paul Touvier, and Maurice Papon, and during the concomitant reflection on French collaboration during the war. At this time, many began to criticize the popular phrase 'devoir de mémoire' or duty of memory, a neologism used in public discourse to designate the responsibility of the French state to recognize and commemorate its own misdeeds. The perception that memory had become a pressing political issue at the forefront of media attention made many scholars feel uneasy about what they perceived as a manipulation of the past for political ends. Thus, in the 1990s, Tzvetan Todorov and others began to write about the 'abuse of memory' (Todorov 2008). In *Memory, History Forgetting*, Paul Ricoeur felt the need to address these debates and – citing the work of Todorov, Henry Rousso and Pierre Nora – shared many of their reservations about the age of memory. Ricoeur argued, with characteristic caution, that when the duty of memory becomes an 'obsession' it is in danger of becoming an 'abuse' of memory, a 'manipulated memory' (2009, 89–91).

Criticisms of the contemporary memory culture grew even more pronounced in the first decade of the twenty-first century and became especially heated after 2005.[6] That year and the years following were marked by much furore around a number of issues, including the so-called *lois mémoirelles* or memory laws, the 50th anniversary of the Algerian war, the question of slavery in the French colonies and the establishment of a museum of immigration.[7] These are but a few of the phenomena that are taken as examples of a memory conflict in France – or even of 'memory wars', as one edited volume on the topic put it – and have led many to condemn the rise of memory (Blanchard and Veyrat-Masson 2008). In 2005, René Rémond and other historians, including Nora, formed a group to defend history against what they saw as an increasingly threatening memory culture in France. The group *Liberté Pour l'Histoire*, or Freedom for History (LPH), was formed after several historians wrote an appeal criticizing a series of laws – which they described as 'memory laws' – because of the threat they ostensibly posed to historians. In their appeal, they proclaim that 'history is not memory', extol the virtues of the former, and demand the repeal of the 'memory laws' (L'appel du 12 décembre 2005). Since then, they have continued to condemn the rise of what they see as 'tyrannical memory' (Nora, 2005).[8] Nora and other influential historians of the LPH have written numerous opinion pieces in the French newspapers on this issue and have also voiced their concerns about memory on the radio, TV, the Internet and in academic publications. Amongst them was the historian and theorist of history, François Dosse who began a polemical opinion piece in the news paper *Le Monde* by stating 'Yes, we are decidedly in the middle of what Pierre Nora has called "the age of commemoration"' (2010). Dosse took aim at what he perceived as a general culture of memory:

> Amongst the *symptoms* of our *pathologies*, we can point to the nasty habit of litigiousness that has pushed political powers to legislate memorial matters. We have witnessed an *acceleration* of this genre [of laws] since 2000. (Dosse 2010, my emphasis)

The critics mentioned above take issue with the memory culture of 'our time' more than with memory itself. Although it is commonly stated that memory has existed in all times and places, it is also pointed out that memory has only recently become so ubiquitous as to justify being characterized as an 'explosion' or an 'obsession'. In the last volume of his *Lieux de Mémoire* trilogy, Nora claimed that we have left behind the historical 'moment' of 'restrained memory' and that 'our age' is one caught up in an 'avalanche' of 'generalized memory' (1997, 4715). In French discussions of memory, memory is almost always historicized. The rise of memory is said to be the result of certain historical developments such as the collapse of future oriented ideologies and the traumatic events of the twentieth-century.

These academic critiques of memory have been very influential. Important voices in French society have formulated similar condemnations of the rise of memory culture in France. For example, the essayist Pascal Bruckner takes inspiration from Nora in his book *Tyranny of Repentance*, and describes the contemporary Western obsession with the duty of memory as a form of Nietzschean *ressentiment* (2006, 182).[9] But by far the most prominent critic of 'repentance' is, without a doubt, former president Nicolas Sarkozy. During the last months of his 2006 electoral campaign, he spoke out several times against what he saw as the growing culture of repentance: he continued to condemn it during his presidency using astonishingly strong language and claiming to 'hate' the culture of repentance and the 'shame' that it brought with it. Sarkozy insisted that it was wrong to force children to correct the 'supposed' faults of their parents (Sarkozy 2006). For Sarkozy the culture of memory and 'repentance' is nothing less than a *falsification of the history of France* (Sarkozy 2006 my emphasis).

In part, as a response to widespread claims that there is too much memory in France, the government set up a special commission – the so-called Accoyer commission – to study the 'memory laws' and rise of state-sanctioned commemorations in the country. In the context of this commission, historian André Kaspi produced a report that warned of the dangers of the current memorial culture, stating that 'it is not healthy that the number of commemorations has doubled' (*Rapport de la Commission de Réflexion sur la Modernisation des Commémorations Publiques* 2008).

A number of political concerns underpin many of these condemnations of memory. Foremost amongst those concerns is the controversial issue of assimilation and *communautarisme*. Memory and *communautarisme* are often spoken of in the same breath. The Kaspi report, for example, warned of 'memorial *communautarisme*' (26). According to some, the competition among memories is really another manifestation of a divisive form of identity politics. Many are convinced that the French Republican model – which emphasizes a universal equality of citizenship without regard to gender, race or ethnicity – will be endangered if different groups are allowed to institutionalize their 'communities'. In other words, the multicultural model, associated by some with the United States and Great Britain, is to be avoided because it leads to exclusion, the crystallization of difference, and hence to the undermining of national cohesion as well as a growth of racism. State-led commemorations of the Holocaust, the slave trade, the Armenian genocide, and so on, are seen as attempts to cater to Jewish, Antillean and Armenian communities respectively. This is criticized as a desperate attempt to gain votes, often at the cost of sacrificing Republican values. Sarkozy, for example, says that the competition of memory is a threat to national unity:

> I hate this repentance that wants to prohibit us from being proud to be French, and which is the open door to a competition of memories that pits the French against one another based on their origins. It is an obstacle to integration because one rarely wants to integrate with something that one has learned to hate. (2006)

Of course Sarkozy's point about integration is a reference to immigration. Sarkozy links memory to French (immigrant) communities, and, as we will see, history is reserved for the nation.

The concepts of 'history' and 'memory' have taken on a supplementary socio-political meaning: memory is associated with community identities, and hence is deemed prone to particularism and division, while history is associated with the French Republic, inclusion and universalism. Memory and *communautarisme* and history and the Republic represent opposing pairs of analogical concepts in this discourse. This distinction between memory and history directly parallels a distinction that is often made between *communautarisme* and the Republic. Communities are said to be divisive while the Republic is universal and inclusive.[10] For Nora the same can be said of memory and history:

> memory arises from the group and brings the group together: which is to say that there are as many memories are there are groups; that [memory] is by nature, multiple, divisible, collective, plural and individualized. History on the contrary, belongs to everyone and no one, and this is what gives [history] its universal character. (Nora 1984, xix–xx)

The distinction between memory and history remains a question that is unresolved in scholarship.[11] But in France there is more of a consensus on the issue of the boundaries between the two than in other countries. The French anthropologist Joel Candau sums up the 'radical' difference between memory and history as it is understood in much French scholarship:[12] Memory, he claims, serves group identity, but the historian does not write *une histoire sur mesure*, as Henry Rousso would say. For Candau both are representations of the past, but only history has the objective of 'exactitude' in representation – memory, meanwhile, is interested in the probable. History aims at 'clarifying' the past and is concerned with putting things 'in order', while memory is characterized by 'disorder' and 'passion', 'emotion' and 'affect'. History tries to put the past at a distance while memory tries to 'fuse' with it (1998, 127–128).

The linking of memory to 'identity', 'emotion' and 'affect' in the writings of many French scholars renders it irrational and prone to error. History, on the other hand, is considered to be scientific, rational and epistemologically superior, something that allows it to, in the words of Paul Ricoeur, 'exercise its corrective function with regard to memory' (2009, 269).

It is easy to see what these claims about the epistemological hierarchy between history and memory imply for the political debate about the respective merits of French Republican universalism and *communautarisme*: Republican universalism is credited not only with being politically more efficient than *communautarisme*, it is also epistemologically superior to it. The former is thought of as a calculated and rational polity while the latter is an emotional form of pseudo-politics and a pernicious form of retrospection. Olivier Lalieu, who has studied the emergence of the key phrase 'duty of memory' in France, claims that one of the main critiques of memory has sought to describe it as a '"new civic religion" that privileges emotion without any content, and which is politically inefficient' (2001, 83). History and French Republicanism, meanwhile, are presented in this same discourse as being efficient and rational.

Just as immigrants are encouraged to integrate into the French Republic, many believe that memories should be integrated into French history. Thus, for example, Pierre Nora reacted to the publication of a historical study of French colonialism by stating that the interest in colonialism is just the latest example of the memorial wave that is sweeping France: 'In a sense, the colonial question is nothing but the latest arrival of the memorial explosions'. He then went on to point out the problem posed by colonial memory:

> In reality the question goes much further, opposing those who think that the colonial part of our history only slightly affected the permanent features of our national identity and those who think it necessary to rethink the entirety of that national identity in post-colonial terms because national identity is not far from revealing its truth in the colonial oppression and in its denial. Thus it is no longer about finding a place for colonialism in the great record of national history but of rewriting this history against the dark light of colonization. (Nora 2011b)

The issue of national identity is thus of central importance to Nora, who claims that while it is acceptable for colonial memory to be integrated into French history, we must not rewrite French history altogether around the issue of colonialism. For Nora, history is threatened when memorial groups try to limit what can be said about the past and impose their own 'particularistic' views on the historians, whose job should be to write a universal and inclusive history that takes into account different views. The excess of memory is also said to pose a danger to the past itself, as well as to history, which remains, according to many, the best tool available for accessing the past. Memory is said to look to the past in the service of present interests, and this is one of the reasons that it remains epistemologically suspect in comparison to history. The problem is that when one looks at the past with a present interest in mind – that is, according to this view, in a memorial rather than historical mode – one is prone to errors of representation, to manipulation of the historical record, to mendacity, and most of all, to anachronism.[13] Nora thus claims to defend history against memory. But because *communautarisme* and memory are so linked, his criticisms could just as easily be understood as a defence of French Republicanism and an attack on *communautarisme*.

This dubious association of memory with communities and history with France can in part be explained by the fact that memory is so often viewed against the background of the 'age of commemoration'. Memory is explained as a sort of panic reaction to historical forces. The rise of *communautariste* memory politics is said to be a direct result of the diminishing influence of future-oriented utopian and inclusive ideologies like French Republicanism and communism, or indeed the decline of grand historical narratives. In this way memory and *communautarisme* are set up in opposition to history and the French Republic. The decline of forward-thinking and inclusive projects apparently left no other options available except to embrace their opposite: backward looking exclusionary politics. As the French historian, and specialist on the Algerian war, Benjamin Stora, put it:

> This global memorial process must be related to the crisis of transnational and international ideologies. The growing memorial overflow thus appears as a *symptom*: confronted with a breakdown of political projects, one turns to the past of one's own group. (2008, 12, my emphasis)

Scholars outside of France have made similar claims about the rise of memory politics, its links to identity, and the abandonment of utopian politics: John Torpey, for example, described the same phenomenon with the phrase 'when the future collapses, the past rushes in' (2006, 24). The Belgian historian Pieter Lagrou, offers a similar assessment of the significance of memorial politics. Lagrou claims that the memorial groups that have sprung up around the holocaust, the Armenian genocide and slavery 'exploit' their memories in order to advance their own identity politics. He argues that this form of politics is the opposite of inclusive politics that aim to achieve an open society and he criticizes them as 'retrospective' without any vision for the future (2013, 112). A recent *Collective Memory Reader* underlined just how common this explanation of the rise of memory has become:

> The story goes something like this: following the decline of postwar modernist narratives of progressive improvement … nation-states turned to the past as a basis for shoring up their legitimacy. The decline of utopian visions supposedly redirected our gaze to collective pasts, which served as a repository of inspiration for repressed identities and unfulfilled claims. Without unifying collective aspirations, identity politics proliferated. (Olick, Vinitzky-Seroussi, and Levy 2011, 3)

Because memory has been construed as a reaction to, or side-effect of, massive historical changes, the diversity of phenomena labelled as 'memory' in this discourse are portrayed not as calculated and rational undertakings but as a cynical and reactive fad. Moreover, attention is drawn from the individual 'memory' in question to the broader crisis that lurks beneath it and of which it is supposed to be a 'symptom'.

4. Conclusion

Rothberg's claim, cited at the beginning of this article, is correct: Nora's account of memory has been widely taken up and subscribed to. The 'age of commemoration' has proven an especially popular way to contextualize, and hence to explain, phenomena labelled as memory. Perhaps more than any other discussion of memory, Nora's 'age of commemoration' has shaped the way in which the significance of memory in contemporary societies is viewed.

Nora's historical explanation of the rise of memory constitutes memory as an historical object, and explains it through emplotment. Nora has constructed a story of crisis in which individual memories stand as symptoms of, and reactions to, the 'acceleration of history'. The significance of memory is supposed to lie in what it tells us about the times in which 'we' live. It construes memory as a panicked reaction to historical changes, as well as the manifestation of an existential crisis in France. To view the memories of minority groups in the historical context of the 'age of commemoration' is to emplot them into this narrative. The speech of those deemed to be engaged in 'memory' is then read allegorically: no matter what so-called memorial groups say, they signify only a crisis of French identity. Rendered as symptoms of a macrocosmic malaise, the content of their discourse is marginalized, ignored and deemed insignificant.

The influence of Nora's account of the rise of memory can, in part, be explained by the fact that he presents his narrative as an objective description of the age in which we are living: a periodization of the present. The question that remains unaddressed throughout Nora's work, however, is what exactly sets his historical account of the rise of memory apart from the memorial approaches that he criticizes? It is impossible to determine what particular methods Nora is employing that would render his approach epistemologically superior to those who, for example, look to French colonial history in order to understand the racism they suffer today. Nora seems to see no incongruity in lambasting others for wallowing in their own victimhood, even as he agonizes over the drama of French national identity. There is, at the very least, a double standard at play in Nora's claim that 'in France we have a national history and group memories' (2007). Moreover, if, as Nora claims, 'the emancipation of memories is a powerful corrosive of history, which was at the centre of French identity,' it is because from the very first moment that memory was constituted as an object of study, it was emplotted into a story of the crisis of French identity.

Notes

1. Maurice Halbwachs is often credited with bringing up the issue of collective memory much earlier. But many scholars view the contemporary fascination with memory in academia as being traceable to a number of works that appeared in the 1980s including the work of Nora, but also *Zakhor* by Yerushalmi (2012).
2. Kalle Pihlainen has argued that in historical narratives, the distinction between the narrator and the author is hard to draw (Pihlainen 2002, 53).
3. 'Sometimes such "images" or "pictures" of the past even get names of their own. For instance, terms like "Renaissance", "Enlightenment", "early modern European capitalism" or the "decline of the Church" are in fact names given to the "images" or "pictures" of the past proposed by historians attempting to come to grips with the past: the connotations given to these terms always embody specific historiographical interpretations of the past. (I hasten to add that it would be more accurate to speak of "Renaissances", "Enlightenment", "early modern European capitalisms", and so on because there are as many of them as we have historiographical narratives on these subjects.) This does not mean, of course, that "images" or "pictures" of the past are not proposed when such generally accepted terms are not in use.' (Ankersmit 1983, 92).
4. I thank Chris Lorenz for drawing my attention to these passages in the English version of Hartog's book.
5. Writing about the publication of *Les Lieux de Mémoire*, Hartog (2003,142) says the book 'registered it like a seismograph and reflected it like a mirror'.
6. Stefan Dufoix claims that 2005 is a turning point in the debates about memory in France and lists the following key events of that year which pushed the issue of memory to the forefront of public attention: First, an announcement by J. P. Raffarin on 8 July 2004 of the opening of the 'Cité nationlale de l'historie de l'immigration in the Porte Dorée, which was formerly the Museum of the Colonies.' Second, on 19 January 2005, the website *TouTEsEgaux.net* published an *appel* called 'Nous sommes les indigenes de la République' which condemned what it described as a persistent colonial logic in France. This produced numerous responses in the media, which in turn were responded to on 24 February 2005. Third, on 25 March 2005, *Le Monde* published a text by historians protesting the Mekachera law. Fourth, on 12 April 2005, the Comité pour la mémoire d'esclavage delivered its first report to the prime minister (Dufoix 2005, 137–138).
7. 'Memory laws' is the name used by the group *Liberté Pour l'Histoire* (LPH) to designate a number of laws including the Gayssot law, the Taubira law, the Law recognizing the Armenian genocide and the Mekachera law.

8. Most of their public interventions are archived on the website of the organization http://www.lph-asso.fr/ (Liberté pour l'Histoire 2016).
9. According to Tin (2013, 50) the most notable critics of repentance are mainly conservative politicians like Christian Vanneste and Jean-Marie Le Pen as well as media pundits like Alain Finkelkraut, Eric Zemmour and Ivan Rioufol.
10. Anthropologist Alain Bertho explains that the concept of the Republic is understood as follows 'Republic: magic of political symbols. For two centuries the Republic has demonstrated its capacity to unite: from the left to the right, from the officer to the Jew, and from the Bourgeois to the socialist worker …' (2005, 14–18).
11. See, for example, Klein (2000) and Kansteiner (2002). Erll (2008, 7) proposes to dissolve this distinction in favour of different modes of memory.
12. Of course, several scholars such as Pierre Vidal-Naquet, Phillipe Joutard and Paul Ricoeur soften this distinction.
13. Marc Bloch described anachronism as 'the most egregious of all sins against the science of time' (Bloch and Le Goff 1997, 98).

Acknowledgements

All translations from the French are my own unless otherwise stated. I would like to thank Kalle Pihlainen, Chris Lorenz, Berber Bevernage and Claire Norton for their criticisms of, and advice on, versions of this piece.

Disclosure statement

No potential conflict of interest was reported by the author.

References

Ankersmit, Frank. 1983. *Narrative Logic: A Semantic Analysis of the Historian's Language*. The Hague: Martinus Nijhoff.
Assman, Aleida. 2010. "Reframing Memory: Between Individual and Collective Forms of Reconstructing the past." In *Performing the Past: Memory, History, and Identity in Modern Europe*, edited by Karin Tilmans, Frank van Vree, and J. M. Winter, 35–50. Amsterdam: Amsterdam University Press.
Bertho, Alain. 2005. "Malaise dans la République." [Malaise in the republic.] *Mouvements* 38 (2): 14–18.
Blanchard, Pascal, and Isabelle Veyrat-Masson, eds. 2008. *Les Guerres de mémoires: la France et son histoire* [The Memory wars: France and its history]. Paris: Découverte.
Bloch, Marc, and Jacques Le Goff. 1997. *Apologie pour l'histoire ou Métier d'historien* [The Historian's craft]. Paris: Armand Colin.

Bruckner, Pascal. 2006. *La tyrannie de la pénitence: Essai sur le masochisme occidental* [The tyranny of penitence: An Essay on Western Masochism]. Paris: Grasset.

Candau, Joel. 1998. *Mémoire et Identité* [Memory and identity]. Paris: Presses Universitaires de France.

Dosse, François. 2010. "Il faut rejeter les abus de mémoire et le brouillage des repères historiques." [We must reject the abuse of memory and the blurring of the traditional standards of history.] *Le Monde*, October 15.

Dufoix, Stéphane. 2005. "La reconnaissance au présent: Les dimensions temporelles de l'histoire et de la mémoire." [Recognition in the present: the temporal dimensions of history and memory.] *Revue Du MAUSS* 26 (2): 137–154.

Erll, Astrid. 2008. *Media and Cultural Memory*. Berlin: De Gruyter.

Ferenczi, Thomas, ed. 2002. *Devoir de mémoire, droit à l'oubli?* [Duty of memory, right to forgetting?] Paris: Éditions complexe.

Garapon, Antoine. 2008. *Peut-on réparer l'Histoire? Colonisation, Esclavage, Shoah* [Can we repair history? Colonization, Slavery, Shoah]. Paris: Odile Jacob.

Gensburger, Sarah, and Marie-Claire Lavabre. 2005. "Entre 'devoir de mémoire' et 'abus de mémoire': La sociologie de la mémoire comme tierce position." [Between 'duty of memory' and 'abuse of memory': the sociology of memory as a third position.] In *Histoire, mémoire et épistémologie. A propos de Paul Ricoeur* [History, memory and epistemology. On Paul Ricoeur], edited by Bertrand Müller, 76–95. Lausanne: Payot.

Hartog, François. 2003. *Régimes d'historicité: Présentisme et expériences du temps* [Regimes of historicity: presentism and experiences of time]. Paris: Seuil.

Hartog, François. 2012. *Régimes d'historicité: Présentisme et expériences du temps* [Regimes of historicity: presentism and experiences of time]. Paris: Seuil.

Hartog, François. 2013. *Croire en l'Histoire* [Belief in history]. Paris: Flammarion.

Huyssen, Andreas. 2003. *Present Pasts: Urban Palimpsests and the Politics of Memory*. Stanford, CA: Stanford University Press.

Kansteiner, Wulf. 2002. "Finding Meaning in Memory: A Methodological Critique of Collective Memory Studies." *History and Theory* 41 (2): 179–197.

Kaspi, André. 2008. *Rapport de la Commission de Réflexion sur la Modernisation des Commémorations Publiques* [Report of the commission of reflection on the modernization of public commemorations]. Available at http://www.ladocumentationfrancaise.fr/rapports-publics/084000707-rapport-de-la-commission-de-reflexion-sur-la-modernisation-des-commemorations-publiques

Klein, Kerwin Lee. 2000. "On the Emergence of Memory in Historical Discourse." *Representations* 69 (Winter): 127–150.

Lagrou, Pieter. 2013. "De l'histoire du temps présent À l'histoire des autres: Comment une discipline critique devint complaisante." [From the history of the present to the history of others: how a critical discipline became complacent.] *Vingtième Siècle. Revue d'histoire* 118 (2): 101–119.

Lalieu, Olivier. 2001. "L'invention du 'devoir de mémoire.'" [The invention of 'duty of memory'.] *Vingtième Siècle* 69 (1): 83–94.

Liberté pour l'Histoire [Freedom for History]. Accessed February 15, 2016. http://www.lph-asso.fr/

Lyotard, Jean-François. 1979. *La Condition Postmoderne: Rapport sur le Savoir* [The postmodern condition: report on knowledge]. Paris: Les Editions de Minuit.

Matsuda, Matt. 1996. *Memory of the Modern*. Oxford: Oxford University Press.

Nora, Pierre, ed. 1984. *Les Lieux de mémoire: Tome 1* [The Places of memory: volume 1]. Paris: Gallimard.

Nora, Pierre. 1989. "Between Memory and History: Les Lieux de Mémoire." *Representations* 26 (Spring): 7–24.

Nora, Pierre, ed. 1997. *Les Lieux de Mémoire: Tome 3* [The Places of memory: volume 3]. Paris: Gallimard.

Nora, Pierre. 2002. "Pour une histoire au second degré." [For a history with a pinch of salt.] *Le Débat* 122 (5): 24–31.

Nora, Pierre. 2005. "La mémoire est de plus en plus tyrannique." [Memory is more and more tyrannical.] *Le Figaro* 22 December.

Nora, Pierre. 2006. "Malaise dans l'identité historique." [Malaise in the historical identity.] *Le Débat* 141 (4): 44–48.

Nora, Pierre. 2007. "Le nationalisme nous a caché la nation." [Nationalism has hidden the nation.] *Le Monde*, March 18–19.

Nora, Pierre. 2011a. *Présent, Nation, Mémoire* [Present, Nation, Memory]. Paris: Gallimard.

Nora, Pierre. 2011b. "La question coloniale: Une histoire politisée." [The colonial question: a politicized history.] *Le Monde*, October 15.

Olick, Jeffrey K., Vered Vinitzky-Seroussi, and Daniel Levy. 2011. *The Collective Memory Reader*. Oxford: Oxford University Press.

Pihlainen, Kalle. 2002. "The Moral of the Historical Story: Textual Differences in Fact and Fiction." *New Literary History* 33 (1): 39–60.

Ricoeur, Paul. 2009. *Memory, History, Forgetting*. Translated by Kathleen Blamey and David Pellauer. Chicago, IL: University of Chicago Press.

Rothberg, Michael. 2010. "Introduction: Between Memory and Memory: From lieux de mémoire to noeuds de mémoire." *Yale French Studies* 118 (119): 3–12.

Rousso, Henry. 1994. *The Vichy syndrome: history and memory in France since 1944*. Translated by Arthur Goldhammer. Cambridge, MA: Harvard University Press.

Rousso, Henry. 2007. "Vers une mondialisation de la mémoire." [Towards a globalization of memory.] *Vingtième Siècle* 94 (2): 3–10.

Sarkozy, Nicholas. 2006. "Je Déteste La Repentance." *L'Humanité*. Accessed June 22, 2015. http://www.humanite.fr/node/371023

Stora, Benjamin. 2008. 'La France et "ses" guerres de mémoires.' *Les Guerres de mémoires: la France et son histoire*, edited by Pascal Blanchard and Isabelle Veyrat-Masson, 8–14. Paris: Découverte.

Tin, Louis-Georges. 2013. *Esclavage et réparations* [Slavery and reparations]. Paris: Stock.

Todorov, Tzvetan. 2008. *Les abus de la mémoire* [The abuses of memory]. Paris: Arléa Poches.

Torpey, John. 2006. *Making Whole What Has Been Smashed: On Reparations Politics*. Cambridge, MA: Harvard University Press.

White, Hayden. 1978. *Tropics of Discourse: Essays in Cultural Criticism*. Baltimore, MD: Johns Hopkins University Press.

Yerushalmi, Yosef Hayim. 2012. *Zakhor: Jewish History and Jewish Memory*. Seattle, WA: University of Washington Press.

Thinking the past politically: Palestine, power and pedagogy

Claire Norton and Mark Donnelly

School of Arts and Humanities, St Mary's University, Twickenham, London

ABSTRACT
This article explores the socio-political, economic and legal implications of what counts as historical knowledge. Academic history has long been practiced *as if* its value and authority reside in its ability to produce truth, but pretending that that history occupies an epistemologically foundational position is an illusion that needs to be abandoned. History is a discourse whose sources of cultural power are ultimately social and institutional. By examining narrations of the *Nakba*, the article focuses attention back on to the political dimensions of historical practices and how hegemonic historical interpretations of Israel's establishment in 1948 are closely intertwined with questions of identity and legitimisation. The second half of the article considers a number of reflexive, vernacular narratives on the subject of Palestinian and Israeli pasts that seek to make a direct ethical or political intervention and challenge the dominant discourse. In many ways, these works foreground how traditional academic histories tend to function as a representative of hegemonic discourses. They are more effective in making clear the issues, framing the arguments, engaging with broader, non-academic audiences and stimulating ethical discussion and political action. The focus on how broader mnemonic and cultural orientations towards 'pastness' have been mobilised effectively as cultural and rhetorical resources in tactical campaigns for socio-political justice culminates with an analysis of the case of the American–Palestinian Rasmea Odeh. This example shows how historicising praxis can be used to both reinforce and challenge state power as manifested by the judiciary.

[H]istory writing is a dialectical process fusing ideological agenda and political developments with historical evidence …. (Pappé 2009, 6)

History and memory are endowed with political meaning, but they are not endowed with one, single meaning: different, viable meanings can be drawn. (Confino 2012, 56)

Introduction

In 'The Vicissitudes of the 1948 Historiography of Israel', Ilan Pappé discusses how 'the writing of history absorbs and represents ideological disputes and political developments' (Pappé 2009, 7).[1] He argues that trends in Israeli historiography are closely linked to political events and societal currents, particularly the changing dynamics of the Israeli–Palestine peace process. Pappé contends that in the context of the Israeli invasion of Lebanon in the 1980s, the first Palestinian uprising and the Oslo peace process there was a development in narratives of the 1948 war by the so-called 'new historians' who began to write what some have termed post-Zionist history. These accounts challenged the classical Zionist meta-narrative and, in common with Palestinian accounts, acknowledged that massacres, ethnic cleansing and war crimes were inflicted on the Palestinian population in 1948 (Pappé 2009, 7–8). This intervention in the 1948 historiographical debate was brought to an end when most of the Israeli media and academia rallied behind the Zionist consensus that emerged as a response to the second intifada in 2000 (Pappé 2009, 8). The emergence of a 'neo-Zionist historiography' at this time, Pappé argues, does not differ significantly 'from a purely factual standpoint' from the history of the earlier 'new historians'; instead it differs in its interpretation of the ethnic cleansing, and the expulsions and massacres of Palestinians. While the new historians saw this as evidence of human rights abuses or war crimes, the neo-Zionist historians interpret the same events as normal, justified, or even commendable acts that facilitated the creation of a secure, predominantly Jewish state (Pappé 2009, 9, 11–12).

Pappé's discussion of the historiography of 1948 epitomises how questions around what gets to count as historical knowledge can matter politically. The procedural norms that have to be observed in order for particular iterations of propositions, narratives, interpretive readings, textual forms and material artefacts to be categorised as 'historical' are always tangled up in networks of other social practices and relations of power. And yet as Kalle Pihlainen has rightly observed, discussions of what constitutes historical knowledge are usually framed as essentially epistemological questions (Pihlainen 2011, 469, 480–1).[2] Historians rarely acknowledge that their institutionally accredited power to regulate what counts as legitimate past-talk might have social or political consequences. They prefer to regard this function of their work as being a kind of ideologically neutral and morally-responsible knowledge audit: more like a referee overseeing agreed-upon rules among players than a coercive policing operation that favours some interests at the expense of others. Todd May saw why this was important when he pointed out that the political effects of historicising praxis can be 'all the more telling because of the mantle of political impartiality in which it cloaks itself' (May 1994, 92).

In this article, we examine discussions of the *Nakba* in Palestine–Israel as a way of focusing attention back onto the political dimensions of historical practices. In doing so, we recognise that what is at stake politically when it comes to historicising past events varies widely between cases. Whereas most historiographical disputes only interest relatively small communities of specialists, it is easy to see how attempts to secure and defend a hegemonic historical interpretation of Israel's establishment in 1948 have important political implications across transnational public spheres. Nevertheless, while 1948 is a particularly useful (and radical) case study for illustrating our central arguments, we do not believe that our critical position on historical practices only holds value when it is applied to similarly politically contentious historical debates. We maintain that history as an academic discipline should always be subjected to general questions about its political responsibilities because it operates, in Martin Davies's description, as a *social practice that not only organises the world in the shape of past events, but imposes its practice as the sole, exclusive way of organising it* (Davies 2006, 3 emphasis in original). Academic history has long been practiced *as if* its value and authority reside in its ability to produce truth, where truth is understood as correspondence of sorts to a noumenal reality. But pretending that history occupies an epistemologically foundational position is an illusion that needs to be abandoned. History is a discourse whose sources of cultural power are ultimately social and institutional (Davies 2006, 2010; Jenkins 2009).[3] True, in our current post-foundational intellectual culture we have learned to be sceptical about epistemological claims in all fields of knowledge. In this respect, we recognise that history is no more or less contingent, positioned and rhetorical than other discourses. But what does make it distinctive is its widespread cultural status as a special kind of discourse that purports to be able to explain features of the world as being an outcome of 'historical processes' or 'developments'. This, we argue, is why historical practices need to be critiqued in terms of their ability to produce or legitimise political effects, and not simply in relation to methodological, formal and other professional criteria.

Advocating a critique of history along these consequentialist lines is another way of making the case that Hayden White has been making since the 1960s about the value of placing historical practices in the service of emancipatory or progressive political projects (White 1978; 2014).[4] His argument that the past should be appropriated in ways that, for example, contribute to serving marginalised and oppressed groups in the present retains an inspirational force. But as White explains in his recent work, there is little reason to hope that academic historians might be capable of performing such a political role. More important, according to White, is what he calls (after Oakeshott) the construction of the 'practical past': the past that is constituted by practices and representational forms that lie outside the borders of academic history's professional codes; a past that often does resonate in the social conversation and which can be used as a store of tactical resources for one's conduct in the world (White 2014, 3–24).

Therefore we also intend to explore in this article how vernacular, popular and public forms of past-talk – the broader mnemonic and cultural orientations towards 'pastness' that characterise most people's sense of the historical imaginary – have been (and can continue to be) mobilised effectively as cultural and rhetorical resources in tactical campaigns for socio-political justice.[5] (In the context of our chosen case study, we would understand 'justice' to involve the necessity of guaranteeing the human rights of all involved in the conflict, adherence to UN resolutions, the end of occupation and a fair division of resources.) We then ask how academic engagement with these examples of past-talk might provide a model for a transformed, reinvented version of 'institutional history' that could provide it with a broader social relevance and with a more openly-acknowledged political orientation towards 'the solution of practical problems in the present' (White 2012, 127, quoted by Pihlainen 2015).[6]

The Tantura massacre: politics and silence

Historical accounts of the 1948 Tantura massacre, including the controversial MA dissertation written by Teddy Katz, provide an apposite example of how state apparatuses, here the educational and judicial systems, as well as the media and academic publishing practices, work via institutional coercion to silence or permit different accounts of the past.[7] It demonstrates the inherently politicised nature of institutional histories and thus challenges the claim of history to being a truth-seeking/truth-establishing discourse. Before exploring these points in more detail it may be useful to provide a brief overview of the case. Teddy Katz submitted a MA dissertation to Haifa University that was awarded a very high mark in 1999. One of the chapters was about the ethnic cleansing of the village of Tantura in 1948. He collected oral testimony from Palestinians and members of the Alexandroni Brigade, which, together with the limited textual sources available, very strongly suggested that there had been a massacre of up to 250 Palestinians after the occupation of the village by Israeli forces. A few months later a local journalist published a story based on Katz's thesis, after which the surviving Brigade veterans decided to sue Katz for libel. The trial, which began in late 2000, concentrated on six occasions where Katz had mis-translated or over-generously interpreted what the witnesses had said. No discrepancies were found in the other 224 references to events that transpired at Tantura. After 2 days of the trial, despite Katz's defence team and supporters looking forward to the subject being discussed in an Israeli court, Katz, following pressure from friends and family, and suffering from health problems, agreed to a request by one of his legal team to sign an agreement in which he apologised for fabricating evidence. Although the following day he withdrew his apology and requested that the trial continue, the judge refused. When the case was taken to the Supreme Court, again the judge ruled against resuming the trial. Subsequently, Haifa University set up a commission of inquiry and investigated Katz's thesis. They ostensibly found faults and recommended that his work should be disqualified. He was later permitted to submit a revised version of his thesis, which now only focused on the case of Tantura. A special panel was organised to assess it. Two members of the panel awarded it very high marks, two failed it, and one gave it an average mark – Katz was eventually awarded a non-research masters' degree as his thesis was deemed to have failed. Lastly, a couple of years later Ilan Pappé (at that time employed by Haifa University) together with a colleague attempted to organise a conference on the historiography of 1948 at Haifa University at which Teddy Katz and Udi Adiv were due to speak. However, the university rector ordered that the conference be cancelled on the grounds that particular bureaucratic forms required for the event to take place had not been completed correctly. After re-describing the event as a departmental symposium (which invoked fewer bureaucratic controls), Pappé and other academics due to take part found that the venue they had booked was locked and security guards were waiting outside to escort them from the site. Eventually the research papers had to be presented by speakers in a very informal way in the university cafeteria (Pappé 2010, ch. 6; Pappé 2007, 133–35).

This example provides a clear illustration of how state institutions, judicial and educational, can act to silence counter-hegemonic narratives. While people may want to believe that academic history as taught in universities and as published in journal articles and monographs is neutral, non-partisan and objective, the example of Teddy Katz's thesis shows that this is not necessarily so.[8] The assumption that academics cannot and do not leave their political beliefs outside the university when they go to work is illustrated by Benny Morris in a 2004 article on the Tantura case. Here, in an off-hand manner, he provides background information on the various examiners involved with Katz's second MA thesis. We presume that Morris expected his readers to interpret these personal details as evidence that explained the examiners' political perspectives on the historic events of 1948, and also their current views on Palestine, the occupied territories, Israel and Palestinian refugees (Morris 2004).[9] The implication is that the examiners' political perspectives determined their evaluation of the thesis: those predisposed to overlook the expulsions and atrocities of 1948 would react negatively to Katz's thesis, while those of Arab background or who worked on the peace process would be more sympathetic to it.

Of course, what is at stake in the Katz case is not simply a challenge to a dominant historiographical discourse; it is also a political challenge, because histories of 1948 directly relate to the legitimacy of claims to disputed land in the present. Moreover, the historiography of 1948 has, for Israeli society, the status of an Althusserian foundational myth that not only legitimises, but also maintains the existing social order. The Katz case does however clearly demonstrate how academia, media and the state's educational and judicial institutions all provide a 'professional and scholarly scaffold' for hegemonic narrations of the past (Pappé 2009, 7–8). Far from achieving hegemonic status because of their purported mimetic resemblance to the past, historical accounts generate cultural authority from the political, ideological and aesthetic values that they embody. People prefer historical narratives that resonate with them ethically, politically and ideologically, and which are composed as stories that persuade them with their aesthetic qualities. Alon Confino's recent article on Tantura exemplifies how a historical account can become part of a historiographical hegemony in this way. Confino argues that '[m]eanings of the past emerge when a historian commingles evidence with an opportunity of art, with a poetic act that brings human life to the course of events. It means to capture the historical sensations of a given past' (Confino 2012, 43). He explains how in his article he tried 'to present one such historical sensation from the war of 1948' in both text and images (Confino 2012, 43).

Rhetorically, Confino locates the ethnic cleansing (he prefers the term forced migration) of Palestinians from the nascent Israeli state/Mandate Palestine within stories of other twentieth-century population transfers, which he argues were ultimately sanctioned by the international community as humanitarian and a means by which minority rights could be protected. He also positions it within stories of miracles that felicitously resolved seemingly intractable problems (Confino 2012, 27, 32, 37, 38–9, 40–42, 25–7).[10] While he acknowledges in part the brutality that was involved in the forced departure of Palestinians from Tantura, he is notably reticent on the subjects of violence and killing. Although he notes that keeping quiet about actual deeds conforms to 'a pattern of silence of the generation of 1948', a 'stillness' that they display with regard to their war experiences that may just be 'the first indicator for the historian that there is something to hide', he employs just such silence or muted stillness to great rhetorical effect in the article (Confino 2012, 29). For example, he mentions that in court Katz retracted his claim that the Alexandroni Brigade had committed a massacre and published an apology, but does not add that Katz subsequently retracted his retraction and (unsuccessfully) asked for the court case on the libel claim to resume. He does not respond to, or discuss, claims that a massacre happened at Tantura and declines to discuss the Alexandroni Brigade's denials of Katz's claims.[11] He does however claim that in the article he will concentrate on 'those events in Tantura the soldiers did not speak openly about', events that they kept silent about, events that generated a 'bottled-up sense of guilt' (Confino 2012, 30). He cites an 'off the record' interview by a Brigade veteran at an event commemorating the Brigade's capture of Tantura in which the veteran states that he would never forget the crying, shouting, and lamentation when the women, children and elderly were forcibly removed from Tantura in 1948 (Confino 2012, 29–30). Confino reproduces the scrap of paper on which the veteran drew a schematic of the expulsion: a piece of paper that accidentally survived, a piece of paper that 'the historian was not supposed to have possession of' (Confino 2012, 30 and 46). Reflecting on this single piece of paper Confino recalls Carlo Ginzberg's rejoinder to Hayden White that 'the voice of a single witness is enough to reach a certain historical reality and therefore some historical truth' (Confino 2012, 30). Confino asks: 'what did the soldiers think they were doing [...] how did it merge with their collective sense of self and of Jewish identity? What images of their personal or collective pasts did the crying of desperate refugees evoke in them'? But what he does not ask is: was there a massacre? (Confino 2012, 30).

Confino wants to move the historiography of 1948 in the direction of cultural history – he wants to explore the 'culture, memories, feelings and sensibilities that made Jews and Arabs behave as they did' (Confino 2012, 38). One way that he does this – one way that he presents a 'historical sensation' – a 'historical sensation' that plays with the form of academic history – is through a series of twenty-two photographs of the expulsion and repopulation of the village. The photos that Confino uses to create his 'historical sensation' of 1948 are fairly benign in the context of an alleged massacre. They show the separation of the women and children and their expulsion to Furaydis. They show the participation of various Red Cross and other officials in the relocation of the inhabitants, soldiers giving water to those being expelled, and then the arrival of Jewish settlers (some of whom are immigrants from Turkey) whose children play in the streets, who make the roads bloom, who work to develop a local fishing industry (Confino 2012, 44–45).

The story of the expulsion of Palestinian women and children and the occupation of Tantura by young Jewish men and women is at the heart of the article. It is used as a means of interrogating the process by which the nascent Israeli state appropriated the lands of Palestinians who fled or were forced out. Confino presents an aesthetically satisfying, superficially critical, narrative of events based on supposedly authoritative sources – photographs, and the drawing and reminiscences of a soldier who was there. He holds back from explaining and interpreting the meaning of this story, leaving it to the reader to give it meaning, to use it as a trigger for thought, to open up discussion (Confino 2012, 57). He argues that 'Israeli Jews should acknowledge their role in the forced migration of the Arabs because [...] it is part of their history [...] it is inextricably linked to their own gaining of home and homeland.' But this 'historical sensation' is endowed with a specific political meaning. It simulates the giving of space to the various, often contradictory, voices surrounding the ethnic cleansing of Palestinians in 1948, but in reality it functions as a further means of silencing the oral testimony of the expelled Palestinian residents of Tantura. Confino claims that we don't 'need to hear another lesson about 1948, from this or that side' but this is exactly what he provides. He creates a morality tale on the anguish and hope arising from early twentieth-century population transfer in times of conflict and in doing so, hopes that it is sufficient to keep the events of 1948 firmly in the past; out of reach of the politics of the present (Confino 2012, 57). His narrative demonstrates that rather than the task of history being to *teach* us how we got here, as he claims, it almost always functions as a *political justification* of a chosen explanation of how we got here (Confino 2012, 56). *Pace* Confino, past-focused narratives can be (and have been) constructed and used in such a way as to 'redeem and justify any action' (Confino 2012, 57).

Yossi Ben Artzi and Benny Morris similarly regard Ilan Pappé's work on 1948 as 'propaganda and the exposition of a personal political ideology' (Ben-Artzi 2011, 165). One of the many issues that arise from the Katz/Tantura debate is the status of oral testimony. Yossi Ben Artzi's review article, much of which is an *ad hominem* attack on Pappé, claims that Katz's 'unsubstantiated claims' of a massacre at Tantura were based on 'hearsay and village folklore', that they ignored 'demographic and historical evidence to the contrary' and that oral testimony is 'of questionable validity as a sole historical source' (Ben-Artzi 2011, 166, 171). However, the debate is not really one about the legitimacy of different types of historical evidence, nor is it concerned with the few minor mis-transcriptions that Katz made. Instead it is about the political use of the past to maintain present claims and control over territory and resources. It is about what constitutes morally acceptable practices. It is about the production and authorisation of explanatory and legitimising narratives, and making sure that the 'right' ones are heard and the 'wrong' ones are silenced. The titles of the journals that have published some of the articles on this debate, to some extent, stand as a synecdoche of the political nature of historical knowledge: Pappé published in *The Journal of Palestinian Studies* while Ben-Artzi and Confino published in *Israel Studies*.[12]

Benny Morris, in a review article on a number of Pappé's books, concludes with an anecdote about a student who took a seminar he taught at Ludwig-Maximilian's University in Munich. The student wrote a paper entitled 'Ethnic Cleansing of Palestine May 1948–January 1949' and used Pappé's *The Ethnic Cleansing of Palestine* among other works. She apparently argued that ethnic cleansing is inhuman and brutal and drew a number of comparisons between the Nazi expulsion and genocide of Jews in Europe and Israel's expulsion or ethnic cleansing of Arabs. For Morris this 'is a fine indication of the measure of Pappé's success, of his reach in polluting Middle Eastern historiography and in poisoning the minds of those who superficially dabble in it. This is unfortunate, even tragic' (Morris 2011).

The cultural politics of historicisation

At one level Morris is simply making Foucault's point that knowledge and power are entangled and embedded in other practices (institutional, judicial, pedagogic, articulatory, and so on). And as Ernesto Laclau and Chantal Mouffe explain, these are the practices that possibilise the temporary stabilisations that constitute a hegemonic fixing within a given social formation. Historical practices are not 'unpolluted'. One of their functions is to combine with other practices to create, circulate and reproduce the 'common sense' that hegemonic stabilisations require. As is well understood, histories in their modern discursive form grew out of nationalist projects of self-legitimisation. Of course the discipline is now more open, pluralistic and multi-directional (and sometimes it aspires to be anti-hegemonic). But equally it remains true that history teaching in schools, and the professionalisation of history as a university discipline, continue to serve nation-state oriented agendas. Formal education is one of the primary means by which national narratives and identities are established and perpetuated (Wertsch 2002, 10, 69, 172, cited in Peled-Elhanan 2012, 2–3). Textbooks, academic writings, lessons and lectures are a powerful means by which states encourage the imagination of particular personal and national collective identities, and encourage the construction and interpretation of public memories. If this were not the case, then history curricula and the content of school history textbooks would not be the subject of political contestation across the world.[13]

In the case of Israel, Pappé notes that in the late 1990s the topic of Palestinian expulsions in 1948 was for the first time considered for inclusion in the national curriculum, but after debate in the Knesset Education Committee it was rejected. However since 2000 the expulsion of the Palestinians has been explicitly discussed in Israeli textbooks, albeit from a Zionist perspective that contextualises it not only as a positive series of events that enabled the establishment of a secure and majority Jewish state free from a Palestinian threat, but also as ultimately the fault of the Palestinians themselves (Pappé 2009, 17–18; Peled-Elhanan 2012, 78–91). Daniel Bar-Tal in his analysis of Israeli textbooks argues that a Zionist interpretation of the conflict predominates with its concomitant negative stereotyping of the Palestinians in contrast to the portrayal of Jews as victims (Bar-Tal 2007, 443, cited in Pappé 2009, 18). Nurit Peled-Elhanan similarly illustrates how the state uses text books to create a 'usable past' that justifies Zionist ideology and de-legitimises Palestinian claims. In particular, she demonstrates how such textbooks intersect with, and reproduce, the hegemonic Israeli–Zionist meta-narrative that presents the Palestinians simply as a problem in the wider context of Israel's need for land and security. As such, she explores the question of interpretive naming, foregrounds the almost exclusive representation of Palestinians in these textbooks as primitive farmers, terrorists, or poor refugees, and deconstructs the 'toponomyc silences' in cartographical representations of Israel where illegal settler colonies are depicted as visually the same as Israeli cities such as Tel Aviv; the occupied West Bank is presented as part of Israel, but renamed as Judea and Samaria; and Palestinian place names are erased or Hebraised (Peled-Elhanan 2012, ch.1 and 119–125).

These examples seem to confirm Davies's argument that history is an 'indispensible information-management technology' whose production makes universities, as well as heritage institutions, the ideal, compliant instruments of socially dominant interests, governmental and cultural policies and neo-liberal ideology (Davies 2010, 57 and 61; Davies 2006, 133). The academic function, says Davies, sponsored as it is by the state, blocks any knowledge that 'won't reproduce the prevailing order' or won't affirm received values (Davies 2008, 464–5). In one sense this instrumental use of history is to be expected. As Keith Jenkins has argued, it would be perverse for government agencies to allocate such sizeable funds to history teaching in schools and (at least until recently in the UK) universities, and to support historical research and heritage activities, unless they believed that in doing so they were helping to reproduce forms of social cohesion and acquiescence in current political arrangements. Sande Cohen occupies a similar critical position, arguing that historians provide the data that give particular social formations present credibility (for example, by anchoring them to perceived traditions or inter-generational shared values), and that they are also able to underscore future-oriented appeals by collectives through their power to exclude contending claims to the future by designating them as (supposedly) historically invalid (Cohen 2006, 118).

Jenkins argues that causes associated with justice, emancipatory ideas and left politics have nothing to gain from academic history as it is conventionally practised (Jenkins 1999, 1–33; Jenkins 2009, 15–6, 107).[14] According to this line of reasoning, institutional history is out-dated at best and politically compromised at worst; it is one of modernity's failed cultural projects, incapable of adding anything specific or useful to arguments about political or ethical issues; if one wishes to counter historical claims that are experienced by a group as oppressive, he argues, one can do so using 'ethics-talk' or politics-talk (Jenkins 1997, 62). But of course Jenkins equally understands that history's professional and politically-supported infrastructure is sufficiently powerful to make its survival a safe bet for many years to come (Jenkins 2009, 16).

Historians' claims that they can apprehend the past as an already-available object of *historical* enquiry (one that precedes the effects of their discursive codings) are epistemologically flawed; moreover, few individual academic histories reach a wide audience. But these generic shortcomings do not stop historians' social authority from running wide and deep. For a host of cultural and material reasons, societies bestow semantic and epistemological authority on certain types of (sedimented) historical practices more or less unquestioningly. This is why critiques of knowledge about the 'historical past' that are articulated using a different language game to history are vulnerable to being dismissed on the grounds that they are irrational, counter-factual or 'unhistorical' (not only by those whose interests such history serves). Defenders of academic history commonly reject critiques of their professional practices by questioning whether non-historians – people who do not produce accounts of the past based on conventional archival sources – are capable of understanding what historians really do.

This is why we believe that productive resistance to history's hegemonic functions has to come from *within* its own institutional practices as well as from outside. This would not simply involve reviewing methodological protocols, allowing new types of source material into what is taken to constitute the historical archive, or resolving to be more adventurous in choices of representational forms (though we do, nevertheless, support each of these). It would involve historians working to challenge our own collective identity as experts who act as if we have been accorded final rights to adjudicate questions of meaning, value and truth in relation to the past. It would involve historians becoming truly self-critical, rather than critical of everything *except* the epistemological assumptions that underpin academic historical practices: using Davies's vocabulary, it would be welcome if more historians became experts in *historics* rather than history.[15]

Chantal Mouffe argued that because any given social configuration lacks a final ground and is 'never the manifestation of a deeper objectivity that is exterior to the practices that brought it into being', it is always susceptible to being challenged by counter-hegemonic practices that attempt to 'disarticulate it in an effort to install another form of hegemony' (Mouffe 2013, 2). In her view such counter-practices could take any form: there is nothing inherent in any articulatory practice that determines how it might be used politically. But in our opinion academic history's potential to be used as a form for challenging dominant power appears pretty weak; as Jenkins observed, it hardly ever does so: 'the present day is rarely *damaged* by mainstream academic historians' (Jenkins 2009, 275 emphasis in original). This is why we believe that 'everyday' or 'vernacular' appropriations of the past are more likely to be (and have been) mobilised effectively *as cultural and rhetorical resources* in tactical campaigns for socio-political justice, countering oppressive claims to knowledge, expanding the scope of personal and social autonomy, and achieving individual or group dignity.

Reflexive, political, vernacular pasts

Recently there has been a profusion of what might be termed reflexive, political and vernacular narratives on the subject of Palestinian and Israeli pasts that seek to make a direct ethical or political intervention or contribution. These works, we argue, might be able to throw into sharper relief – and thus contribute to circumventing – the ways in which history tends to function as a representative of hegemonic discourses. In many ways, we think that these works are more effective than traditional academic histories in making clear the issues, framing the arguments, engaging with broader, non-academic audiences and stimulating ethical discussion and political action. They provide a space in which plural voices are more likely to be heard on their own terms, invoking multi-layered temporalities, and perhaps permitting a degree of dialogue that is absent from academic histories. Of course there are numerous plays, films, novels, political posters and works of art that deal with issues of socio-political injustice in Israel and the occupied territories, but in this article we focus briefly on just three examples.[16]

Footnotes in Gaza by journalist and graphic artist Joe Sacco is an investigation into, and narration of, two Israeli massacres of Palestinians that occurred in Khan Younis and Rafah in 1956, during the Suez Canal Crisis (Sacco 2009).[17] Sacco employs an unconventional historical form: the graphic novel. However, the research process, the analysis, and the interpretive processes he undertakes are in line with both journalistic and historical praxis. While he does use archival and textual sources (and extracts from these are included in an appendix), much of the research is based on an oral history approach. The format Sacco chooses to use to narrate events permits a degree of polyvocality and also makes explicit the contradictory, overlapping and contingent nature of historical knowledge. Moreover, he situates his discussion of the 1956 massacres in a present context of the essential incarceration of Gaza and its residents, punitive and discriminatory house demolition on a large scale, and the human rights abuses of Gazans. His past-focused narrative is here used to draw parallels with a present situation and to encourage ethico-political debate on a variety of issues. It also effectively gives voice to those who are rarely heard. Sacco's work can be read as an example of engaged journalism, but equally it can be seen as an instance of a 'democratised history'.[18] He has been able to find a wide audience for work that discusses historic massacres, current hardships, the inhumane treatment of Palestinians in Gaza, and self-reflexive discussion about the evidential value of his sources. His work is popular, sold at reasonable prices, and available in public libraries, not locked away behind journal embargos.

The work of photographer Paul Antick is similarly reflexive and engaged with issues of current ethico-political relevance. His 'documentary-fiction' projects explore experiences of dark tourism and highlight issues of socio-political injustice through the device of the fictional photographer Smith and his companion, the equally fictional anthropologist Willing, whose research involves observing how Smith behaves in challenging situations and difficult environments.[19] His recent work 'Smith in Palestine (to be read aloud, in its entirety)' is a screenplay interspersed with photos. It is described as 'what remains of a film that was shot in Palestine, by Willing between 12 and 17 August 2009' (Antick 2012, 3). Like Confino his work on Palestine is a mixture of text and photos, but there the similarity ends: Antick has constructed his narrative in an explicitly self-reflexive way that draws attention to (and problematises) questions of meaning, authorial authority, the power of the reality effect, and the ways in which we narrate and perceive on-going conflict. The author (Antick) instructs the reader to vocalise the text in its entirety, including technical instructions. In doing so our attention is drawn to the way in which the work has been put together; it foregrounds the form as a construct and as part of the means by which meaning is produced. By vocalising the technical instructions the reader's participation in the construction of meaning is emphasised: meaning is not found, it is performed. Simultaneously, however, the authorial instruction to read the text in its entirety engenders a tension; if we obey, do we prioritise the authority of the author? Do they, should they, or can they ultimately determine how we read and respond to a text?[20]

However, the presence of photographs frustrates a reader's attempt to carry out the author's instruction – how can one read aloud a photo? They cannot be translated in the same way that one translates a written word into a spoken one. They remind us that language never transparently and unproblematically conveys *the* meaning. Another effect of the photographs is to remind the reader that 'part of the text will always apparently remain beyond them' reminding us that meaning is never simply given and fixed forever, it is situated, contested and politicised (Antick 2012; 3). Reading aloud, the reader-as-performer 'is corporeally propelled by the rhythms of the text.' Perhaps, Antick suggests, we are analogously propelled through the enduring conflict in Palestine and Israel by the 'aural, visual and narrative rhythms' of news broadcasts, the sentiments of politicians, the sounds of war (Antick 2012, 2). Perhaps the shape that the conflict is given by news broadcasts and academic histories gives it a sense of inevitability and inures us to the many injustices – it is the 'same old thing' playing out endlessly as background noise.[21] However, reading aloud the technical instructions acts as an interruption to the rhythmical speech of the characters. This dissonant irregularity interrupts and disturbs, jolting us out of a complacency that figures the conflict as inevitable and unending.

'Smith in Palestine' also engages obliquely with a range of ethical issues, and instances of injustice both past and present, including the massacres of refugees at Sabra and Shatila; the difficulty and brutality of daily life in the Occupied Territories; and Pappé's argument that the 1948 *Nakba* was a deliberate policy of ethnic cleansing designed to forcibly remove Palestinians from what would become Israel, rather than an accidental consequence of war. The work also deliberately confuses and confronts our ontological notions of self and other. Discussing life in a *moshav*, Smith outlines the hierarchy of workers from the settlers at the top and Israelis working as part of their national service, to European volunteers and Palestinian workers. While one might assume that Israelis and Palestinians would imagine or construct radically different identities, in some ways the Palestinians, in comparison to the European volunteers, have more in common with the Israelis: they often speak Hebrew (as the language of power and authority in the state) and they have a very personal relationship of belonging to the land they farm.

Lastly, the unusual form (from the perspective of history writing) of Antick's work actively engages and inspires readers. His earlier work 'Bhopal to Bridgehampton' motivated students at his university to dramatise and perform his work, and to send messages of support to those fighting for justice for the residents of Bhopal.[22] Antick's work, we argue, is an instructive example of how vernacular, non-traditional forms can be used to narrate past events in such a way that they explicitly and directly engage with current ethico-political issues and inspire reader reflection and action.

Our third example is a counterfactual history by International Relations specialist Tony Klug: *How Peace Broke out in the Middle East: a short history of the future* (Klug 2007). This short hypothetical history provides a narrative of how 'peace finally came to the Middle East' at some future date 'to be determined' (Klug 2007, 3). It is a clever work that contextualises a future peace deal against a background of actual events and key players. Of interest for us here is not only the unusual form that this 'history' takes, but the political aspect of Klug's work. The counterfactual peace deal functions as a means of outlining a way for the different sides in this conflict to end the bloodshed, oppression and occupation, while guaranteeing security and access to resources for all concerned as well as a fair and equitable settlement. Klug has previously made these arguments in a number of other works in an international relations context, but by presenting them as 'already having happened' he foregrounds the viability and possibility of the solution while not underestimating any of the problems.[23] Furthermore, by arguing that a peace deal is not reliant on some ever-elusive 'auspicious moment' nor that it is a 'mere pipe dream' but it is 'a matter of political will' he implies that not making peace is equally a political decision (Klug 2007, 27).

Political activism, engagement and the case of Rasmea Odeh

Activists, journalists, educators, aid workers, and refuseniks, – people – working in various ways to oppose the Israeli occupation, to defend the human rights of Palestinians and Israelis, and to seek a fair and just solution for both peoples, frequently use past-focused narratives of some form in their work. From the journalists writing for +972, to activists and campaigners involved with Zochrot, Palestine Solidarity Campaign, Jews for Justice for Palestinians, and the Electronic Intifada – to name but a few – appropriations of the past are used to contribute to the framing contexts of their work.[24] The Palestine Solidarity Campaign offers factsheets on its website that explain the *Nakba*, Britain's role in the establishment of the state of Israel, as well as time-lines and a series of maps illustrating the disappearance of Palestine as a geo-political entity.[25] Jews for Justice for Palestinians and the Electronic Intifada have sections on their website that provide a context to the occupation and the ethnic cleansing of Palestinians from Palestine/Israel. They also engage in debate with, and respond to, works by Israeli and other historians writing about the expulsion of Palestinians and the occupation. The NGO Zochrot as part of its goal to 'promote Israeli Jewish society's acknowledgement of and accountability for the ongoing injustices of the Nakba' hosts tours to the sites of destroyed Palestinian villages and localities, and employs past-focused narratives in the workshops, lectures, teacher training and the other educational courses that it provides as part of its political programme to persuade and educate.[26] They have also designed the trilingual I-Nakba app that maps Palestinian localities that have been destroyed, ruined or depopulated since 1948.[27] The interactive app provides information, photographs and videos and it allows users to upload their own images, share comments, follow updates and provide information on destroyed villages. I-Nakba is, just like all cartography, a political tool. It is a digital response to the material, toponomyc and cartographic erasure of Palestinian settlements. Despite the political, military and historiographical efforts to silence Palestinians it asserts an effective counter-narrative that engages and informs its users.[28]

Contextualising how material conditions and physical forces are configured on the ground is a fundamental part of the political work of numerous activists and campaigns seeking justice and peace in Palestine/Israel. As part of this, past-focused narratives are often *chosen* by activists as favoured contextual frames within which other discourses about rights, dignity, resources and territory are then brought into play. The contextual frames within which such discourses are positioned do not so much imply that injustices in Palestine/Israel result from a logics of history. Rather they point towards the value of understanding asymmetries of power on the ground in terms of genealogical processes: the question is not so much 'what is the truth of the matter?' as 'how have regimes of truth in specific conditions been used to legitimise coercive and oppressive acts?' Bearing this in mind, we want to discuss the case of a American-Palestinian activist in Chicago, Rasmea Odeh.[29] She is a refugee whose family was expelled from their village in 1948 and who grew up in the occupied West Bank. She is a Palestinian–American and an associate director at the Arab American Action Network, a community-based organisation that supports, through advocacy and education, the Arab–American community in Chicago. She is also a Palestinian activist. Odeh moved to the USA in 1995 and in 2004 applied to become an American citizen. However, in 1969, aged 21, she was arrested by the Israeli military in the Occupied Territories and tortured. After beatings, electric shocks and the subsequent torture of her father she was coerced into confessing to involvement in two bombings. Although she renounced her confession before an Israeli military court less than a month later, she was convicted by the court and sentenced to life in prison. She was subsequently released after 10 years as part of a prisoner exchange and following her release she testified to the UN about her torture. While resident in America, she also spoke on occasion in public about her torture, her treatment in Israeli custody and her conviction. However, when she completed her application for US citizenship she was asked if she had ever been arrested or imprisoned. Not understanding that the US immigration authorities were inquiring about imprisonment in the US and overseas, Odeh failed to mention her political detention in the Occupied Territories by an Israeli military court. Odeh was arrested in 2013 and charged with 'Unlawful Procurement of Naturalization'; in November 2014 she was convicted of immigration fraud and the following

March she was sentenced to 18 months in prison and deportation. She is currently appealing her sentence.[30]

Her lawyers and supporters are arguing that although she was found guilty of immigration fraud for failing to disclose a conviction on her naturalisation form, the conviction was handed down by an illegitimate regime that extracted a confession, and thus secured a conviction, through torture. Therefore, they argue, it does not constitute a valid conviction and as such she did not commit immigration fraud. Israel's military court system oversees all court cases in the Occupied Territories and nearly all (99.74%) of the court cases end in conviction – most of which are based solely on signed confessions. There is also significant documentation from human rights organisations including Human Rights Watch as well as Israel's High Court of Justice that the interrogation process that leads to these confessions includes the kind of torture that Odeh describes.[31] Moreover, Odeh testified at her trial that had she understood that the immigration forms were inquiring about her political detention in the Occupied Territories she would have volunteered the information.[32] Her defence had hoped to use her trial as an opportunity to scrutinise in a public forum the illegitimacy of Israel's military judicial regime in the Occupied Territories, but the judge in the case refused to allow the defence to introduce most of its evidence and kept the parameters of the case extremely narrow. Specifically, evidence about her torture was deemed inadmissible and the defence was not allowed to explain the compromised nature of the court that convicted her. In contrast, the judge did allow more than 100 official Israeli documents asserting that she confessed to, and was convicted of being involved with, two bombings. Despite the judge's claim that the case is not 'political', the decision to allow evidence from an Israeli military court in occupied territory, but not evidence of their human rights abuses and regular use of torture to extract confessions, *is* political. It clearly illustrates how state institutions including the judiciary facilitate the telling of narratives about the past that affirm and uphold the interests of the state while silencing counter-hegemonic narratives. The defence team and supporters argue that this case is part of a wider political attack on the Palestinian–American community and Palestinian solidarity supporters that since 9/11 has become intertwined with the 'war on terror' rhetoric.[33] Odeh's case exemplifies Foucault's point about the need to problematise epistemologies of all kinds – including, from our perspective, those that produce and delimit the genre that we recognise as academic history. In Foucault's words:

> There is a battle 'for truth', or at least 'around truth' – it being understood once again that by truth I mean not 'the ensemble of truths to be discovered and accepted' but, rather, 'the ensemble of rules according to which the true and the false are separated and specific effects of power attached to the true', it being understood also that it's not a matter 'on behalf' of the truth but of a battle about the status of truth and the economic and political role it plays. (Foucault 2002, 132)

Final thoughts

Academic history culture is committed to long-dominant epistemologies, methodologies and representational forms. As we have shown, these can function politically to authorise certain past-focused narratives and to find others wanting in the 'court of history' – and thus to exclude or silence them. We see little evidence that the political consequences of how historicising practices are mobilised and regulated are given due academic attention –based on our reading of texts such as UK history degree curricula, articulations of history departments' aims, criteria for research 'excellence', and adverts for academic history jobs (Donnelly and Norton 2015). In a post-foundational (or post-1968) intellectual culture, we cannot take seriously history's epistemic claims to being a unique authority on past-focused matters, or *the* arbitrator between competing narratives about past events. Instead the discourse of history is just another politicised contribution to conversations about how we live and what we should do. In order to stop it being used to function in oppressive ways, histories (and 'pastifying' practices generally) have to be more open, democratic, plural and accessible. Institutional barriers should not be used to impede forms of past-talk operating in ways similar to a 'cinema of advocacy' or 'journalism of attachment' – as a vehicle for critical voices that speak to wide audiences. History as-discourse, we have argued here, claims for itself the right to be the benchmark against which other forms of knowledge about the past are tested; but this 'right' rests on fragile grounds. History is not a discursive instrument that explains 'how the past has caused the present', and the idea that it constitutes a collective enquiry into the actuality of what happened in the past raises significant (and now well-traversed) problems about epistemology, ontology, metaphysics, narrativity, and the status of the archive. Of course, historians invoke empirical procedures for making statements about the past that cohere with surviving traces of information, traces which the profession chooses to regard as specifically 'historical evidence'. And we recognise that these empirical *procedures* are often vital, particularly in circumstances in which matters of human rights violations, criminal conduct, justice, restitution, and so forth are involved. But there is no reason why we should believe that (we) historians are more adept at practising these empirical procedures than, say, journalists, lawyers, screenwriters, historical novelists, social activists or academics in other disciplines. While history often succeeds in subjecting the past to its controlling disciplinary gaze, this simply confirms its elevated institutional status as a certain kind of articulatory practice. Moreover, this status means that it has the discursive power to contribute to marking out the boundaries of 'legitimate knowledge' that are required for temporarily fixing hegemonic social formations.

Where does this leave projects that seek to instrumentalise past-knowledge for emancipatory political objectives? Can forms of past-talk contribute to challenging those temporary fixings of the social that are experienced as unjust and oppressive? Laclau and Mouffe would suggest that they can, because they understood the social to be a contingent, open and never-to-be-completed effect of linguistic and extra-linguistic articulatory practices, marked by the infinite play of differences. As they stated: 'The social *is* articulation insofar as society is impossible' (Laclau and Mouffe 2014; 100 emphasis in original). Antagonism was an irreducible feature of their model of the social; as such, they argued, there will always be adversaries. In what Mouffe calls a model of 'agonistic pluralism', articulatory practices of varying types are understood to be part of a politics that provides a framework for managing differences between adversaries *as* adversaries, and not as enemies (accepting that there could never be a final reconciliation). Vernacular, cultural mnemonic and non-institutional forms of past-talk are better suited than academic histories to contribute to this agonistic pluralism, because the latter – while purporting to take the past conceived as a whole as its referent – works within narrowly limited methodological and evidential boundaries. This is why we believe that historians should cease subjecting all forms of past-talk to their own communally-agreed criteria for making truth claims. However, in more positive terms, perhaps Ilan Pappé's and Jamil Hilal's discussion of how historians can produce 'bridging narratives' that would help rival communities to 'distance themselves critically from the reigning nationalist ideologies' shows that a politically-engaged historiography can still aspire to perform a constructive discursive-political role. In *Talking to the Enemy,* they defined bridging narratives as 'a conscious historiographical effort taken by historians in societies wrought with long internal and external conflicts, to cross over conflicting narratives and historiographies' (Moses 2005, 329). This exemplifies the kind of constructive political function that historical practices can be used to perform.[34] But unless historians themselves work to constitute those practices in less coercive ways, history will continue to serve the interests of state and/or dominant powers in most circumstances. Is this what we want historical learning, research and writing to do? Is this the role of an engaged historian?

Notes

1. Pappé explained and defended his ideas about the ideological positioning of historians' work in a televised interview with Stephen Sackur, *HARDtalk,* BBC News channel, 30 June 2014.
2. Arguing that history should be, and can be politically neutral is as disingenuous as insisting that medicine and health is not a political issue. For the debate surrounding the *Lancet*'s coverage of the 2014 Gaza conflict see http://www.independent.co.uk/news/uk/politics/major-medical-journal-lancet-under-attack-for-extremist-hate-propaganda-over-its-coverage-of-the-israelipalestinian-conflict-10199892.html [last accessed April 28, 2015].

We also owe our discussion that institutionalised history is circumscribed by a commitment to truth-seeking as opposed to practical use to Pihlainen (2015).

3. While Davies might argue that there is something particular about the historical perspective that engenders its socio-political appropriation by hegemonic powers, we would argue that it is perhaps the institutionalised nature of history produced within and disseminated by the educational, broadcasting and heritage organisations of the state that means it can so readily be employed by dominant interests. We also acknowledge that the state itself does not represent a singular, identifiable entity or collection of interests and that it can be more profitably seen as a site of contestation between various influential, authoritative and powerful groups.

4. Other historians have also argued that history as a genre of writing may have relevance today as a means of facilitating ethical debates not only on our society today but on possibly different futures: Harlan (2003); Southgate (2005); Munslow (2010); Rigney (2007); and Pihlainen (2012).

5. Here we are stretching White's usage of the term 'practical past' beyond the way he discusses it in his published text.

6. Such a future for a reinvented form of institutionalised history would be dependent on a recognition that it does not have mimetic properties and an acknowledgement that it does not possess a unique, foundational socio-political authority as *the only* accurate or truthful guide to the past. In its engagement with other forms of past-talk it would need to actively encourage the agonistic pluralism outlined by Mouffe (2013) rather than simply evaluate or police such narratives and practices against its own communally-agreed and thus contingent genre protocols.

7. The case has been written about extensively by Pappé (2000–01a), (2007), (2010). Morris (2004), 21 also provides an overview of the 'atrocities' that happened there while doubting that events can be 'reconstructed' on the basis of oral testimony as a result of faulty memories and political interests. Much later, Ben-Artzi (2011) and Morris (2011) wrote hostile review articles of Pappé's work with particular focus on the Katz/Tantura case. Accounts of the massacre at Tantura in 1948 can be found in Pappé (2007), (2000–01b). See also Confino (2012).

8. The collusion between academia, the judiciary and politicians in silencing counter-hegemonic narratives occurs in all political systems to varying degrees as illustrated by the last minute cancellation by the University of Southampton of a conference 'International Law and the State of Israel' initially approved by the University in 2014 and scheduled to be held 17–19 April 2015 at the University. It was cancelled ostensibly on health and safety grounds, but after significant political pressure from government ministers, Conservative members of parliament and pro-Israel lobby groups. The decision was upheld by the High Court in a judgement issued on 8th April 2015 refusing permission to bring a judicial review of the decision at the request of the organisers of the conference. See http://www.southampton.ac.uk/israelpalestinelaw/index.page, http://www.theguardian.com/uk-news/2015/mar/31/southampton-university-cancels-event-questioning-israel-existence, https://www.timeshighereducation.com/news/southampton-cancels-controversial-israel-conference/2019499. article, http://artistsforpalestine.org.uk/2015/05/10/uk-high-court-backs-shutdown-of-israel-conference/, http://www.thejc.com/news/uk-news/133033/southampton-university-confirms-it-considering-cancelling-anti-israel-conference [all last accessed on December 24, 2015].

9. Morris writes 'In September 1998 Katz's supervisor, Firro, and two examiners – Yair Hirschfeld (who was involved in the secret Israeli-PLO talks that resulted in the 1993 Oslo agreement), and Israeli Arab historian Muhammad Yazbek – gave Katz 97%. […] Katz resubmitted his thesis […] in September 2002. […] The University appointed five examiners who, by a 3:2 margin, failed the thesis. [….] The other two who failed it, giving it 40 and 50, were Dr Avraham Sela (Hebrew University) and Dr Arnon Golan (Haifa University). Three years ago […] these two scholars authored "The Conquest of Lydda, July 1948" published by the Israel Defense Ministry Press. The slim volume, apologetic in focus and intent, argued that the Israeli Army had carried out only a "partial expulsion" of the populations of the Arab towns of Lydda and Ramish and dismissed the charge that the troops had massacred Lydda townspeople […] In fact, according to IDF records from 1948, in the IDF archive, what was ordered and carried out was a full-scale expulsion; and Yiftah Brigade troops killed some 250 townspeople.' 2004, 20–21.

10. Confino, in this regard, follows neo-Zionists such as Golan (2004), 912 cited in Pappé (2009), 13 who argue that expulsion is just something that happens in times of war.

11. Indeed when he mentions the conquest of Lydda and the expulsion of the civilian population, unlike Morris (2004), 21 he does not mention the massacre of 250 Palestinians.

12. It is worth noting that there is a journal entitled *Palestine–Israel: Journal of Politics, Economics and Culture* http://www.pij.org/index.php founded by two Palestinian and Israeli journalists in 1994. The journal is produced locally in East Jerusalem and is staffed by a joint team of Palestinians and Israelis with two chief editors and two managing editors. It aims to provide 'background material and in-depth analysis of various aspects of the conflict from the perspective of both sides, thus helping to shed light on the complex issues dividing Israelis and Palestinians and the relationship between the two peoples.' Its aims include the promotion of rapprochement and understanding between the two peoples by fostering active dialogue on the issues at the heart of the conflict from both perspectives in a climate of constructive criticism and respect. Past issues have focused on the environment, the media, settlements, Jerusalem, national identities, water, human rights, peace education, etc. http://www.pij.org/about.php The current issue is on the subject of natural resources and the Arab–Israeli conflict http://www.pij.org/current.php [last accessed May 08, 2015].

13. For a couple of recent examples in Russia and America of political interference in school history curricula see: http://www.ecfr.eu/article/commentary_ vladimir_putin_historian_in_chief346 [last accessed April 28, 2015]; http:// www.theguardian.com/commentisfree/2014/sep/30/high-school-history- classes-colorado-school-board [last accessed April 28, 2015]. See also Loewen (2005) for America; Donnelly and Norton (2011), 125–129 for examples from France, Greece and Turkey.

14. This parallels recent debates among radical political theorists about the merits of 'withdrawal' from existing institutions.

15. See Davies (2006), 18 for his point that if universities really were places for critical intellectual reflection there might be here or there departments of historics rather than history. He defines historics as an examination of what history does in an already historicised world in which history is the socially dominant idea. Historics exposes and examines the unconscious ideological

effects of history including the way in which academic consensus is fabricated. See pp. 5, 7, 16.

16. We could mention the recent wall art by Banksey in Gaza and the West Bank http://www.theguardian.com/arts/pictures/0,1543331,00.html [last accessed April 30, 2015] as well as the art of Mohammad Saba'aneh who uses cartoons as a means of informing people about the Palestinian situation http://mondoweiss.net/2015/04/political-cartoonist-palestine [last accessed April 30, 2015] and http://www.cartoonmovement.com/p/148 [last accessed April 30, 2015]. The exhibition by Emily Jacir, *Europa,* at the Whitechapel Gallery, http://www.whitechapelgallery.org/exhibitions/emily-jacir-europa/ [last accessed November 06, 2015]. See also the Palestinian Museum http://www.palmuseum.org/language/english [last accessed November 06, 2015]. For films about Palestine see http://www.palestinecampaign.org/films-about-palestine/ [last accessed November 06, 2015].

17. Sacco has produced work about a number of conflicts that are historically contested, including the war in Bosnia, the Chechen War, and Iraq, as well as pieces about marginalised communities such as India's 'untouchables' and Saharan refugees. See, for example, Sacco 2000; 2003, 2010, 2012.

18. We see engaged journalism as another term for Martin Bell's 'journalism of attachment', Bell (1998).

19. Like Sacco, Antick has produced work on a number of complicated, politically resonant events: the Bhopal Disaster, Palestine, former Nazi death camps, and Rio's favelas. Antick (2012); (2013a) and (2013b). He is currently working on another documentary-fiction project provisionally entitled 'Smith at Batang Kali: a short history of little value' that explores the 1948 British massacre of 24 unarmed civilians in Malaysia. A topic of current political relevance as relatives of the victims continued a 66-year battle for justice by taking the case to the UK Supreme Court in late April 2015, see http://www.independent.co.uk/news/uk/home-news/batang-kali-killings-britain-in-the-dock-over-1948-massacre-in-malaysia-10187309.html [last accessed April 30, 2015].

20. We find Wittgenstinian theories of meaning as use more persuasive and coherent than those predicated on the authority of the author. Wittgenstein (1973), 42 'the meaning of a word is its use in a language'. We would argue that meaning is always, and only, constructed within and by 'interpretive communities' we can never, therefore ascertain *the* authorial meaning, never mind prioritise it. The term is from Fish (1980, 14) – '[i]nterpretative communities are made up of those who share interpretive strategies [... A]n interpretive community is [...] a bundle of interests, of particular purposes and goals.'

21. The phrase 'the same old thing' recalls Davies' argument that history is not simply the intellectual instrument of dominant socio-economic interests in an already historicised world, but that it also affirms and legitimises violence in general as well as specific conflicts in particular as historically normal. The *latest* human rights abuse in the Occupied Territories, the *latest* house demolition, extra-judicial murder or bombing is really just the *same old thing.* Davies (2006), 4–5 and 7.

22. A review of the performance can be found here. https://bhopalfacing30.wordpress.com/2014/05/05/comments-on-bhopal-to-bridgehampton-performance-by-university-of-roehampton-stp-drama-students-2-may-2014/ [last accessed April 30, 2015] and the students' message

of support can be seen here https://www.youtube.com/watch?v=q5S8UZCfMAY [last accessed April 30, 2015].

23. Klug has been arguing for a two-state solution since the 1970s. Specifically, in a thoughtful Oxford Research Group policy paper (Klug 2009) he outlines three moves by which the international community, having set clear goals and with effective enforcement, could resolve the conflict.

24. For +972 see http://972mag.com/ [last accessed April 30, 2015]; for Zochrot see http://zochrot.org/ [last accessed April 30, 2015]; for the Palestine Solidarity Campaign see http://www.palestinecampaign.org/ [last accessed April 30, 2015]; Jews for Justice for Palestinians http://jfjfp.com/ [last accessed April 30, 2015]; for the Electronic Intifada see http://electronicintifada.net/ [last accessed April 30, 2015].

25. http://www.palestinecampaign.org/information/factsheets/ [last accessed April 30, 2015].

26. http://zochrot.org/en/content/17 [last accessed April 30, 2015].

27. http://zochrot.org/en/keyword/45323 [last accessed April 30, 2015].

28. In the first week since its launch in May 2014 there were approximately 12,000 downloads http://www.washingtonpost.com/world/middle_east/with-inakba-palestinians-delve-into-their-history/2014/05/14/7c2a8026-db8d-11e3-a837-8835df6c12c4_story.html [last accessed April 30, 2015].

29. https://plutopress.wordpress.com/2014/11/25/criminalizing-the-victim-the-life-story-of-rasmea-odeh/ [last accessed November 06, 2015].

30. http://www.thenation.com/article/188033/will-rasmeah-odeh-go-prison-because-confession-obtained-through-torture [last accessed April 30, 2015] http://electronicintifada.net/blogs/ali-abunimah/judge-sentences-rasmea-odeh-insisting-case-not-political [last accessed April 30, 2015].

31. http://www.thenation.com/article/188033/will-rasmeah-odeh-go-prison-because-confession-obtained-through-torture [last accessed April 30, 2015].

32. Torture expert Dr Mary Fabri was prepared to testify that torture survivors living with post-traumatic stress disorder frequently and unintentionally narrow their focus and supress recollection. However, evidence concerning the rape and torture of Odeh was disallowed by the judge and she was not able to testify at the trial. Odeh's legal team believe this to have been a legal error. http://justice4rasmea.org/news/2015/10/14/defense-attorney-hits-it-out-of-the-park-in-appellate-court/ [last accessed November 06, 2015].

33. For example the case of Sami Al-Arian and the Holy Land Five http://www.thenation.com/article/188033/will-rasmeah-odeh-go-prison-because-confession-obtained-through-torture see also http://mondoweiss.net/2012/10/holy-land-five-appeal-could-set-precedent-on-using-secret-evidence-in-u-s-courts [last accessed April 30, 2015].

34. We are here mindful of Pihlainen's persuasive argument that blurring the boundaries between institutionalised histories and more practical appropriations of the past may lead to history, through its preoccupation with an ultimately unobtainable search for truth, contaminating more progressive ways of thinking about our relation to the past and undermining their political and social efficacy. Pihlainen (2015). We discuss this issue in more depth in our forthcoming book, *Liberating Histories* (Routledge, forthcoming).

Acknowledgements

We would like to thank the editor of this special edition and the two reviewers for their extremely helpful comments – their suggestions have significantly improved the finished article.

Disclosure statement

No potential conflict of interest was reported by the authors.

References

Antick, Paul. 2012. "Smith in Palestine (to be Read Aloud, in its Entirety)." *Visual Communication* 11 (4): 443–460.

Antick, Paul. 2013a. "Bhopal to Bridgehampton: Schema for a Disaster Tourism Event." *Journal of Visual Culture* 12 (1): 165–185.

Antick, Paul. 2013b. "Smith's Tour Favela." In *Transcultural Montage*, edited by Christian Suhr and Rane Willersley, 106–130. New York: Berghahn Books.

Bar-Tal, Daniel. 2007. *Living with the Conflict, Socio-Psychological Analysis of the Jewish Society in Israel*. Jerusalem: Carmel.

Bell, Martin. 1998. "The Journalism of Attachment." In *Media Ethics*, edited by M. Kiernan, 15–22. London: Routledge.

Ben-Artzi, Yossi. 2011. "Out of (Academic) Focus: On Ilan Pappe, Out of the Frame: The Struggle for Academic Freedom in Israel." *Israel Studies* 16 (2): 165–183.

Cohen, Sande. 2006. *History Out of Joint: Essays on the Use and Abuse of History*. Baltimore, MD: The John Hopkins University Press.

Confino, Alon. 2012. "Miracles and Snow in Palestine and Israel: Tantura, a History of 1948." *Israel Studies* 17 (2): 25–61.

Davies, Martin. 2006. *Historics: Why History Dominates Contemporary Society*. London: Routledge.

Davies, Martin. 2008. "Institutionalized Nihilism: An Outline of the Academic Function." *Rethinking History* 12 (4): 463–481.

Davies, Martin. 2010. *Imprisoned by History: Aspects of a Historicized Life*. London: Routledge.

Donnelly, Mark, and Claire Norton. 2011. *Doing History*. London: Routledge.

Donnelly, Mark, and Claire Norton. 2015. "In the Service of Technocratic Managerialism? History in UK Universities." *Educational Philosophy and Theory*. doi:10.1080/0013 1857.2015.1104232.

Fish, Stanley. 1980. *Is There a Text in this Class?*. Cambridge, MA: Harvard University Press.

Foucault, Michel. 2002. "Truth and Power" interview with Alessandro Fontana and Pasquale Pasquino [1976]. In *Foucault. Power: Essential Works of Foucault 1954–1984*, edited by James D. Faubion, Translated by Robert Hurley and others, 111–133. London: Penguin.

Golan, Arnon. 2004. "The Reshaping of the Ex-Arab Space and the Construction of an Israeli Space (1948–1950)." [in Hebrew]. In *Israel's War of Independence, 1948–1949* [in Hebrew], edited by I. Kadish. Tel-Aviv: Israeli Ministry of Defence Publications.

Harlan, David. 2003. "Ken Burns and the Coming Crisis of Academic History." *Rethinking History* 7 (2): 169–192.

Jenkins, Keith. 1997. "Why Bother with the Past? Engaging with some Issues Raised by the Possible 'End of History as We Have Known it." *Rethinking History* 1 (1): 56–66.

Jenkins, Keith. 1999. *Why History: Ethics and Postmodernity*. London: Routledge.

Jenkins, Keith. 2009. *At the Limits of History: Essays on Theory and Practice*. London: Routledge.

Klug, Tony. 2007. *How Peace Broke out in the Middle East: A Short History of the Future.* Fabian Society. Accessed May 08, 2015. https://www.fabians.org.uk/wp-content/uploads/2012/04/HowPeaceBrokeOutInTheMiddleEast.pdf

Klug, Tony. 2009. *Visions of the End Game: a strategy to bring the Israeli-Palestinian conflict swiftly to an end*. Fabian Society. Accessed May 09, 2015. http://www.oxfordresearchgroup.org.uk/sites/default/files/endgame.pdf

Laclau, Ernesto, and Chantal Mouffe. 2014. *Hegemony and Socialist Strategy: Towards a Radical Democratic Politics*. London: Verso.

Loewen, James W. 2005. *Lies my Teacher Told Me: Everything Your American History Textbook got Wrong*. New York: Simon and Schuster.

May, Todd. 1994. *The Political Philosophy of Poststructuralist Anarchism*. Pennsylvania: The Pennsylvania University Press.

Morris, Benny. 2004. "The Tantura 'Massacre." *The Jerusalem*, Report (09/02/2004): 18–22. Accessed April 29, 2015. http://www.ee.bgu.ac.il/~censor/katz-directory/04-02-06morris-the-jerusalem-report-tantura.pdf

Morris, Benny. 2011. "The Liar as Hero." *New Republic*, March 17, 2011. Accessed April 29, 2015. http://www.newrepublic.com/article/books/magazine/85344/ilan-pappe-sloppy-dishonest-historian

Moses, Dirk. 2005. "Hayden White, Traumatic Nationalism, and the Public Role of History." *History and Theory* 44 (3): 311–332.

Mouffe, Chantal. 2013. *Agonistics: Thinking the World Politically*. London: Verso.

Munslow, Alun. 2010. *The Future of History*. Basingstoke: Palgrave MacMillan.

Pappé, Ilan. 2000–01a. "The Tantura Massacre, 22–23 May 1948." *Journal of Palestine Studies* 30 (119): 5–18.

Pappé, Ilan. 2000–01b. "The Tantura Case in Israel: The Katz Research and Trial." *Journal of Palestine Studies* 30 (119): 19–39.

Pappé, Ilan. 2007. "Historical Truth, Modern Historiography and Ethical Obligations: The Challenge of the Tantura Case." In *The Israel/Palestine Question: A Reader*, edited by Ilan Pappé, 115–138. London: Routledge.

Pappé, Ilan. 2009. "The Vicissitudes of the 1948 Historiography of Israel." *Journal of Palestinian Studies*, 39 (1): 6–23.

Pappé, Ilan. 2010. *Out of the Frame: the Struggle for Academic Freedom in Israel*. London: Pluto Press.

Peled-Elhanan, Nurit. 2012. *Palestine in Israeli School Books: Ideology and Propaganda in Education*. London: I.B. Tauris.

Pihlainen, Kalle. 2011. "The End of Oppositional History?." *Rethinking History* 15 (4): 463–488.

Pihlainen, Kalle. 2012. "Towards a Post-problematic History." Paper given at the Philosophy of History seminar at the Institute of Historical Research, University of London, November 22nd, 2012.

Pihlainen, Kalle. 2015. "What can history Do?" paper presented at the *Ethos of History* conference Sigtuna, Sweden, September 10–12, 2015.

Rigney, Ann. 2007. "Being an Improper Historian." In *Manifestos for History*, edited by Keith Jenkins, Sue Morgan, and Alun Munslow, 149–159. London: Routledge.

Sacco, Joe. 2000. *Safe Area Goražde: The War in Eastern Bosnia 1992–95*. Seattle: Fantagraphics Books.

Sacco, Joe. 2003. *Palestine*. London: Jonathan Cape.

Sacco, Joe. 2009. *Footnotes in Gaza*. London: Jonathan Cape.

Sacco, Joe. 2010. "The Unwanted." *Virginia Quarterly Review* 86 (1 and 2). Accessed April 29, 2015. http://www.vqronline.org/vqr-gallery/unwanted-part-1http://www.vqronline.org/vqr-gallery/unwanted-part-1 and http://www.vqronline.org/vqr-gallery/unwanted-part-2

Sacco, Joe. 2012. *Journalism*. New York: Henry Holt and Company.

Southgate, Beverley. 2005. *What is History For?*. London: Routledge.

Wertsch, James V. 2002. *Voices of Collective Remembering*. Cambridge: Cambridge University Press.

White, Hayden. 1978. "The Burden of History." In *Tropics of Discourse: Essays in Cultural Criticism*, 27–50. Baltimore, MD: John Hopkins University Press. First published in 1966.

White, Hayden. 2012. "Politics, History, and the Practical Past." *Storia della Storiografia* 61: 127–133.

White, Hayden. 2014. *The Practical Past*. Evanston, IL: Northwestern University Press.

Wittgenstein, Ludwig. 1973. *Philosophical Investigations*. Translated by G. E. M. Anscombe. 3rd ed. New York: Pearson.

The ideal of objectivity and the public role of the historian: some lessons from the *Historikerstreit* and the History Wars

Anton Froeyman

Department of Philosophy and Moral Sciences, Centre for Logic and Philosophy of Science, Ghent University, Ghent, Belgium

ABSTRACT

In this paper, I attempt to offer some new insights into an age-old question: what is the public usefulness of history and historians? More specifically, I discuss the role of the ideal of the disinterested and objective historian in two different and very important public historical debates: the German *Historikerstreit* and the Australian History Wars. My analysis is not so much aimed at analysing the outcome of these debates, but rather at the way these debates were held, and the specific ways in which the participants argued with each other. I combine a rhetorical analysis of these debates with a method from analytic philosophy of science to arrive at the following conclusion: both the *Historikerstreit* and the History Wars were haunted by a misguided ideal of historical objectivity that in the end had a negative influence on the quality of these debates. Finally, I also suggest an alternative view on the public role of the historian, which is based on Chantal Mouffe's distinction between agonistic and antagonistic pluralism.

Introduction

The aim of this article is to assess the public utility of history and historians. The central question is, quite simply: What is the usefulness of history and historians? What can historians and history contribute to present-day society? This is an age-old question, and has pervaded the historical profession since Classical Antiquity. Nevertheless, today, in an age in which humanities departments are continuously expected to justify their existence, it has become more important than ever to have an answer to the question 'What is history for?'

The traditional answer, of course, is *Historia Magistra Vitae Est* – history is the teacher of life. From Antiquity to roughly the eighteenth century, history was thought of as a reservoir of examples that orators could use for rhetorical purposes, or that might provide princes, generals and politicians with experience (Koselleck 2004, 27). As the historical consciousness of the West changed and 'history' as a collective singular took shape, the idea of history as a teacher of life changed. It became associated with the idea of a single grand narrative, a large-scale course of history that could be known and analysed by historians and philosophers. (Koselleck 2004, 41) This meant that *Historia Magistra Vitae* became associated with substantial philosophy of history, and, in the end, also with nationalist or otherwise politically inspired grand narratives.

During the second half of the twentieth century, historians abandoned the grand narratives of the nineteenth and early twentieth centuries, and with it, also the classical conception of the relevance of history for life. As an alternative, many historians sought refuge in the scientific and epistemic view of history as a way of telling the truth about the past. In this sense, the relevance of history stems from its participation in the more encompassing project of scientific inquiry in general. If the writing of history possesses a scientific status – so it is often thought – we need not worry about its relevance any longer. After all, is it not self-evident that science is relevant and important? And does this not mean that history, as a scientific enterprise, is relevant too?

The resulting view is one in which the scientific status of the work of the historian is the single most important reason, perhaps even the *only* reason, for its relevance to society. Historians are useful only if they pledge unconditional loyalty to historical truth. This also entails that, when entering into a public discussion, historians should never take sides or express their own political or ideological sympathies, but simply stick to the facts. In exchange, they can expect to be judged solely on the basis of their work and the truth-claims they make, and never be subjected to personal attacks.

We do not often see the view that I have sketched above expressed explicitly. The reason is that, as Peter Novick already noted several decades ago, it is not an explicit methodology but an informal creed, a set of (often rather unconscious) ideas about what it means to be a historian in present-day society. (Novick 1988, 2) Nevertheless, it is quite prominent in the theoretical and more general writings of practising historians. It is not a coincidence, for example, that Joyce Appleby, Margaret Jacob and Lynn Hunt's famous work on the nature of the historical profession and the relevance of history is called *Telling the Truth About History* (1995). For what they claim is exactly this: the contribution historians have to make to society consists of supplying that society with historical truth, and the more truth there is, the better off society will be. (Appleby, Hunt, and Jacob 1995; 289 and 308) The reason for this is that truth is thought to have a unifying effect. By gathering around a common historical truth, different social groups are thought to be able to overcome their differences. Whereas most public representations and uses of the past are supposed to be partial and driven by motivations and social divisions outside history itself, professional historians can supposedly bridge these gaps by sticking to the facts and representing the past in a more balanced and impartial manner. (MacMillan 2009) In an important edited volume on the same matter (the social responsibility of history), François Bédarida adds the converse: whenever the past seems to generate controversy or strengthen social divisions, this is inevitably the consequence of a lack of understanding of historical truth. (Bédarida 1995, 4–6) This general view is nowhere clearer than in Richard Evans' best-selling *In Defence of History* (1997). Evans takes it that history needs defending, because its status is being attacked by postmodern theorists. What is striking is that Evans interprets the postmodernist and post-structuralist view as a strictly epistemological critique of history writing – as the claim that historical knowledge is impossible to obtain (Evans 1997, 9) – and that he presupposes that this is also automatically an attack on its public relevance. (Evans 1997, 223) This means that the public relevance of history writing is proportional to its ability to tell the truth. In short, the more truth historians produce, the bigger their contribution to society, and *vice versa*.

Of course, since the end of the end of the 1970s, another view has also been present. As insights from post-structuralist theory began to find their way into history and historical theory, narrativists such as Hayden White and Frank Ankersmit challenged the objectivist presumptions of traditional history and historians. (White 1972, 1978; Ankersmit 1983; Jenkins 2003; Cohen 2006; Munslow 2007) They argued that, even if we can unearth all kinds of factual historical knowledge, there still is no clear route from historical facts to a historical representation. For every given set of facts, there are always several possible narratives that are equally true. Hence, the choice of one narrative over another – both for the historian deciding how to frame her subject and for the reader deciding which book to read – is always determined by personal, ideological preferences.

This debate has had important consequences for our conceptions of the social relevance of history, precisely because many historians' positions are based on the possibility of a neutral and objective view of the past. Hence, their preferred role is that of the neutral expert, the myth-buster or the fact-checker, not that of the activist or the partisan. (Kalela 2011, 148) Historians will tend to present themselves as the voice of reason, as guardians of truth and scholarship. If, however, we follow the narrativists and argue that the idea of a single objective view of history is an illusion, this takes away the foundation on which the 'objectivist' view of the public role of the historian is based. Instead, we arrive at a view of historians as engaged intellectuals, partisans of a political cause

What is interesting now is that these two different views regarding the public role of the historian also imply two very different views of contemporary society. As noted, for the objectivist view sketched above, the idea is that history and historians can create a sense of community, gather diverse groups around a common historical past, and in this way contribute to a more harmonious and consensual society. Of course, this view is untenable from the narrativist position. After all, how can we expect people to gather around a single story when there are always numerous alternative stories available? Hence, the view of the public relevance of history and historians that follows from the narrativist or post-structuralist positions is very different. It is a view of society as a multi-coloured collection of views, ideas and interests. The ideal, then, is not a consensual society where everyone agrees with one another, but an arena in which different people from different backgrounds are allowed to have their say, without the obligation to come to an agreement. What is to be protected is not a sense of social unity but quite the opposite: the right of every individual or social group to protest against the status quo and to be heard.

So, in short, the discussion between the narrativist and the objectivistic views of history is not just an epistemological discussion about the capacities of historical texts to refer to the past. It is also a discussion about the social relevance of history, the public role of the historian, and, ultimately, the kind of society we wish to inhabit. One the one hand, we have the historian as a neutral expert, contributing to a more harmonious polis from a bird's-eye, scientific point of view. (This, I believe, remains more or less the orthodox view for the majority of professional historians.) And on the other hand, there is the historian as an engaged intellectual, a partisan for a political and ideological cause, speaking up for a specific social group. Although there are some groups of historians who seem to have adopted this view already (postcolonial and gender historians are the clearest examples, but one could also mention many cultural historians), it is still much more popular among theorists than among historians.[1]

As stated, up until now, the discussion has been mostly carried out on a fairly abstract and epistemological level, and less on a more practical and public one.[2] My aim now is to contribute to the debate in the latter register, the debate on the public role of history and historians. More specifically, I will do so by means of a close reading of two important public discussions on history: the German *Historikerstreit* and the Australian History Wars. My idea is to take a look at the role that actual historians played in these discussions about history, and try to find out which of the two models outlined is better suited for accounting for the public role of the historian. It should be noted here that I am not so much interested in the outcome (or lack thereof) of these debates. This has already been discussed extensively by others. Rather, I want to make a point about how the debates were held, and how the ideals of the historical profession played a role in them.

The argument consists of two parts. First, I will argue that both discussions were personal, politically laden, and far from neutral and objective. This, of course, will not come as a surprise to most people. Both narrativists and objectivists will surely admit that the discussions surrounding these two controversies were messy, that historians did not assume the role of neutral experts, and that the end result was not a single story that was commonly accepted but rather an affirmation of already existing social divisions. The difficult question is: What should we learn from this? For the narrativists, this will simply demonstrate that history, and therefore historians too, are not neutral. For objectivists, however, it means something different. Their reply would be that this is (public) history at its worst: Historians may have behaved like partisans of an ideological cause, but this is not how things should be. If historians would have behaved as they are supposed to, as serious, disinterested scholars, the outcome would have been different. The discussions would have been more rational, and a consensual historical narrative, or at least something close to such, would have been possible. The second part of my argument will be directed against this reply. Using a method from contemporary philosophy of science, I will show that the debates of the *Historikerstreit* and the History Wars *could not have proceeded otherwise*. In these discussions, a rational consensus was not simply absent – it was, from the beginning, impossible.

Part 1: The *Historikerstreit* and the History Wars: a brief description

The Historikerstreit

The *Historikerstreit* took place in the second half of the 1980s in Germany. In essence, it was a discussion about the nature and causes of the Holocaust and the question of whether the Germans and Germany should bear some exceptional burden of guilt. The public controversy began in the aftermath of an opinion piece by historian Ernst Nolte in the *Frankfurter Allgemeine*, in which Nolte claimed that it was time to 'historicize' the Holocaust; by which he meant that we could stop seeing it as a sudden manifestation of absolute evil, and compare it to other events of the nineteenth and twentieth centuries. (Nolte 1993a) Nolte claimed that, although the scale and ruthlessness of the Holocaust might be unprecedented, the mind-set behind it was not. Rather, it was just another instance of a way of thinking that had already existed for a century or so – the belief that it was justified to eradicate entire groups of people in the service of a totalitarian utopia. The Holocaust was neither the first nor the last of such large-scale massacres, and was preceded by Stalin's mass murder of the kulaks and followed by the Cambodian genocide, among others. Provocatively, Nolte also stated that the Holocaust was a copy, not an original, and somewhat vaguely seemed to suggest that Hitler might have taken many of his ideas from Stalin. Around the same time, another historian, Andreas Hillgruber, argued that the Second World War should not be seen exclusively through the eyes of the victims and published a book in which the Jewish perspective was placed beside the tragic situation of the Germans fighting on the

Eastern front to protect what was left of Germany. Hillgruber made the point that the Allied victories were not seen or experienced as a liberation by many of the common Germans and backed this up by referring to the (perceived or real) horrors committed by the Red Army and the Allies.

Nolte's piece was followed by a sharp article from the philosopher Jürgen Habermas (1993a), who accused Nolte and Hillgruber of apologetic tendencies and viewed their writings as part of an attempt, prevalent since the conservative political turn in the early 1980s, to establish a new German nationalist consciousness that was hostile to Western Europe and the values of the Enlightenment. The Holocaust, Habermas argued, should continue to be seen as unique because only in that way could Germany develop into a tolerant and pluralist (Western European) society

Both Nolte and Hillgruber as well as Habermas were joined by numerous historians and public intellectuals, and two camps soon formed. On the conservative side, the most important actors were the historians Nolte, Hillgruber, Michael Stürmer, Klaus Hildebrand and Joachim Fest. On the progressive side, Habermas was joined by historians such as Jürgen Kocka, Martin Broszat and Hans Mommsen.

One of the most striking features of the *Historikerstreit* as a discussion is its unsatisfactory nature. Instead of being a constructive debate about a specific subject, it was a piece of intellectual trench-warfare that ended in a stalemate. The two sides were vehemently opposed and the few attempts to formulate a compromise or a middle way were not recognised as such (for some attempts at compromise, see Meier 1993 and Geiss 1993). Moreover, it was never clear what the discussion precisely involved. The various actors did not really engage with each others' claims and often argued by ascribing hidden intentions to their opponents, at times almost hinting at conspiracy theories. (Fleischer 1993, 80; Habermas 1993a, 42; Mommsen 1993b; Sontheimer 1993, 185; Winkler 1993, 169–170) In the end, this resulted in a situation where the majority of attention was directed at the debate itself rather than focusing on history or the Holocaust: many pieces included extensive arguments about how person X had misrepresented, misquoted or misread person Y, and of how those on the other side set up straw men instead of engaging with real positions. (See, for example, Mommsen 1993, 104; Habermas 1993b, 169–170; Hillgruber 1993, 222; Meier 1993) At a certain point, Nolte and Habermas even resorted to what can only be described as gossip: Nolte by stating that Habermas used his influence to prevent him from speaking at a conference and Habermas by accusing Nolte of chasing away Saul Friedländer at a reception. (Nolte 1993b, 39)

With respect to the argument of this article, the most important thing about the *Historikerstreit* is that historians blatantly failed to take up the role of the neutral and disinterested expert. Despite the fact that the majority of the participants were academic historians (for example, Nolte, Hillgruber, Stürmer, Fest, Meier, Hildebrand, Wolfgang as well as Hans Mommsen, Möller, Bracher,

Jäckel, Kocka, Schulze, Broszat, Nipperdey, Geiss and Winkler), this fact did not result in a dispassionate, scholarly discussion. Moreover, the participating historians did not limit themselves to fact-checking or myth-busting, but freely drew political and moral conclusions. As Karl Dietrich Bracher notes, it was remarkable that there could be so much disagreement when all the relevant historical facts had already been known for thirty years. (Bracher 1993, 72)

The obvious conclusion would be that, at least in the *Historikerstreit*, the classic idea of the historian as an impartial guide to the truth does not correspond with how historians actually behave in public debates. However, when we take a closer look at the discussion itself, we can see that the classic, scholarly role of the historian is very much present, albeit not as a description of what is happening but as a rhetorical instrument instead. The most common rhetorical strategy in the *Historikerstreit* seems to have been to represent one's opponents as partisans who force the historical facts into the straightjacket of their own moral and political preconceptions. Protagonists of one's own group, on the other hand, were generally represented as serious scholars whose only interest was to do their job and advance historical knowledge. Generally, the conservative rightist side was represented by the leftists as a group of nationalist historians who wanted to force Germany into a new, restricted form of nationalism. The leftist side, on the other hand, was portrayed by the rightists as an overly politically correct and moralising thought police that wanted to foist its own political preferences onto other people. Nolte, for example, referred to the political (leftist) consensus as an impediment to historical knowledge (Nolte 1993a; 3–4, 13 and 15), while Habermas saw himself as defending historical objectivity against the particularist nationalism of Nolte and Hillgruber. (Habermas 1993a; 42) Jürgen Kocka claimed that Nolte's and Joachim Fest's writings did not have anything to do with the 'sober' historical analysis of motivations and causes'. (Kocka 1993, 87–88) Martin Broszat accused Nolte of arrogant disdain for empirical and historical procedures'. (Broszat 1993, 126) Heinrich August Winkler stated that a comparison between Hitler, Stalin and Pol Pot was not serious historical scholarship. (Winkler 1993, 175) Imanuel Geiss argued that Hillgruber had crossed the boundaries of his profession by abandoning sober explanation. (Geiss 1993, 256) Finally, Walter Euchner made this same claim regarding Nolte, accusing him of resorting to 'philosophical speculations' (Euchner 1993, 241) – such speculation clearly meant in a derogatory sense. Klaus Hildebrand and Thomas Nipperdey, on the other hand, stated that Habermas had let politics come in the way of scholarship (Hildebrand 1993, 50), and that historical research was best conducted with soberness and distance. Joachim Fest agreed, stating that, contrary to social scientists (like Habermas), historians always base their statements on the secure footing of historical facts. (Fest 1993, 70) Both sides also made clear statements about the value of truth: Hildebrand argued that historians can fight totalitarian regimes by telling the truth about the past (Hildebrand 1993, 50), while Wolfgang Mommsen claimed that scholarly consensus among (leftist) historians actively benefits democratic values. (Mommsen 1993, 207–208)

As can be seen, the ideal (or spectre) of the dispassionate scholar interested in historical truth and the advancement of knowledge was, after all, very much present in the *Historikerstreit*. Nevertheless, it had little to do with how historians actually behaved. Ironically, the ideal of dispassionate and objective historical scholarship was mainly used to create the exact opposite of what it represented: a polarised and partisan situation based on a rigorous distinction between 'us' and 'them' in which the 'we' were serious, dispassionate, sober and balanced, and the 'they' were partisan, dogmatic, politically motivated and not open to serious scholarly discussion.

The History Wars

The Australian 'History Wars' were an even bigger and more influential public debate about history than the *Historikerstreit*. In essence, the dispute was about the place of Aboriginals in Australian history: Should Australian history be seen as a triumphant March of civilisation, or rather as an imperialist story of conquest and crimes against the native people of Australia? In the course of the late 1980s, Australian history became an important topic in the political battle between conservatives and progressives. Public disputes about Australian history have been going on for about two decades, flaring up around significant landmark events such as the celebration of the Australian bicentenary in 1988, Paul Keating's Redfern Park Speech (1992), the release of the final report of the national inquiry into the Stolen Generations (1997), the opening of the National Museum of Australia (2001), prime minister Kevin Rudd's apology to indigenous Australians (2008) and the announcement of a new history curriculum (2010).

Up until the 1960s Australian history was generally portrayed as an extension of that of the British Empire and part of the Western process of civilization, in which brave white men succeeded in turning a barren wasteland into a modern democratic welfare state. The point of view of the Aboriginals, viewed as remnants of the Stone Age, was simply seen as irrelevant. In the course of the second half of the twentieth century less positive national narratives emerged, and the crimes against the Australian natives gradually came to be recognized. The most prominent figure in this process was the historian Manning Clark, who, no doubt wrongly (see MacIntyre and Clark 2004, 50–71), came to be seen as a symbol of the negative, leftist and politically correct view of Australian history. Clark's opposite was the right-wing historian and public intellectual Geoffrey Blainey. In 1993, Blainey coined the term 'Black Armband History' in his Sir John Latham Memorial Lecture (1993), using it to refer to the supposed leftist consensus among professional historians that downplayed Australia's achievements and attempted to burden present-day Australians with a sense of guilt for crimes that they themselves had not committed. In addition to being one of the most important voices on the right wing side of the History Wars, Blaney became the symbol for this position. Other important figures on the right were the conservative politician John Howard (prime minister from 1996 to 2007) and the conservative writers and journalists Keith Windschuttle, Kevin Donnelly and Padraic McGuinness, all closely connected to the conservative journal *Quadrant*. The most important figures on the left were Labour politician Paul Keating (prime minister from 1991 to 1996), his speech writer Don Watson, historians Stuart MacIntyre, Anna Clark, Dirk Moses, Henry Reynolds and political scientist and historian Robert Manne.

Just like the *Historikerstreit*, the History Wars were more or less the exact opposite of a respectful, scholarly debate. Again, large parts of the debate were more about the debate itself than about its content. Participants continually searched for hidden motives and accused each other of ignorance and hypocrisy instead of engaging with each others' arguments. This is particularly visible in the rhetoric of the right, which was based on a theory (possibly inspired by American neo-cons; see MacIntyre and Clark 2004, 134; Bonnell and Crotty 2004, 231) about the invasion of the academic and political world by leftists with an aversion for reality and truth. Importantly, the debate was never resolved and left a bitter aftertaste. Graeme Davison deplored the way in which history functioned as a source of social division and opposition rather than of social unity (Davison 2000, 2) and Anthony Mason expressed the hope that the discussion might become less sharp, more scholarly, and hence more beneficial to society as a whole. (Mason 2004, viii)

As in the *Historikerstreit*, it is remarkable that historical facts did not play a significant part in the History Wars. Neither the historian Geoffrey Blainey nor the politician and prime minister John Howard initially denied the occurrence of crimes against Aboriginals. (Howard 1996) The debate was not so much about whether Aboriginals had been wronged or not, but about who, if anyone, should be held responsible. Especially during its first years, the debate was more about the perspective one should take on Australian history and Aboriginal suffering than about that suffering itself. However, the situation changed dramatically following the publication of Keith Windschuttle's first volume of *The Fabrication of Aboriginal History* (2002). Windschuttle challenged the orthodox view on aboriginal history, basically stating that there had been a huge conspiracy by academic leftists to invent past crimes against aboriginal Australians in order to spread their own politically correct ideological agenda. Although this turn in the debate seemed to bring historians back to their home ground – by refuting Windschuttle, historians could again argue over archives, sources, research methods, evidence, argumentation and historical facts – the result was not what they might have hoped for. No matter how extensively and meticulously they refuted his claims (or a least the large majority thereof), many politicians still continued to take him seriously and large parts of the media treated him as on a more or less equal level with professional historians such as Henry Reynolds or Dirk Moses, and continued to view the debate as a discussion between two opposing camps rather than as an intellectual skirmish between the community of serious historians and a lone, quasi-negationist outsider. (Manne 2003, 7) Again, the idea of the objective historian bringing the historical truth to the general public did not seem to apply. The general public seemed much more inclined to see a continuing debate with two equally serious opposing views rather than a single, true consensus built by professional historians. Part of this can of course be ascribed to the mainstream media's craving for polemics, but I do not believe that this is the whole story. As Anna Clark's research seems to suggest, the general public is much more accepting than professional historians of the idea that one's view of the past is never neutral and that there will always be different perspectives. (Clark 2009)

Part 2: The *Historikerstreit* and the History Wars: an analysis

Of course, even though both the *Historikerstreit* and the History Wars were messy, personal and ideological as debates, and hence far from neutral, this will not be likely to impress objectivists. As noted, they have recourse to an obvious reply: This is simply not how historians are supposed to behave. The *Historikerstreit* and the History wars were an embarrassment for the profession precisely because historians were tempted to involve themselves in political in ideological matters, and forgot their true role of neutral experts only interested in the past itself. If they would have held on to that role, things would have looked quite different and a common history that could help bridge social divisions might have been created. However, as I said in the introduction, the second part of my argument is devoted to denying this reply.

I will do this in the following way: I will construct what can be called a 'rational reconstruction' of both discussions. A rational reconstruction of a debate or argument involves stripping something of its context, leaving only the bare logical structure. This results in a highly artificial situation, an abstract model in fact, and is by no means something that can happen in the real world. Nevertheless, such a model can offer insight into the general logical and linguistic framework of a debate. The logical structure of a debate limits the possible routes a debate can take: it does not determine who is right or wrong, but it does determine what kind of claims are at stake, and hence also what a given participant should prove or disprove to make her point.

Hence, by creating such a rational reconstruction of the two debates discussed here, we can investigate whether there were other possible outcomes. Was it even possible for the debate to end in a more satisfying way, for example by one party convincing the other by a specific piece of evidence, or following a specific line of argumentation? Or was there perhaps a possible compromise that could have been reached if both parties had behaved more as disinterested scientists, and less as partisans?

I will use a slightly modified version of the so-called erotetic model of explanation, developed by Dutch philosopher of science Bas Van Fraassen (1980). The central claim of this model is that scientific (or more broadly, scholarly) explanation consists of giving answers to why-questions. Hence, if we want to understand a certain claim, hypothesis or theory, we should first identify the question to which it is an answer. This may sound trivial, but it is not. As Van Bouwel and Weber (2008) have shown, allegedly contradictory claims can turn out to be answers to very different questions and hence not contradict each other after all. For Van Fraassen, all questions should be why-questions and clarifying the question should also consist of clarifying its contrast class. In my modified application of his model, I will, however, also use other questions and other forms of clarification. Justification for doing so can be found in a previous article where I argue that how-questions, the basis of historical narratives, can also be viewed as causal claims and hence carry explanatory value. (Froeyman 2009)

Without giving too much away in advance, I want to reveal that the specific nature of the questions that were asked is the central issue in both the *Historikerstreit* and the History Wars. In both debates, the participants claimed to be answering one question while actually offering answers to another.

The Historikerstreit II

Let us start with the *Historikerstreit*. According to the erotetic model, if we want to reformulate the debate in abstract and logical terms, we need to find the question that the participants pretend to to answer. In essence, the most important question in the *Historikerstreit* looks like this:

Q1: *What was the cause of the Holocaust?*

At first sight, it seems as if both parties are attempting to answer this question. Both Nolte and Habermas want to explain the Holocaust and understand its causes rather than simply describe it. Nevertheless, on a closer look, Nolte is in fact answering a somewhat different question:

Q1': *Why did the Nazi's decide to annihilate the Jews and gypsies?*

What Nolte and his supporters wanted to do, was to recreate the thought-processes that made it seem rational to the Nazi's to annihilate all Jews and gypsies. Their answer is that the Nazi ideology did not fall from the sky. Rather, it was (either directly or indirectly, Nolte is rather vague about this) modelled after other mass murders aimed at the annihilation of entire social groups, and not simply aimed at troublesome individuals. Hence the Holocaust was not the prototype of this kind of criminal action but only one example in a series. It was preceded by, among others, the Stalinist mass murders and the Armenian genocide, and followed by the atrocities of the *Khmer Rouge*. Of course, the scale of the Holocaust was larger and its methods more systematic. Nolte never denied this. Nevertheless, in terms of answering this more specific question, the ruthlessness or scale of the Holocaust do not really matter; what matters is what drove the Nazi's to see the annihilation of entire social groups as a realistic and legitimate possibility.

Habermas and his supporters, on the other hand, sought answers to a very different question:

Q1": Why was the Holocaust so ruthless and methodical?

Contrary to Nolte, the left side of the debate, to which Habermas belonged, did not want to know why the Nazi's actually *decided* to annihilate the Jews and gypsies but instead asked why the scale was so large and the methods so ruthless, and why there was so much cooperation and so little protest. The answer, of course, appeals to circumstances that were particular to Germany in the 1930s and 1940s: racism, anti-Semitism and general intolerance were more prominently present in Germany than in other countries, especially among the bureaucratic elite. Hence, it was no coincidence that the deadliest and most horrible mass murder of the twentieth century was committed by Germans.

Alongside the question of the origin of the Holocaust, there is another question that was discussed in the *Historikerstreit*, as a consequence of Andreas Hillgruber's book *The Twofold Fall* (1984). This question can be formulated as follows:

Q2: Why was there so much support for, and so little resistance against, the Nazi regime?

However, when we look at Hillgruber's argument closely, his question looks more like this:

Q2': Why did the German soldiers fight the Russians rather than surrender or oppose the Nazi regime?

Hillgruber claims that this had to do with the gruesome reputation of the Red Army, as well as (but to a lesser extent) with the imperialistic ambitions of the Allied forces. He argues that the (possible) defeat of Germany and the Nazis was not seen by common Germans as a liberation. Germans were afraid of the (partly perceived, but also partly justified) horror of the Red Army, as well as of the Allies' perceived intentions to erase Germany from the world map. Hence they had little choice: it was either fighting for the Nazi's or risking the lives of their families and friends.

Q2": Why did the Germans support the Holocaust?

For the leftist side, however, this did not really matter. For them, it was immoral to take the perspective of the common German soldier since this was the perspective of the perpetrators, hence easily appearing as a justification. One should, instead, take the perspective of the persecuted and ask why so few people helped them and why so many Germans willingly assisted in their annihilation. Here the answer is again racism and anti-Semitism: most Germans did not regard the Jews and gypsies as true German citizens and hence did not see their annihilation as problematic.

The History Wars II

As already noted, the History Wars revolved around the question of whether Australian history should be seen as a triumph or a tragedy. Thus it may be somewhat more artificial to reformulate it in explanatory terms, as an answer to a question. Nevertheless, this is precisely what must be done to analyse it as a scientific discussion. The general question goes as follows:

Q3: How did Australian society become what it is now?

Again, however, when we look at the precise argument of Paul Keating and the leftist camp, we can formulate the question in more specific terms:

Q3': How did different groups of Australians live together?

Here, the answer is not a happy one. Since the arrival of Western colonizers, Australia has had a long history of racism, crimes and discrimination against the Aboriginal population and – although Australians have managed to overcome the worst of these practices – discrimination against Aboriginals and against a new generation of Asian immigrants is still very much present.

Q3": How did the welfare of Australians develop over the past few centuries?

For the rightists on the other hand, the question is very different – as is the answer. People like John Howard compared the way Australia looked at the end of the eighteenth century with the way it looks now. Obviously, the comparison is favourable to the modern era: Australia developed from a barren wilderness to a modern, democratic welfare state, with modern housing, medicine, transport, entertainment, and so on. There were of course some speed bumps on the way, and not everything went as smoothly or as fairly as it should have, so there is still much room for progress. But in the end, the balance sheet should be positive.

A second central topic in the History Wars were the so-called 'Stolen Generations': A substantial part of aboriginal children were removed from their mothers at birth and placed with white, middle-class foster parents as part of the Australian child removal policy in the first half of the twentieth century. Here, the question is the following:

Q4: Why were Australian children taken away from their families?

In the arguments of the right-wing side of the debate, however, the central question is implicitly posed as follows:

Q4': What were the intentions of the people who took away aboriginal children?

Here, the answer is the following: policy makers, nurses, doctors and midwives simply thought it was in the children's best interest to be removed from their biological parents and handed over to foster parents who held a higher position on the social ladder, and who could thus offer these children a better upbringing. It is of course true that, in itself, this is a case of severe racism. But this way of thinking was common at the time and the people involved in the removal of Aboriginal children should not be seen to bear any special responsibility. They simply did what they thought was best for the children, according to the standards of their time.

Q4": What was the rationale behind the removal of aboriginal children from their mothers?

According to the majority on the leftist side, however, the forced removal of children was nothing less than an attempt at genocide: the intent was to destroy aboriginal identity and society by making sure aboriginal children were raised according to Western standards. It may be that many of the people involved did not have these specific intentions in mind, but this does not really matter: this is not about the intentions of specific individuals, but rather about a general rationale that lies behind a collective activity.

Conclusion: Could it have gone differently?

As noted, the point of this analysis was to offer a reply to the objectivist's statement that the misunderstandings and personal attacks in the *Historikerstreit* and the History Wars were merely the consequence of the fact that historians did not behave as they should have, that is, as disinterested and objective scientists. Hence, I have undertaken a rational reconstruction of the debate, with the aim of making its underlying logical structure visible. With this, we can determine whether an 'objectivist' debate, with one party convincing the other by rational argument, or with two parties reaching a consensus, was possible at all.

The result is quite clear: neither dispute was a scientific debate about how a certain historical phenomenon should be explained. Strictly speaking, the participants actually never denied that the explanations of their opponents were valid. When confronted with an argument from the opposing party, they did not try to question this argument. Rather, they offered a different argument instead, an answer to a question that was actually very different. No one really engaged with an argument of the opposing party. Nolte, for example, never denied the leftists' claim that the Holocaust was unique in scale and method. And Habermas and Kocka never contested Hillgruber's statements about the reasons that German soldiers might have had for fighting the Russians. Similarly, in the History Wars, John Howard and Geoffrey Blainey never denied that the early colonizers held racist views, nor did the left side deny that Australian society is, economically and materially speaking, better off now than it was 200 years ago.

What in fact happened was that the parties disagreed less about the correct answer to a given question and more about what question should be posed in the first place. This explains the feeling that both camps were constantly talking past each other: They assumed that they were trying to provide contradicting explanations for the same phenomenon when, in fact, they were not. The important thing for us to understand now is that *the discussion about which question should be posed is not a scientific discussion*. When a given question is posed, within a specific context, there can be a scientific argument about what is the best answer. But when the question (or the context that determines the precise nature of the question) is not given, there is that nothing science can do. The choice of a certain question, like the presuppositions that underlie the specific form in which the question is posed, is determined by what one believes to be relevant and important. The choice of which question to ask in the History Wars, for example, depends on what one deems most important in society: economic welfare or peaceful coexistence? The choice of which question to ask in the *Historikerstreit* depends on who's perspective one is willing to take: that of the victims, the perpetrators, or both?

The conclusion, then, is clear: The fact that historians did not assume a neutral point of view is not a coincidence or a failure or misjudgement. It is a necessary and unavoidable consequence of the nature of the discussion itself and the questions that were posed. To take part in a discussion is to take a stance and become embroiled in political and ideological debates. There is simply no way around this.

There is one possible final reply from the objectivist that might still be an option. 'Fine', she might say, 'these debates were clearly political and ideological from the outset, and there is no way historians could have fulfilled their role as neutral experts. But this just means that they they should have kept out of them altogether.' This is, of course a viable choice, and if one wants to hang on to the ideal of the public role of the historian as a neutral and objective expert, it is the only available one. But there is a high price to pay. The *Historikerstreit* and the History Wars were not just any discussions. They were arguably occasions where history mattered more for many more people than it usually does. And if we as historians say that we don't want to be a part of this, we are refusing to intervene on precisely those occasions when history matters the most – and when historians could prove their relevance to society. As stated at the beginning already, in an age in which humanities scholars in general are continuously asked to prove their utility for society, this is a very dangerous thing to do.

So, the social, political and ideological divisions in the *Historikerstreit* and the History Wars – and most likely in a lot of other public debates about history too – could never have been bridged by disinterested historians creating a consensus by means of their expert knowledge of the historical facts. But what does this mean for the debates themselves? Does it follow, then, that there was actually nothing wrong with them? And does this mean that the general feeling that these discussions were an embarrassment to the historical profession is unjustified?

Not quite. Although it seems that at least part of the frustration surrounding these debates was the consequence of a misguided ideal of neutrality and objectivity, I believe that there was something wrong with them. In general, it is quite clear that the quality of the debates was poor: Participants did not take each other seriously, and large parts of the debates were devoted not to content, but to 'uncovering' one's opponent's ideological partisanship while presenting oneself as an objective and serious scholar. In the end, this rhetorical strategy could only have negative consequences. On the one hand, if both parties use it, it loses all credibility to the undecided observer. On the other, it also encourages members of one side not to listen to the arguments of the other side in the first place. In Chantal Mouffe's terminology, it creates antagonism rather than agonism: the idea that the opponent is an enemy to whom we should not listen but only try to defeat. (Mouffe 2000)

This brings us to an ironic final conclusion. I began this paper by claiming that ideals of objectivity and of historians as disinterested and neutral scientists still pervade the historical profession. And indeed, we have seen they are abundantly present in the *Historikerstreit* and the History Wars as well. But, and this is crucial, the historians involved did not do what they were supposed to do. The ideals of neutrality, disinterestedness and objectivity did not guide these historians in a process of rational argumentation. They did the exact opposite. Participants in both debates went out of their way to present themselves as as objective scholars and their opponents as political partisans, and while doing so, they forgot to argue and listen to each other. Although it was quite clear that the opposing camps found themselves more or less in a stalemate situation, they never acknowledged this as such. Rather, they still pretended that there was a very real possibility of a single, objective overarching truth (which obviously was to be found on their side of the argument). Through this, they, and through them the ideal of the 'objective and rational historian', actually had a negative influence on the quality of the debates. In short, it seems that the more the idea of the rational and objective scientific historian is present in a public historical debate, the less scientific or rational the actual debate can be.

Notes

1. Nevertheless, the idea of postcolonial, gender and cultural historians as by definition engaged historians needs some nuancing. I agree with Kalle Pihlainen (2011) that these approaches did have a true, oppositional edge at the time when they originated, but that this edge has become much more blunt during the last decades. What used to be radical and oppositional ways of writing history, have now sometimes, under the influence of a specific interpretation of postmodern theory, turned into mainstream undertakings that actually preserve the status quo.
2. With the exception of Sande Cohen's *History out of Joint* (2006).

Disclosure statement

No potential conflict of interest was reported by the author.

References

Ankersmit, F. 1983. *Narrative Logic. A Semantic Analysis of the Historian's Language*. The Hague: Nijhoff.
Appleby, J., L. Hunt, and M. Jacob. 1995. *Telling the Truth about History*. New York: Norton.
Bédarida, F., ed. 1995. *The Social Responsibility of the Historian*. Providence, RI: Berghahn Books.

Blainey, G. 1993. "Drawing up a Balance Sheet of Our History." *Quadrant* July-August 10–15.

Bonnell, A., and M. Crotty. 2004. "An Australian "Historikerstreit"? Review Article." *Australian Journal of Politics and History* 50 (3): 425–433.

Bracher, K. 1993. "Letter to the Editor." In *Forever in the Shadow of Hitler?*, translated by J. Knowlton and T. Cates, 72–73. Atlantic Highlands, NJ: Humanities Press.

Broszat, M. 1993. "Where the Roads Part: History is not a Suitable Substitute for a Religion of Nationalism." In *Forever in the Shadow of Hitler?* translated by J. Knowlton and T. Cates, 125–129. Atlantic Highlands, NJ: Humanities Press.

Clark, A. 2009. "Teaching the Nation's Story: Comparing Public Debates and Classroom Perspectives on History Education in Australia and Canada." *Journal of Curriculum Studies* 41 (6): 745–762.

Cohen, S. 2006. *History out of Joint. Essays on the Use and Abuse of History*. Baltimore, MD: Johns Hopkins University Press.

Davison, G. 2000. *Use and Abuse of Australian History*. St Leonards: Allen & Unwin.

Euchner, W. 1993. "The Nazi Reign – A Case of Normal Tyranny? On the Misuse of Philosophical Interpretations." In *Forever in the Shadow of Hitler?* translated by J. Knowlton and T. Cates, 237–242. Atlantic Highlands, NJ: Humanities Press.

Evans, R. 1997. *In Defence of History*. London: Granta Books.

Fest, J. 1993. "Encumbered Remembrance: the Controversy about the Incomparibility of National-Socialist Mass Crimes." In *Forever in the Shadow of Hitler?*, translated by J. Knowlton and T. Cates, 63–71. Atlantic Highlands, NJ: Humanities Press.

Fleischer, H. 1993. "The Morality of History: On the Dispute on the Past That Will Not Pass." In *Forever in the Shadow of Hitler?* translated by J. Knowlton and T. Cates, 79–84. Atlantic Highlands, NJ: Humanities Press.

Froeyman, A. 2009 "Concepts of Causation in Historiography." *Historical Methods* 42(3): 116–128.

Geiss, I. 1993. "Letter to the Editor of Der Spiegel, October 20, 1986." In *Forever in the Shadow of Hitler?* translated by J. Knowlton and T. Cates, 147–148. Atlantic Highlands, NJ: Humanities Press.

Habermas, J. 1993a. "A Kind of Settlement of Damages: The Apologetic Tendencies in German History Writing." In *Forever in the Shadow of Hitler?*, translated by J. Knowlton and T. Cates, 34–44. Atlantic Highlands, NJ: Humanities Press.

Habermas, J. 1993b. "On the Public Use of History: The Official Self-Understanding of the Federal Republic is Breaking up." In *Forever in the Shadow of Hitler?*, translated by J. Knowlton and T. Cates, 162–170. Atlantic Highlands, NJ: Humanities Press.

Hildebrand, K. 1993. "The Age of Tyrants: History and Politis: The Administrators of the Enlightenment, the Risk of Scholarship, and the Preservation of a Worldview. A Reply to Jürgen Habermas." In *Forever in the Shadow of Hitler?*, translated by J. Knowlton and T. Cates, 50–55. Atlantic Highlands, NJ: Humanities Press.

Hillgruber, A. 1993. "Jürgen Habermas, Karl-Heinz Janssen, and the Enlightenment in the Year 1986." In *Forever in the Shadow of Hitler?*, translated by J. Knowlton and T. Cates, 222–236. Atlantic Highlands, NJ: Humanities Press.

Hillgruber, A. 1984. *Zweierlei Untergang. Die Zerschlagung des Deutschen Reiches und das Ende des europäischen Judentums*. Berlin: Siedler.

Howard, J. 1996. *The Liberal Tradition, Sir John Menzies Lecture 1996*. http://menzieslecture.org/1996.html

Jenkins, K. 2003. *Re-thinking History*. New York: Routledge.

Kalela, J. 2011. *Making History*. London: Palgrave Macmillan.

Kocka, J. 1993. "Hitler Should Not Be Repressed by Stalin or Pol Pot: On the Attempts of German Historians to Relativize the Enormity of the Nazi Crimes." In *Forever in the Shadow of Hitler?* translated by J. Knowlton and T. Cates. Atlantic Highlands, NJ: Humanities Press.

Koselleck, R. 2004. *Future's Past. On the Semantics of Historical Time.* [*Vergange Zukunft. Zur Semantik Gesichtlicher Zeiten*]. New York: Columbia University Press.

MacIntyre, S., and A. Clark. 2004. *The History Wars.* Melbourne: Melbourne University Publishing.

MacMillan, M. 2009. *The Use and Abuse of History.* London: Profile.

Manne, R. 2003. "Introduction", In *Whitewash. On Keith Windschuttle's Fabrication of Australian History*, edited by R. Manne, 1-16. Sydney: Black.

Mason, A. 2004. "Foreword", In *The History Wars*, edited by S. MacIntyre and A. Clark, vii-viii. Melbourne: Melbourne University Publishing.

Meier, C. 1993. "Keynote Address on the Occasion of the Opening of Thirty-Sixth Conference of German Historians in Trier, October 8, 1986." In *Forever in the Shadow of Hitler?* translated by J. Knowlton and T. Cates, 135–142. Atlantic Highlands, NJ: Humanities Press.

Mommsen, H. 1993a. "Search for the "Lost History"? Observations on the Historical Self-Evidence of the Federal Republic." In *Forever in the Shadow of Hitler?* translated by J. Knowlton and T. Cates, 104–112. Atlantic Highlands, NJ: Humanities Press.

Mommsen, W. 1993b. "Neither Denial nor Forgetfulness will free us from the Past: Harmonizing our Understanding of History Endangers Freedom." In *Forever in the Shadow of Hitler?* translated by J. Knowlton and T. Cates, 202–215. Atlantic Highlands, NJ: Humanities Press.

Mouffe, C. 2000. *The Democratic Paradox.* London: Verso.

Munslow, A. 2007. *Narrative and History.* New York: Palgrave Macmillan.

Nolte, E. 1993a. "The Past that Will not Pass: A Speech that Coud be Written but not Delivered." In *Forever in the Shadow of Hitler?*, translated by J. Knowlton and T. Cates, 18–23. Atlantic Highlands, NJ: Humanities Press.

Nolte, E. 1993b. "Letter to the Editor of Die Zeit, August 1, 1986." In *Forever in the Shadow of Hitler?*, translated by J. Knowlton and T. Cates, 56–57. NJ: Humanities Press.

Novick, P. 1988. *That Noble Dream. The "Objectivity Question and the American Historical Profession.* Cambridge: Cambridge University Press.

Pihlainen, K. 2011. "The End of Oppositional History." *Rethinking History* 15 (4): 463–488.

Sontheimer, K. 1993. "Makeup Artists are Creating a New Identity." In *Forever in the Shadow of Hitler?*, translated by J. Knowlton and T. Cates, 184–187. Atlantic Highlands, NJ: Humanities Press.

Van Bouwel, J., and E. Weber. 2008. "*A Pragmatist Defense Of Non-Relativistic Explanatory Pluralism In History And Social Science.*" *History and Theory* 47 (2): 168–182.

Van Fraassen, B. 1980. *The Scientific Image.* Oxford: Clarendon Press.

Winkler, H. A. 1993. "Eternally in the Shadow of Hitler? The Dispute about the Germans' Understanding of History." In *Forever in the Shadow of Hitler?*, translated by J. Knowlton and T. Cates, 171–176. Atlantic Highlands, NJ: Humanities Press.

White, H. 1972. *Metahistory: The Historical Imagination in Nineteenth-Century Europe.* Baltimore, MD: Johns Hopkins University Press.

White, H. 1978. *Tropics of Discourse: Essays in Cultural Criticism.* Baltimore, MD: Johns Hopkins University Press.

Windschuttle, K. 2002. *The Fabrication of Aboriginal History. Volume One: Van Diemen's Land 1803-1847.* Sydney: Macleay Press.

Calliope's ascent: defragmenting philosophy of history by rhetoric

Rik Peters

Faculty of Arts, Department of History, University of Groningen, Groningen, The Netherlands

ABSTRACT

In order to find a cure against the pandemic fragmentation in current theory of history this paper aims at uniting experience, narrative, and action from a rhetorical perspective. Developing a pragmatics of speech acts about actions and events from the most simple to the most complex, according to the rhetorical situation in which they occur, the paper presents the notions of retrospective and prospective historical narrative as expressions of historical experience. In the end, it appeals to historians and philosophers of history to take rhetoric more seriously in order to make historiography practically more relevant.

E qui Calliopè alquanto surga

Seguitando il mio canto con quel suono.

Dante, *Purgatorio*, I, 9–11.[1]

1. Eppur si muove

Theory of history is suffering from pandemic fragmentation. In the past decade, 'the field' has been talking of memory, trauma, historical experience, hermeneutics, presence, narrative, epistemic virtues and the practical past without being able to indicate how all these things hang together. Symptomatic of the ailment was the opening conference of the International Network for the Theory of History in Ghent in July 2013. In the call for papers, the organizers, signalling an enormous 'diversity in theory of history', explicitly asked 'where the unity in this field is to be found. Is it a field at all?'[2] After 4 days of discussion in dozens of parallel sessions on topics varying from the covering law model to hermeneutics, from historical experience to narrativism, and from the use of digital media to historical ethics, no answer to the question of the unity of theory of history was found.[3]

In spite of this disappointing result, the organizers of the conference still saw a bright future for the theory of history. In the introduction of a special issue of the *Journal of the Philosophy of History*, based on the conference papers, they claim that this future should no longer be sought in the discipline of history, but outside it, because, in the words of Ricoeur, 'historians no longer have hegemony in the space of retrospection' (Bevernage et al. 2014, 147). For this reason, the authors claim, the future of the theory of history lies in the reflection on 'public engagements with the past' which may vary from 'the use of the past, in court rooms, video games, and personal identity'. In this vein, the organizers appeal to their colleagues to 'engage more with the public outside of academia' in order to make theory of history practically more relevant (Bevernage et al. 2014, 147).

This appeal sounds heartening, but it is far from clear how a focus on the practical aspect of history outside the discipline of history can cure the fragmentation inside the theory of history. Indeed, it is to be feared that indiscriminate reflection on 'uses of the past' will only worsen the disease; in the end every 'use of the past' will have its own theory. To some, this disintegration of theory is not a serious problem, and some may even welcome it under fashionable headings like 'multidisciplinarity' or 'metatheoretical reflection', but in my view further fragmentation will eventually complete the deplorable estrangement between theory of history and the historical discipline, which began some four decades ago.

Whereas the first post-war philosophers of history still discussed problems directly issuing from historical inquiry, narrativists, inspired by the linguistic turn of the 1960s, began to focus on its end-product, the historical narrative. Initially, this shift of focus was most innovative, but eventually it developed into a new creed. Its first commandment was to brush problems concerning historical inquiry away as 'trivial', in order to study the problems of historical writing. For two decades, theorists thus studied the historical narrative in great detail, without greatly bothering about the other aspects of the historical discipline. In its latter days, when narrativism had completely exhausted its field, some of its practitioners solemnly declared that the discipline of history had come to an end (see, e.g. Jenkins 1999), like unfaithful lovers who reproach their loved ones for having become old.

By that time, theory of history had already gone through the 'experiential turn' that further widened the rift between theorists and historians. Like the linguistic turn, it began with an innovative approach to memory, trauma, historical experience and presence, and ended with the old credo that historical inquiry can be dispensed with. In the beginning, theorists were frank enough to admit that their explorations of experience of the past and presence had no implications for historical inquiry (Ankersmit 2005, xiii–xvi). But soon, some of them became so infatuated with the deep secrets of the presence of the past, that they began to distance themselves from 'ordinary history'. The absolute low point in this estrangement between theorists and historians has recently been reached with the claim that 'historians do not think' (Runia 2014, xi).

For several reasons, this estrangement between theory of history and the historical discipline is completely counter-productive. In the first place, despite the 'turns' in theory of history, and the dismissals of the historical discipline by some theorists, 'ordinary historians' have continued to do their jobs. Many of them have been highly successful; in the past four decades, historians have not only developed many new approaches to history, but they have also found vast audiences for their publications that have been disseminated in all modern media (Iggers and Wang 2008, 364–402). Secondly, unlike the majority of theorists, historians have indeed become more practically engaged. Sub-disciplines like public history, applied history and learning histories flourish, and have firmly been institutionalised, both inside and outside history departments. Historians have increasingly become involved in matters of politics and policy and their publications are widely read as, for example, the site *History and Policy* attests (see http://www.historyandpolicy.org/). Thirdly, and most importantly, historians have become increasingly aware of the practical use of their discipline. The recent *History Manifesto* speaks for all of them when it calls upon historians to 'speak truth to power' by offering a general audience long-term analyses of the pasts that have given rise to our present global crises of climate, governance and inequality (Guldi and Armitage 2014).

The recent development in historiography calls for a strong philosophical basis but, since many theorists of history are even more allergic to the idea of the practical use of history than to the historical discipline itself, this has not yet been provided. The main aim of this paper is therefore to outline a philosophical basis for the practical use of history. Fully endorsing the recent initiatives to make the historical discipline more relevant for practice, I propose not yet another 'turn' in the theory of history, but a return to the question: In what sense is history a practical form of knowledge? From this perspective, I will focus on repairing the relationship between historical experience, narrative and action, because it is here that the fragmentation in the philosophy of history now hurts most. Practicing historians tend to recognise the strong relationships between experience, narrative and action, but theorists of history have so far not been able to provide a coherent account of these.[4]

In order to fill this gap, I first return to classic historicism because this tradition explicitly based its view of the practical value of history on all of its aspects, from experience and inquiry to narrative and action. Next, I will pursue the classic view to its ultimate consequence by arguing that if history is to be practically relevant, it must first be persuasive; or in other words: history must be rhetorical in order to be practically relevant. Since even the most pragmatic classic historicists eschewed the identification of history with rhetoric, I will merge phenomenology and speech act theory into a pragmatics of historical language. On this basis, I will claim that speaking about our experience of events from the simplest to the most complex is intrinsically rhetorical in the sense that it effects the audience's perspectives on the relationship between past, present and future. By this linking of experience, language, and change of perspectives on reality, I will 'subsume history under the general concept of rhetoric' (to paraphrase the title of Croce's first paper on the philosophy of history) more radically than has been done before in the theory of history.[5] More importantly, this pragmatist rapprochement between rhetoric and history will provide a basis for defragmenting theory of history in order to provide a philosophical basis for the practical use of history both inside and outside the historical discipline.

2. The philosophical foundations of practical history

The best place to begin the defragmentation of contemporary theory of history is classic philosophy of history. The abiding relevance of philosophers of history like Droysen, Weber, Meinecke, Croce, Gentile, Gramsci, Oakeshott, Collingwood, Ortega y Gasset and O'Gorman lies in the fact that they were all active as historians themselves. In contrast to many contemporary theorists of history, the classic philosophers of history were not outsiders but insiders to the historical craft. Unlike contemporary theorists, therefore, the classic thinkers did not limit themselves to either contemplations of immediate historical experience, sublime or not, or to dissections of finished products, varying from monuments to narratives. For them, history, from experience to inquiry, and from narrative to action, was not something for the ivory tower, but it was for life itself.

This principle of the immanence of history to life had profound implications for the way these classic thinkers conceived of the relationship between historical experience, historiography and action. Firstly, it obliterated sharp distinctions between professional historians' discipline and so-called 'laymen'. Being convinced that all human beings make their lives by reflecting on their past, classic philosophers of history saw all human beings as historians. From this perspective, professional historians are only specialists in a form of experience that is common to humanity. Since it was always this common experience, and not the historical discipline, that had the last word in historical matters, the classic thinkers never claimed any hegemony for historians in the field of retrospection.

Secondly, unlike the so-called scientific historians of the nineteenth century who strove for 'objective histories' of a remote past, the classic philosophers of history held that all true history is contemporary history. This did not mean that historians should no longer study remote pasts but that they always study the past from the perspective of contemporary problems.

Thirdly, and most importantly, the classic thinkers, deeply convinced that human life is historical, saw the historian's activities themselves as constituting history. The philosophical implication of this idea is that historians never merely describe a past that lies outside themselves but, rather, a process of which they themselves are a part. Or, to say it in classical terms, *res gestae* and *historia rerum gestarum coincide in medias res*. Or as the Italian historicists said: history is 'atto in atto', act in act, that is, in thinking and writing about the past, historians make history. History is therefore 'pensiero e azione', 'thought and action' (Peters 2013).

This view of the unity between thought and action formed the backbone of a practical historicism to which classic philosophers of history subscribed, though they did not explicitly use that term for their philosophies.[6] It took a convinced pragmatist like John Dewey who, harvesting the fruits of his predecessors, stated in 1938:

> A further important principle is that the writing of history is itself an historical event. It is something which happens and which in its occurrence has existential consequences. (Dewey 1949, 237)

Giving Athenian ancient historiography, nineteenth-century national history, and Marxist historiography as examples, Dewey argued that 'historical inquiry and construction' are 'agencies in enacted history' that modify the course of history they are describing. Interestingly, this pragmatist view of history was shared by many historians at that time, both inside and outside the English-speaking world. In the U.S., pragmatism inspired historians from Frederick Jackson Turner, Carl Becker and Charles Beard to Thomas Haskell, David Hollinger and Joyce Appleby to make history practically relevant (Kloppenberg 2004; Wilkins 1959), and Mexico's leading historian Edmundo O'Gorman demanded that a new 'historiology' should take into account that historiography has always been a 'tool' to serve practical interests (O'Gorman 1947, 131–132).

In spite of this acceptance of pragmatist principles among historians, few classic philosophers of history have been willing to draw the ultimate conclusion of identifying historical writing with rhetoric. Though they recognised that historians *do* something to reality when they deal with the past, they did not explicitly acknowledge that their dealings with the past require rhetoric in order to be persuasive. Among the German historicists, only Droysen dedicated an entire chapter to the rhetoric of historiography in his 1857 *Historik*; his successors did not follow in his footsteps (Droysen 1967, 273–317, 359–367). The English and Italian idealists explicitly rejected rhetoric in their aesthetics, even though they implicitly accepted it in their philosophies of history (Maggi 1989, 162–163; Peters 2013, 369). Pragmatists, for all their interest in the practical value of knowledge, never discussed rhetoric at length (Bacon 2012; Hildebrand 2003; Misak 2013).[7] In his 1944 lecture on the philosophy of history, Ortega y

Gasset explicitly identified 'razón historica' with 'razón narrativa', claiming that both were essential to practical life, but without identifying historiography with rhetoric (Ortega y Gasset 1983, 237). Likewise, O'Gorman elaborated his idea that the function of historical narrative is to change the representations of the past into a pragmatist view of historical knowledge – one that did not include rhetoric, however (O'Gorman 1947, 269, 2007, 57–60).

In hindsight, the classic thinkers' neglect of the rhetorical aspect of historical language is not so surprising given that even modern narrativists, who never eschewed the notion of rhetoric, have never fully employed it in the study of the practical effects of historical writing. Hayden White, for all his interest in the rhetoric of historical writing, has not extensively dealt with its pragmatics (Megill and McCloskey 1987, 224; Williams 2002, 242). Arthur Danto, who was very sensitive to the rhetoric of art, does not discuss the rhetoric of history in his seminal *Analytical Philosophy of History*. Louis O. Mink, who coined the phrase 'narrative form as a cognitive instrument' did not show how this instrument is to be used in practice. Finally, the subtitle of Ankersmit's (1983) *Narrative Logic* shows that he was primarily interested in the semantics of the historian's language, not in its pragmatics. And, in his most recent book, Ankersmit, speaking for mainstream narrativism, most clearly states its credo as: 'whoever tells a story does not act' (Ankersmit 2012, 40).

Only a small minority of theorists have discussed the pragmatics of historical language. Interestingly, but not surprisingly, among them were some practicing historians as well. The best known theorist who dealt with the pragmatic effect of historical language is perhaps the philosopher W. B. Gallie, who discussed it under the concept of 'followability' without relating it to rhetoric, however (Gallie 1964, 39–43). J. H. Hexter, a paradigmatic 'ordinary historian', wrote a classic article on the rhetoric of history in which he maintains that all aspects of history, from inquiry to writing, contribute to the communication of historical knowledge so that 'the advancement of historical knowledge depends to a considerable extent on the quality of the historian's rhetoric, on the efficacy of his historiography, and is almost inseparable from it' (Hexter 1971, 27). In his *Comment on écrit l'histoire*, historian Paul Veyne recognises the 'praxeological significance of rhetoric' and uses the rhetorical notion of 'topics' in order to show how historical knowledge can make progress by extending its arsenal of questions (Veyne 1978, 145–153). In a chapter on the rhetoric of history, in their seminal *The Rhetoric of the Human Sciences*, Allan Megill and Donald McCloskey opt for a full rhetorical approach to history, arguing that historical writings can best be read as 'orations' (Megill and McCloskey 1987, 221). However, concerning the pragmatics of historical writing, they only discuss how historians create audiences, without elaborating on this view (Megill and McCloskey 1987, 231–232). In *History, Rhetoric and Proof*, Carlo Ginzburg explicitly dealt with the practical effect of historical writing, but in his zeal to secure historical truth, he limited his analysis to the efficacy of logical proof, thus leaving the two other traditional rhetorical 'proofs', pathos and ethos undiscussed (Ginzburg 1999, 45–48). Against this background, the most important theorist of the pragmatics of historical language is the historian and philosopher Nancy Struever, who in a long series of books and articles, has elaborated her view that a truly pragmatic historiography can offer insight in the temporal dimensions of action only hand-in-hand with rhetoric (Struever 1970, 199). Together, rhetoric and history form a 'valuable civil inquiry' which is not engaged in finding philosophical certainties, but 'in finding and posing political or civic possibilities' (Struever 2009, 117)

In this context, Hayden White's latest book, *The Practical Past*, may be seen as a breakthrough. Referring to J. L. Austin, White claims that we must think of all discourses, of which historiography would be one, as speech acts. In saying something about the world, White points out, speech acts 'seek to change the world, the way one might relate to it, or the way things relate to one another in the world' (White 2014, 34). According to White, the theory of speech acts may therefore fruitfully be employed to analyse historiography as a 'praxis', which he defines as 'an action intended to change or have an impact on the world by the way it says something about it' (White 2014, 34).

From the perspective of practical historicism, this proposal is most welcome because it expresses its central principle that making history and writing about history coincide. However, from the perspective of historical practice, White's proposal needs further elaboration on three points. Firstly, Austin distinguished between 'constatives' which can be true or false and 'performatives' which are neither true or false but 'do' something. When one says 'it is one o'clock' or it is 'good weather today' one is using constative language, which differs from performative language, which one uses when saying, for example, 'I do' when marrying another, or when one says 'I name this ship the Queen Elisabeth' (Austin 1962, 5). John Searle rightly criticised Austin's classification of speech acts, but his analysis needs further elaboration, before it can be applied to historical narratives (Searle, 1970, 68–69). Secondly, it is not entirely clear how speech act theory applies to historiography since it has primarily been applied to short sentences, or 'utterances', but not to large-scale narratives (Beale 1987, 82–83, 2009, 87ff; Wallace 1970, 3–5, 72ff). The relationship between speech acts and narratives therefore needs further elaboration. Finally, even if we accept the performativity of historical narratives, it is not exactly clear what practical effects narratives can actually have. More specifically, it is not clear how narratives about the past can make a difference for the future. As Nancy Struever pointed out, this problem of future possibilities is of the highest interest to show how historical inquiry and narratives relate to action (Struever 2009, 117). But before proceeding to extend speech act theory to historical narratives, it is necessary to investigate how experience and language are related since this is the foundation of persuasion.

3. Experience and language in rhetoric

Classical rhetoric located the performative force of discourse in the completion of the rhetorical argument, the enthymeme, or the 'incomplete syllogism'. In his *Rhetoric*, Aristotle famously argued that when an audience is being confronted with an enthymeme, it will fill in the missing premises on the basis of their memory. As Aristotle pointed out, a speaker does not have to say that Dorieus won a garland when he won an Olympic contest since everybody knows that the prize is a garland (Aristotle 1991, 1357a15). The enthymeme thus typically functions as an invitation for the audience's collaboration in supplying the missing premises of an argument for itself. From this it follows that the most important task of a speaker is to estimate the foreknowledge of his audience in order to construct the most effective enthymemes for a given rhetorical situation.

In the past four decades, modern rhetoricians have considerably expanded this ancient completion theory. Starting from the view that rhetorical arguments are not merely logical, but broadly experiential, modern rhetoricians argue that audiences can complete utterances beyond the logical. For example, the use of rhetorical presence, or the foregrounding of certain elements to represent something absent – think of Marc Anthony words in Shakespeare's Julius Caesar 'you all know this mantle' showing Caesar's blood stained toga to the audience – has strong emotional effects on his audience (Perelman 1982, 35). Likewise, the antithesis 'Don't ask what your country can do for you, but what you can do for your country', said by a particular speaker, at a particular moment and in a particular tone, elicits a strong emotional response in the audience. Figures of speech, modern rhetoricians claim, are both 'proto-arguments' and 'signs of emotion in speakers and triggers of emotion in the audience' (Fahnestock 1999, 19). By using figures of speech, speakers solicit the collaboration of audiences who thus 'experience' both the logical and the emotional force of discourse (Tindale 2004, 70–1). Speakers 'do things with words', in the sense that they change audiences' experiences of reality.

Though modern rhetoricians have fruitfully explored the experiential effects of arguments, they have not yet provided a theory that explains them. In particular, they have not yet provided a theory that expounds the conditions for experiential completion. Such a theory is necessary if we want to understand how experience relates to language. In order to fill this gap, I will borrow from Husserl's theory of experiential meaning, 'Sinn', and from Collingwood's philosophy of mind.

Husserl's theory of experiential meaning starts from the principle of intentionality, which says that conscious is always directed toward an object. At the same time, consciousness also transcends its object by educing other possible acts of consciousness. When I see a vase, for example, I am also conscious of its backside and bottom, even if I do not perceive these. An act of consciousness thus both intends an actual object and also goes beyond that object by pointing to other, possible experiences:

> Every experience has its own horizon; every experience has its core of actual and determine cognition, its own content of immediate determinations which give themselves; but beyond this core of determinate quiddity, of the truly given as 'itself-there, it has its own horizon'. (Husserl 1948, 27; translation by Ludwig Landgrebe p. 32).[8]

Distinguishing between the actual object as the core of experience and the experience that goes beyond it, Husserl distinguished between an internal horizon of consciousness, which comprises the experiences which belong to the object itself, and an external horizon which comprises all possible experiences that go beyond it. To return to the vase, its form, a certain roundness, an opening on the top, and so on, belong to the internal horizon of experience, its capability of containing roses or lilies to the external horizon of experience. On this basis Husserl defined experiential meaning as the combination of the internal and external horizons of an intended object: for an observer, the meaning of the vase is the combination of all actual and possible experiences.

It is important to note, firstly, that this is not a semantic view of meaning; since actions and events are not a form of language, they do not have a linguistic but an 'experiential meaning'. For example, we can experience an invitation as pleasant, a gesture as inviting, or the traffic as dangerous. Secondly, it must be emphasized that Husserl does not exclude any object from consciousness; objects may vary from actual to imagined objects. Therefore, my consciousness of an imaginary unicorn may be as concrete as my experience of a real traffic light. Finally, when experience is expressed in symbols it receives a social dimension: given our customs and traditions we experience some gestures as inviting and others as not, some traffic as dangerous and other traffic as not.

Although meaning is not primarily linguistic, language is one of the most important media, if not the most important medium, by which we convey meaning to others. According to Husserl, the meaning-giving act of consciousness can be expressed by words that function as signs or indications for the hearer's understanding:

> All expressions in communicative speech function as indications. They serve the hearer as signs of the 'thoughts' of the speaker, i.e. of his meaning-giving [sinngebenden] mental experiences [psychische Erlebnisse]. (Husserl 1968, 277 par. 7; translation by Smith and McIntyre 1984, 179)

According to Husserl's interpreters Smith and McIntyre, this expression of meaning in words is to 'perform an action', because it relates a bodily behaviour to an underlying intentional process of consciousness (Smith and McIntyre 1984, 179). The speech act thus always has an intentional aspect; to speak is to give meaning to things in the sense of eliciting acts of consciousness in a hearer. Stated in Husserl's terms, this means that a speaker's utterance opens a range of internal and external horizons of experience in the hearer.

When you employ the word 'vase', for example, you open in my consciousness a horizon of actual and possible meanings such as 'breakable', 'may contain flowers', 'a good gift item', and so on. In this way, meanings open 'horizons of expectations'.

Linguistic behaviour, Smith and McIntyre point out, depends on what speakers hope to bring about with their utterances. By asserting, speakers typically try to get hearers to believe or to know what they say; by questioning, they try to elicit an informative response from the hearers; and by commanding, they try to prompt specific actions from the hearer (Smith and McIntyre 1984, 179–180). All this 'works', so to speak, because hearers are able to relate the speech acts to their own experience that is therefore the *conditio* sine qua non for the performative force of speech acts. Intentional consciousness of experience is the alpha and omega of all effective communication.

4. Emotions and language in communication

Husserl's theory of meaning is useful in understanding why speakers can do things with words in the sense of changing the experience of reality; however, it needs two further emendations to explain how audiences can complete the experiential import of words. Firstly, whereas both classical and modern rhetoricians stress the importance of emotions, or pathos in persuasion, Husserl does not explicitly address the role of emotions in linguistic behaviour. Secondly, though Husserl makes clear what it is that a speaker does to a hearer, it is not entirely clear what the hearer is doing in the communicative act. In order to clarify both points, I will borrow from Collingwood's philosophy of mind which explicitly deals with emotions and the role of the hearer in communication.

Collingwood is usually not ranked among the phenomenologists, yet his conceptual idealism was firmly based on the principle of intentionality (D'Oro 2003; 40–41, 45–46, 149n13). In his philosophy of mind, this comes most clearly to the fore in the theory of 'selective attention' which says that we only become conscious of something by attending to it. It is therefore by selective attention that we become conscious of our emotions. Focussing on one part of them, and leaving other parts in 'the penumbra', we become conscious of our emotions by expressing them in 'ideas'. Collingwood calls this selective activity 'imagination', which he distinguishes from 'thought', the main function of which is to relate ideas. Accordingly, the first function of language is not to make statements but to express emotions; following Vico, Collingwood claims that poetic use of language precedes symbolic language (Collingwood 1938, 225–226).

Collingwood's theory leads to a parallel distinction in his analysis of the relation between speaker and hearer. Before we understand intellectually by thinking the same thought, we first understand aesthetically, that is, by imagining things. In this context, Collingwood discusses the case of a child who expresses his satisfaction at throwing his bonnet off by exclaiming 'hattiaw'

(Collingwood 1938, 239). According to Collingwood, the expression 'hat-tiaw' is a form of speech because the speaker is his own first hearer and conscious of his own emotions and of himself as expressing them. The person to whom the expression is addressed, in Collingwood's example the child's mother, constructs in herself the idea which the words express. On this basis Collingwood locates the act of understanding in the hearer: 'Understanding what someone says to you is thus attributing to him the idea which his words arouse in yourself; and this implies treating them as words of your own' (Collingwood 1938, 250).

Since the hearer treats the words of the speaker as her own, that is, she treats the speaker's words as expression of her own emotions to which she can attend selectively, the speaker can never control what the hearer's experience will be. Yet, this does not exclude speakers choosing words with the aim of arousing emotions in their audiences. Collingwood does not deny the rhetorical use of language but he only refuses to identify art with rhetoric (Collingwood 1938, 275–280).

To sum up. Husserl and Collingwood agree on the principle of intentionality: when we are conscious, we are always conscious of *something in experience*, and it this consciousness of something that we express in language. But whereas Husserl equates language with symbolic language which expresses thought, Collingwood also recognises poetic language which does not express thoughts in concepts and statements but emotions in ideas. Speakers therefore not only open horizons of conceptual meaning in their audiences, but by doing so, they can also arouse the emotions inherent in these meanings, because hearers are able to treat the words they hear as expressions of their own emotions. The words 'Do not ask what your country can do for you, but what you can do for your country' thus invite hearers to complete the argument and its emotional charge for themselves. To do something with words is therefore to do something with emotions in the sense that speakers can effectively change hearers' emotions. Speech acts speak both to hearts and minds or, as the ancients already knew: pathos and logos are one.

5. Communication about simple events

As a starting point for an analysis of the performativity of historiographical speech acts, I take Oakeshott's analysis of descriptions of simple events, or in his terms, 'going-ons'. According to Oakeshott, consciousness of actions and events in the present can be qualified by an awareness of future or past, or a combination of both. To give Oakeshott's own example: when I see a man on the kerb as trying to cross the street, my experience is qualified by an awareness of a particular future, in this case, reaching the other side of the road. Likewise, by attending to specific elements of a going-on, awareness of a particular past may be evoked. For example, when I see a man with a wooden leg hobbling, I may infer that he has lost his own leg (Oakeshott 1983, 8). As Oakeshott rightly stresses, this awareness is not 'evoked' by neglecting the present or past, but precisely by attending to them. For example, by noticing the way the first man stands on the kerb, we direct our attention to the present, and by noticing how the man with the wooden leg hobbles by, we direct our attention to the past. Moreover, present experiences are not necessarily qualified by either an awareness of the past or the future or a combination of both. Combining Oakeshott's examples, I may see the man with the wooden leg crossing the street, and either say 'He is crossing the street' or 'He lost his leg' or, even, 'The man who is crossing the street lost his leg'. None of these descriptions is necessary, and all depend on what I attend to.

On this point, I wish to extend Oakeshott's analysis by noticing that the effect of an evocation of awareness depends on what we attend to in experience. In this directing of attention lies the performative force of descriptions of events. This force comes clearly to the fore in conversations. For example, when you see the man with the wooden leg, you can evoke my awareness of the future by saying to me 'He is crossing the street' or of the past by saying 'He lost his own leg'. You may also admonish me to pass by carefully by exclaiming 'he has a wooden leg', or try to evoke my pity by saying 'the poor guy!' I write 'you may', because, as Collingwood pointed out, in all these cases the effect of your words depends on the way I treat them.

When we differ about the use of words, we disagree about the meaning of a going-on. For example, when I say that the man lost his way, you may counter with 'No he is just crossing the street', in order to convince me of your view. Or I may counter a remark of pity at his lost leg by saying 'Well, at least he can walk'. These examples show that in situations of disagreement the choice of words becomes more delicate and even strategic with a view toward convincing each other. At this level, speech acts become manifestly rhetorical in the sense that they become attempts to change someone's view of reality in Husserl's sense of opening a new horizon of actual and possible meanings. Such attempts can be strengthened by using figural language. For example, as when I say to you, pointing at the man with the wooden leg, 'Look at Captain Ahab over there', thus opening a new perspective on the situation. Likewise, when I want to stress the swiftness with which someone crosses the street, I may say, 'He's flying'. In the case of the man with the wooden leg, you may take that as too ironical, and combined with a comparison to Captain Ahab, it might even arouse a feeling of disgust in you. All this exemplifies the first rule of rhetoric that speakers must adjust their choice of words to their audiences. This adjustment is not a priori given because the reaction to speech-acts is contingent; an audience may react in one way or another, but none is predictable. However, since audiences tend to react in certain ways to certain words, both logically and emotionally, the use of figural language may help to steer their reactions.

6. Communication about complex events

The performative effect of descriptions of events becomes more varied and complex once we have to describe events that extend over a longer stretch of time, and which do not have a particular past or future in view, as in Oakeshott's examples, but instead a range of points in time. It is descriptions of this more complex kind that Arthur C. Danto analysed under the heading of project verbs. Danto chose this name because such descriptions typically describe temporal wholes in view of their results. To take his example: When we see Jones putting seeds into a hole, we may describe this as 'Jones is planting roses', or when we see someone going to their desk late at night, we may describe this action with 'He is writing a book' (Danto 2007, 159–169). Project verbs can cover a range of activities by relating them to past and future events. The verb 'planting roses' thus describes all activities involved in the planting: digging, fertilizing, sowing, purchasing shovels and seeds before putting the seeds into the hole, and throwing the earth back in the hole, collecting the gardening instruments, and bringing the wheelbarrow back to the barn after putting the seeds into the hole.

As Danto correctly notes, the use of project verbs does not presuppose any continuity in these activities; Jones may have a cup of tea to mark a break and we can still describe his activities as 'planting roses'; and if the writer interrupts the writing of the book for some months, we can still say that he is writing a book. Moreover, the description of the activities need not be identical with the actor's intentions. Jones may think of himself as planting roses, but we may describe him as 'taking a rest'. Finally, the use of project verbs is not restricted to the activities of individuals since we may describe several people planting roses as 'the gardening club is planting roses'.

According to Danto, project verbs form the kernel of 'narrative sentences' by which we describe temporal wholes. Narrative sentences therefore always refer to at least two events separated in time (Danto 2007, 164). So, if we describe someone who is putting seeds into a hole as 'planting roses', we refer both to the present and to the future, that is, in this case, to the result of roses coming forth. It is important to see that the choice of these two events in time is free, and that there is no a priori limit to the number of narrative sentences by which we describe them. To give Danto's own example, we may describe Jones' putting of seeds into a hole as 'planting roses' or as 'Jones is planting prize winning roses', according to the expected outcome we wish to evoke awareness of (Danto 2007, 164). Likewise, though Danto does not explicitly discuss this, we may, along the lines Oakeshott indicated, evoke awareness of past events by saying that 'Jones is planting consoling roses' thus referring to the death of a loved one.

When we proceed to analysing narrative sentences about the past we enter a realm of new performative possibilities. So far, we have analysed situations in which speakers and hearers more or less share the same time horizon as the situations about which they communicate. But things change as soon as speakers start to describe actions and events in the past. Firstly, speakers and hearers no longer directly perceive the actions and events about which they communicate. Secondly, since the time horizon of the speakers and hearers differs from the time horizon of the actors, multiple time horizons are involved, as Koselleck pointed out (Koselleck 2003, 249). The first problem has led to an interminable literature about the problem of how historians can have experience of the past. The second problem led to an equally interminable literature about the function of narrative sentences in historical writing. Both problems can be solved on the basis of the theory of intentionality as expounded above.

Concerning the problem of the experience of the past, it follows from Husserl's principle of intentionality that 'evidence', from footprints to books, opens various horizons of experiential meaning. As Collingwood pointed out, the interpretation of evidence does not begin with an act of inferential reasoning, but with the aesthetic act of understanding. The starting point of a historical argument is not 'This person, or this printed book, or this set of foot prints, says so-and-so' but 'I, knowing the language, read this person, or this book, or these footprints, as saying so-and-so' (Collingwood 1999, 54). This 'so-and-so' does not lie on the level of thought but on the level of the imagination; the evidence forms a language which first speaks to the imagination of the historian, who is therefore in the position of the hearer, or in this case, the reader of a language. When we read Martin Luther King's 'I have a dream' speech, we treat his words as our own, that is, as expressions of our own ideas. And since all language is expressive of emotion, his words may arouse emotions in us.

This emotional impact of reading evidence is a fact which historians know from practice; most often studying the sources is not a cold-blooded affair but a highly exciting experience. To speak for myself: when I studied the trial against Marie-Antoinette, I was swept off my feet when she responded to the accusation of incest with the dauphin with the words: 'Si je n'ai pas répondu, c'est que la nature se refuse à répondre à une pareille inculpation faite à une mère. J'en appelle à toutes celles qui peuvent se trouver ici!' [If I have not replied, it is because nature refuses to reply to such a charge made against a mother. I appeal to all those (mothers) who are here!] These words so much evoked my admiration for the former Queen of France that I completely revised my views of the woman, whom I, like so many others, had formerly despised as l'Autrichienne (Moniteur octobre 1793, 139; Peters 2009, 19–20).

It is important to note that in all these cases readers are both active and passive. They are active, because they make the evidence speak; without the activity of reading, it would remain silent. But when the evidence speaks to them, or better, through them, readers may undergo its performative force: they can be surprised to find footprints going in a certain direction, be thrilled by the pathos used by the Comité du salut public which condemned her, or moved by Marie Antoinette's reply. All such 'moving' experiences challenge historians to make sense of them. This sense-making amounts to producing narrative sentences that evoke horizons of experience in an audience. Interestingly, different historians can open different horizons of experience in order to elicit different intellectual and emotional responses. So, one historian may write that 'Marie Antoinette's execution marked the end of the Monarchy in France', whereas another may write 'Marie Antoinette's execution opened the repression of women in the French Revolution.' In each case, the historian plays with, or, if you wish, manipulates, the horizon of expectations of his readers by relating the execution of Marie Antoinette to a different moment in time, each evoking different ideas and emotions in the readers.

Given the indefiniteness of the future, these 'retroactive realignments of the past', as Danto calls them, can be multiplied infinitely; we can name and place an event in an infinite number of futures; including not only the past's future, but also our own (Danto 2007, 168). Writes Danto: 'To be alive to the historical significance of events as they happen, one has to know to which later events these will be related, in narrative sentences, by historians of the future' (Danto 2007, 169). Likewise, to establish the meaning of past events, it is equally important to relate them to real and possible events prior to them. For example, a historian who wishes to portray Napoleon as the defender of the values of the French revolution who was finally defeated by the reactionary coalition at Waterloo will stress that the wars preceding the Russian campaign were not initiated by the French Emperor but by the coalition forces.

Following the lead of Dutch philosophers Blom and Nijhuis, we can generalise Danto's theory by saying that historians give meaning to an event by locating it in contexts of a selection of real and possible events both prior to, subsequent to and synchronic with the event they study. By interpreting an event as a 'declaration of war', historians situate it synchronically with, for example, the gathering of troops at the frontier and generals pointing at maps, and diachronically with, for example, the growing tension between nations prior to the event and the outbreak of a war subsequent to it. As Blom and Nijhuis point out, every interpretation involves the collaboration of the audience: 'step by step, the narrative mobilizes and exploits the everyday expectations and intuitions of the imaginary public with respect to what is and what is not probable' (Blom and Nijhuis 1989, 44). In historical inquiry and writing, interpretation and evocation go hand in hand – and both address an audience.

7. The rhetoric of historical narratives

The question now is whether this analysis exhausts the rhetorical possibilities of historical writing. This question amounts to asking whether we are entitled to identify historiography with narrative sentences, or collections of narrative sentences. According to Danto and many of his interpreters we are, since the essence of historical writing lies in narrative sentences about the past. But, according to Mink and Ankersmit, this is not enough because history not only describes but also explains or interprets, and this is only possible when we order the narrative sentences into a comprehensive or configurational whole that enables us to see all the events together; in other words, historical explanation or understanding is only possible in a narrative (Ankersmit 2007, 386; Mink 1987, 139–140). My position is that narrative sentences do explain by giving meaning to actions and events, although their explanatory force is relative to the extent they are organised into a comprehensive perspective. As soon as situations become more complex, and *ipso facto* our experience of them become more inscrutable, narrative sentences no longer suffice to explain. When our partner comes home late at night once, he or she may explain the situation by saying 'I am late'. But after several times, more is needed. 'It's not what you think' will not convince us; only a complete story sometimes does. The more complex a situation grows, the more a story is needed to harmonize our hearts and minds.

What kind of experience gives rise to historical narratives? Obviously, experience of situations that are more complex than observing a man with a wooden leg or Jones planting roses – or even reading Marie Antoinette's appeal to the mothers attending her trial. In order to answer this question, I will contrast two kinds of experience: historical experience which is oriented toward the past and kairotic experience which is oriented toward the future. These are not mutually exclusive but represent two extremes on a scale which covers a range of experiences that partake of both past and future.

To begin with historical experience. In most literature on this subject, language and experience are thought to be incommensurable. For this reason, the connection between historical experience and historical narratives has not been made explicit. The most important philosopher in this field, Frank Ankersmit, repeats in all his works that experience and language mutually exclude each other. However, in his *Sublime Historical Experience*, he says that historians are able to 'translate' their experience into narratives. Johan Huizinga thus translated his sublime historical experience of Jan van Eyck's triptych 'Lamb of God' into *The Waning of the Middle Ages* (Ankersmit 2005, 133–135). But the metaphor of translation is not very helpful because, as Ankersmit himself says, it presupposes some commensurability between experience and language. Probably for this reason, Ankersmit has shifted to the notion of the 'expression of experience' in his latest book. Giving the same example of Huizinga and the 'Lamb of God', he argues that the representational language in the opening chapter of *The Waning of the Middle Ages* expresses the 'moods and feelings' Huizinga had while observing the triptych. Moreover, Ankersmit claims that by using representational language, Huizinga pulls his readers into the 'vertical axis of historical experience'. Finally, it was this experience that Huizinga later summarized in one sentence that 'captures the impression the book makes on its (well-informed) readers' (Ankersmit 2012, 203–205).

Ankersmit's analysis of the 'birth' of the *Waning of the Middle Ages* can be coherently rendered in terms of a rhetorical reading of Husserl's and

Collingwood's theory of the relationship between experience and language. Through its shapes, colours, forms, and figures the 'Lamb of God' opened internal and external horizons of meaning for Huizinga. Each of these meanings had an 'emotional charge' for him, which he tried to convey to his readers by expressing them in words that were organized from a single perspective and which he captured in the title of his book. As Ankersmit pointed out in his narrativist theory, the title of the book embodies Huizinga's representation of the late middle ages; it is his proposal to see this period from a certain perspective (Ankersmit 1983, 188–192). If we ask ourselves to whom did Huizinga propose his view of the Middle Ages, the answer cannot be but 'the audience'; like all historians, Huizinga not only intended his books to be read, but he also wanted to convince his readers.

Historical experience and historical writing are part of an ongoing rhetorical process. As the example of Huizinga shows, there was the rhetorical force of the 'Lamb of God', which Huizinga underwent as a viewer. Rhetoric traditionally identifies this 'undergoing' as 'pathos'. Next, several years later, Huizinga expressed this pathos in the language of the *Waning of the Middle Ages*. By a careful use of language, or 'logos' in rhetoric, Huizinga tried to evoke new horizons of experience in his readers, who thus undergo the effective force of his language: pathos again. From a rhetorical point of view, Huizinga's attempt is not effective because his readers have the same experiences he had, let alone the experiences that Jan van Eyck had. Instead, it is effective because they are able to take Huizinga's words, or more precisely, his narrative organization of words, as a narrative of their own. It is this narrative that pulls readers into an experience of a past which is completely foreign to the present.

Ankersmit's discussion of historical trauma can be analysed along the same lines. According to Ankersmit, Francesco Guicciardini wrote his *Storia d'Italia* in order to understand the traumatic event of the sack of Rome in 1527. In Ankersmit's view, it was the rift between his intentions and the terrible outcome of the event's consequences that awakened Guicciardini's historical awareness, which then eventually induced him to understand the unintended consequences of his own advice to the Pope. Given the fact that Guicciardini himself was involved in the event, his *Storia d'Italia* can be seen as an expression of the experience of a historical trauma. As Ankersmit notes, the narrative grew out of the traumatic experience it tried to account for (Ankersmit 2005, 356–358).

It is important to note that this account can never be made by merely retroactively aligning the past because, after the sack of Rome, mere redescriptions of past events would not have convinced Guicciardini's readers. As Ankersmit writes, the sack of Rome caused Guicciardini so much pain that it was too great for him to permit assimilation in his mind (Ankersmit 2005, 358). A dissociation between past and present thus came into bein and, with this, the traumatic past became an object for investigation. It was thus the dissociation

between past and present that made Guicciardini realise that his entire conception of the situation before 1527 was false. In Mink's terms, the sack falsified
his entire conceptual mode of interpretation and analysis, or, in Collingwood's
terms, his absolute presuppositions (Collingwood 1940; Mink 1987). In order
to tell the story of the sack of Rome, Guicciardini had to reorganise his entire
conception of Italian history, which amounted to finding a new configuration
to comprehend the events – or in rhetorical terms, to invent a new frame to
describe the past. Unexpectedly, all had changed, therefore, an entirely new
narrative was necessary.

Both Huizinga's and Guicciardini's histories are examples of what I wish to
call 'retrospective historical writing' because they focus on making sense of
experiences of the past that present themselves to the historian. Retrospective
historical writing is an important genre in historiography, but it is not the only
genre. At least as important is the genre at the other end of the scale, which
I would like to call 'prospective historical writing', because it focuses on proactively realigning historical events towards the future. Prospective historical
writing typically occurs in situations that we experience as 'historical', that is,
in situations in which we make important decisions – indeed, historical ones,
because, when making them, we feel that they will have an enormous impact
on the future. The most typical examples of prospective historiography can be
found in political orations from Pericles to Obama. In moments of *kairos*, that is
in view of taking crucial decisions for the future, orators do not passively experience an overwhelming distance to the past, but actively create this distance
themselves. 'Now is the time …' is the motto of the prospective orator-historian.
Again, in situations like these mere redescriptions of the past will not suffice
because the narrative sentences are no longer experienced as 'fitting' to reality.
Only by opening new horizons of past and future can historical narratives
change audiences' perspectives on the present in which they act.

This view of the rhetoric of historical narratives has important implica-
tions for periodisation, the most basic form of creating perspectives on time.
In most historical writing, periodisation is predominantly retrospective. As
Danto writes:

> It is a period solely from the perspective of the historian, who sees it from with-
> out; for those who lived in the period it would be just the way life was lived. And
> asked, afterwards, what it was like to have lived then, they may answer from the
> outside, from the historian's perspective. From the inside there is no answer to
> be given; it was simply the way things were. So when the members of a period
> can give an answer in terms satisfactory to the historian, the period will have
> exposed its outward surface and in a sense be over, as a period. (Danto 1981, 207)

Danto accounts here for the normal case in which historians create *post facto*
perspectives on history. But in moments of *kairos*, historian-orators create new
perspectives on time *in medias res*. No longer satisfied with the way things
are, they raise and answer the question what a new reality must look like. By

proactively realigning past and present to the future, they close a period to open a new one. In this way, prospective historiography literally makes history by speaking about it, and in speaking about it, it incites its audience to leave the past behind and to enter a new era in history.

As in retrospective historical writing, metaphor plays an important role in this making of history, but it has a different function: by using metaphor, the speaker proposes a new perspective on reality; not primarily in order to come to terms with the past, but in order to come to terms with the future. For example, Elisabeth I, in sight of the approaching Armada, removed doubt in her leadership by saying: 'I have the heart and the stomach of a King' (MacArthur 1995, 40–41). Or take Saint-Just, who convincingly framed his accusation of Louis XVI with the metaphor that 'the King is the enemy of the people', referring to the future with famous words: 'cet homme doit régner ou mourir' (Walzer 1974, 120–127). Finally, Churchill famously introduced the metaphor of the 'iron curtain', which, in hindsight, became a self-fulfilling prophecy.

Prospective history is not the monopoly of politicians; in decisive moments in history practicing historians are engaged to write prospectively. To give one example: Guido de Ruggiero's seminal *Storia del liberalismo europeo*, written in 1924, the year of the Matteotti crisis, opens with: 'In France, liberty is ancient; despotism is modern', and it ends with: 'Thus recent experience affords a proof of the vitality of the Liberal State, hard beset, yet issuing victorious from the battle' (De Ruggiero 1925). De Ruggiero's readers immediately sensed the emotional force of these words that frame the entire book, and, as long as Fascism lasted, the book encouraged them in their battle against dictatorship. Likewise, readers experiencing the global crises of these days, immediately understand how the first line of the *The History Manifesto* – 'A spectre is haunting our times: the spectre of the long term' – relates to current problems of climate change, governance and inequality. After reading the *Manifesto*, they will also understand its last line: 'Historians of the World unite!' since the *Manifesto* is a most eloquent, and consciously eloquent, appeal to historians to contribute to the solution of global crises. 'The mission for history as a guide to life never entirely lapsed', the *Manifesto* claims, and all classic philosophers of history would have applauded (Guldi and Armitage 2014, 10).

8. Calliope's ascent

In this paper, I have attempted to subsume history under the general concept of rhetoric. Starting from the principle of the immanence of history to life, and its corollary, that historians always describe a process in which they participate themselves, I have developed practical historicism to its ultimate consequence by showing that all forms of historical writing are forms of rhetoric.

On this foundation the defragmentation of the theory of history can begin. First, historical experience and historiography can no longer be severed. The

ultimate consequence of the classic historicist principle of immanence, according to which historians make part of the historical process they describe, is
that all historical writing must also be seen as a part of the same process. To
write history is therefore a form of making it, and making history is a form
of experiencing it. The main task of the historian is to express this experience
in words, from the level of narrative sentences describing simple actions and
events to the level of retrospective and prospective histories that describe highly
complex events. Second, the gap between historical writing and action can be
bridged because historians do things with words; they do not merely describe
and explain the past, but they always do this with a view to the future. From a
rhetorical point of view, historians are 'time-tellers', they tell us what time it is,
not in the ordinary sense of those words, but in the more specific sense of where
we are now from the perspective of the past and the future. Most importantly,
such a rhetorical view of history will make theory of history more relevant to a
broader audience. When historians tell us the time, they do not merely follow
their personal interest in the past 'for the sake of the past', but write about the
past for the sake of the future and in the interest of the audiences they address.

To many historians and theorists, this identification of history and rhetoric
blurs the distinction between history and propaganda. Following Oakeshott,
some of them will say that rhetoric blurs the distinction between the historical
past that we study for the past's sake, and the practical past that we use for practical reasons (Oakeshott 1933, 102–108). Others will object that rhetoric, in its
pursuit of effect, does not do justice to historical truth (Ginzburg 1999, 21–25).
To the first group of objectors, my answer is that the distinction between the
historical and the practical past is not valid from the perspective of practical
historicism. Once we acknowledge that historical writing itself is a form of
action, that we acknowledge that historians do something when they write,
that historians make a difference to the history in which they participate, then
we must acknowledge that the historical past is also a practical past. From this
perspective, I propose to give up the notion of the practical past altogether and
to speak of practical history instead.

To the second group of objectors, my answer is that from the beginning
rhetoric has been reverent to the notion of truth; under the concept of logos
rhetoricians have explored all the techniques by which assertions could be
warranted on the basis of evidence (Ginzburg 1999, 21–24, 38–50; Perelman
1982, 1–8; Struever 2009, 1–7). My plea for a rhetorical view of history is therefore not a plea for propaganda. It is, on the contrary, an attack on propaganda,
because the weapon against propaganda is rhetoric itself. Only if historians
and their audiences are aware of the rhetorical function of historiography will
they be able to distinguish propaganda from history. In rhetoric, the ability to
distinguish between propaganda and rhetoric is part of phronesis, or prudence,
which is the practical wisdom obtained from long experience of deliberation

about particular actions and events (Struever 1970, 193–199). The paradigmatic figure of prudence is the judge who reaches a verdict only after careful considerations of the case at hand and of existing jurisprudence (Gadamer 1979, 292–297). Following this example, prudent historians will carefully judge the rhetoric of different histories before writing their own. So, indeed, let Calliope ascend; her cures for Clio will be many.

Notes

1. 'And let here Calliope somewhat ascend, my song accompanying with that sound.' Translation by Henry Wadsworth Longfellow.
2. http://www.inth.ugent.be/conferences/conference-2/conference/ Accessed July 7, 2015.
3. Despite the success of the conference, the question of the unity of the field remained contested, see INTH Conference, day 4, Round Table Discussion, https://www.youtube.com/watch?v=etJDwSzDz64. Accessed, July 7, 2015.
4. During the preparation of this paper I asked over 100 historians in Mexico, Italy, England and the Netherlands four questions: (1) Have you ever had an historical experience? (2) Have you used that experience in your work? and (3) Do you think that your writing has some practical value? The great majority answered all these questions affirmatively. Only question (4), Do you think that history is a form of rhetoric? led to strong disagreement.
5. So far, many theorists of history have discussed both the rhetorical and pragmatic aspects of history, but they have not identified rhetoric and history on a pragmatist basis. Recently, some theorists have most fruitfully employed the linguistic notion of pragmatics, without identifying history with rhetoric however (Pihlainen 2010, 2014; Tamm 2014).
6. 'Practical' or 'pragmatic historicism' is a term that I have coined for the philosophies of Croce, Gentile, de Ruggiero and Collingwood (Peters 2013).
7. Since these overviews of the pragmatist tradition do not mention the words 'rhetoric' or 'persuasion' it seems that pragmatists did not take rhetoric into account, even when they dealt with the problems of history.
8. 'Jede Erfahrung hat ihren Erfahrungshorizont; jede hat ihren Kern wirklicher und bestimmter Kenntnisnahme, hat ihren Gehalt an unmittelbar selbstgegebenen Bestimmtheiten, aber über diesen Kern bestimmten Soseins hinaus, des eigentlich als "selbst da" Gegebenen hinaus, hat sie ihren Horizont'.

Acknowledgements

I thank Rodrigo Diaz, two anonymous reviewers, and the Amsterdam and Groningen sections of the Dutch Network for the Philosophy of History for their comments on earlier versions of this article. I dedicate this article to Nancy Struever.

Disclosure statement

No potential conflict of interest was reported by the author.

References

Ankersmit, F. R. 1983. *Narrative Logic. A Semantic Analysis of the Historian's Language.* The Hague: Martinus Nijhoff.

Ankersmit, F. R. 2005. *Sublime Historical Experience.* Stanford, CA: Stanford University Press.

Ankersmit, F. R. 2007. "Danto's Philosophy of History in Retrospective." In *Narration and Knowledge*, edited by Arthur C. Danto, 364–395. New York: Columbia University Press.

Ankersmit, F. R. 2012. *Meaning, Truth, and Reference in Historical Representation.* Ithaca, NY: Cornell University Press.

Aristotle. 1991. *The Art of Rhetoric.* London: Penguin.

Austin, J. L. 1962. *How to Do Things with Words.* Oxford: Clarendon Press.

Bacon, Michael. 2012. *Pragmatism. An Introduction.* Cambridge: Polity Press.

Beale, Walter H. 1987. *A Pragmatic Theory of Rhetoric.* Chicago, IL: Southern Illinois University Press.

Beale, Walter H. 2009. *Learning from Language: Symmetry, Asymmetry, and Literary Humanism.* Pittsburgh, PA: University of Pittsburgh Press.

Bevernage, Berber, Broos Delanote, Anton Froeyman, and Kenan Van De Mieroop. 2014. "Introduction: The Future of the Theory and Philosophy of History." *Journal of the Philosophy of History* 8 (2): 141–148.

Blom, Tannelie, and Ton Nijhuis. 1989. "Contingency, Meaning and History." *Philosophica* 44: 33–59.

Collingwood, R. G. 1938. *The Principles of Art.* Oxford: Oxford University Press.

Collingwood, R. G. 1940. *An Essay on Metaphysics.* Oxford: Clarendon Press.

Collingwood, R. G. 1999. *The Principles of History and Other Writings in Philosophy of History.* Oxford: Oxford University Press.

D'Oro, Giuseppina. 2003. *Collingwood and the Metaphysics of Experience.* London: Routledge.

Danto, Arthur C. 1981. *The Transfiguration of the Common Place. A Philosophy of Art.* Cambridge, MA: Harvard University Press.

Danto, Arthur C. 2007. *Narration and Knowledge.* New York: Columbia University Press.

De Ruggiero, Guido. 1925. *Storia del liberalismo europeo* [The History of European Liberalism, Translated by R. G. Collingwood, 1927]. Bari: Laterza.

Dewey, John. 1949. *Logic: The Theory of Inquiry.* New York: Holt.

Droysen, Johann Gustav. 1967. *Historik: Vorlesungen über Enzyklopädie und Methodologie der Geschichte* [Historik: Lectures on the Encyclopedia and Methodology of History]. München: R. Oldenbourg.

Fahnestock, Jeanne. 1999. *Rhetorical Figures in Science.* New York: Oxford University Press.

Gadamer, Hans-Georg Gadamer. 1979. *Truth and Method.* London: Sheed and Ward.

Gallie, W. B. 1964. *Philosophy and the Historical Understanding.* London: Chatto and Windus.

Ginzburg, Carlo. 1999. *History, Rhetoric and Proof. The Menahem Stern Jerusalem Lectures.* Hanover: University Press of New England.

Guldi, Jo, and David Armitage. 2014. *The History Manifesto*. Cambridge: CUP.

Hexter, J. H. 1971. *Doing History*. Bloomington, IL: Indiana University Press.

Hildebrand, David. L. 2003. *Beyond Realism and Anti-Realism. John Dewey and the Neopragmatists*. Nashville, TN: Vanderbilt University Press.

Husserl, Edmund. 1948. *Erfahrung und Urteil: Untersuchungen zur Genealogie der Logik* [Experience and Judgment: Investigations in a Genealogy of Logic]. Hamburg: Claassen und Goverts. Edinburgh Gate: Pearson Education Limited.

Husserl, Edmund. 1968. *Logische Untersuchungen* [Logical Investigations]. Tübingen: Meiner Verlag.

Iggers, George G., and Edward Wang. 2008. *A Global History of Modern Historiography*. Harlow: Pearson Education Limited.

Jenkins, Keith. 1999. *Why History?* London: Routledge.

Kloppenberg, James T. 2004. "Pragmatism and the Practice of History: From Turner and Du Bois to Today." *Metaphilosophy* 35 (1–2): 202–225.

Koselleck, Reinhart. 2003. *Zeitgeschichten* [Times' Histories]. Frankfurt: Suhrkamp.

MacArthur, Brian. 1995. *The Penguin Book of Historic Speeches*. London: Penguin.

Maggi, Michele. 1989. *La filosofia di Benedetto Croce* [The Philosophy of Benedetto Croce].. Firenze: Il Ponte alle Grazie.

Megill, Allan, and Donald McCloskey. 1987. "The Rhetoric of History." In *The Rhetoric of the Human Sciences. Language and Argument in Scholarship and Public Affairs*, edited by John S. Nelson, Allan Megill, and Donald McCloskey, 221–238. Madison, WI: University of Wisconsin Press.

Mink, Louis O. 1987. *Historical Understanding*. Ithaca, NY: Cornell University Press.

Misak, Cheryl. 2013. *The American Pragmatists*. Oxford: Oxford University Press.

O'Gorman, Edmundo. 1947. *Crisis y porvenir de la ciencia histórica* [Crisis and Future of the Science of History]. México: Impr. Universitaria.

O'Gorman, Edmundo. 2007. *Ensayos de Filosofía de la Historia* [Essays in the Philosophy of History]. México: U.N.A.M.

Oakeshott, Michael. 1933. *Experience and Its Modes*. Cambridge: Cambridge University Press.

Oakeshott, Michael. 1983. *On History and Other Essays*. Oxford: Basil Blackwell.

Ortega y Gasset José. 1983. *Obras Completas. Tomo XII* [Complete Works. Volume XII]. Madrid: Alianza Editorial.

Perelman, Chaïm. 1982. *The Realm of Rhetoric*. Notre Dame: Notre Dame University Press.

Peters, Rik. 2009. "Torturing the Torturer. Interpretation of Evidence as Metarepresenation." In *Metarepresentation, Self-Organization and Art*, edited by Wolfgang Wildgen and Barend van Heusden, 13–27. Bern: Peter Lang.

Peters, Rik. 2013. *History as Thought and Action: The Philosophies of Croce, Gentile, De Ruggiero, and Collingwood*. Exeter: Imprint-Academic.

Pihlainen, Kalle. 2010. "On History as Communication and Constraint." *Ideas in History* 4 (2): 63–90.

Pihlainen, Kalle. 2014. "There's Just No Talking with the past." *Rethinking History* 18 (4): 575–582.

Runia, Eelco. 2014. *Moved by the Past*. New York: Columbia University Press.

Searle, John. 1970. *Speech Acts. An Essay in the Philosophy of Language*. Cambridge: Cambridge University Press.

Smith, David Woodruff, and Ronald McIntyre. 1984. *Husserl and Intentionality: A Study of Mind, Meaning, and Language*. Dordrecht: Reidel.

Struever, Nancy. 1970. *The Language of History in the Renaissance*. Princeton: Princeton University Press.

Struever, Nancy. 2009. *Rhetoric, Modality, Modernity*. Chicago, IL: The University of Chicago Press.

Tamm, M. July 18, 2014. "Truth, Objectivity and Evidence in History Writing." *Journal of the Philosophy of History* 8 (2): 265–290.

Tindale, Christopher W. 2004. *Rhetorical Argumentation Principles of Theory and Practice*. Thousand Oaks, CA: Sage.

Veyne, Paul. 1978. *Comment on écrit l'histoire suivi de Foucault révolutionne l'histoire* [How We Write History Followed by Foucault Revolutionises History]. Paris: Éditions du Seuil.

Wallace, Karl R. 1970. *Understanding Discourse. The Speech Act and Rhetorical Action*. Baton Rouge, LA: Louisiana State University Press.

Walzer, Michael. 1974. *Regicide and Revolution. Speeches at the Trial of Louis XVI*. Cambridge: Cambridge University Press.

White, Hayden. 2014. *The Practical past*. Evanston, IL: Northwestern University Press.

Wilkins, Burleigh Taylor. 1959. "Pragmatism as a Theory of Historical Knowledge: John Dewey on the Nature of Historical Inquiry." *The American Historical Review* 64: 878–890.

Williams, Bernard. 2002. *Truth and Truthfulness. An Essay in Genealogy*. Princeton: Princeton University Press.

We are history: the outlines of a quasi-substantive philosophy of history

Zoltán Boldizsár Simon

Bielefeld Graduate School in History and Sociology, University of Bielefeld, Bielefeld, Germany

ABSTRACT

In times of a felt need to justify the value of the humanities, the need to revisit and re-establish the public relevance of the discipline of history cannot come as a surprise. On the following pages I will argue that this need is unappeasable by scholarly proposals. The much desired revitalization of historical writing lies instead in reconciling ourselves with the dual meaning of the word history, in exploring the necessary interconnection between history understood as the course of events *and* as historical writing. Despite the general tendency of the last decades to forbid philosophizing about history in the former sense (at least in departments of history and philosophy), I think that to a certain extent we already do so without succumbing to substantive thought. We already have the sprouts of a speculative although only quasi-substantive philosophy of history that nevertheless takes seriously the postwar criticism of the substantive enterprise. In this essay I will first try to outline this quasi-substantive philosophy of history that attests to the historical sensibility of our times; and second, I will try to outline its consequences regarding history as historical writing. Finally, in place of a conclusion I will suggest that historical writing is not as much a contribution to public agendas as it is the very arena in which public life is at stake.

The logic of proposals and the task of understanding

For as long as I can remember, history (understood as historical writing) has been in crisis. True enough, it was said to be in crisis even before I was born. It was said to be in crisis throughout the entire postwar period, and generally speaking there has been plenty of crisis-talk surrounding history since its institutionalization. What this series of felt crises betrays is, I think, a constant urge for change that, even more generally speaking, might characterize the entire modern period. But regardless of whether these crises are reasonably felt, regardless of whether the changes they evoke are only overdecorated bagatelles as they often prove to be, one thing looks certain: the constant urge for change these crises evince, craves satisfaction.

Within academia, a customary route to satisfaction seems to be to come up with proposals that 'challenge' received wisdom by putting forth 'bold' and 'provocative' ideas in order to achieve 'radical' conceptual shifts. I will call this customary route the logic of proposals, which informs both our academic debates in general and our debates regarding history in particular. As for debates about history, the current flow of proposals reflects a present crisis of history, revolving around the desire to turn history into a valuable contribution to public life.[1] To be clear, at issue is not the contribution of *the past* to present-day cultural, social, environmental and political concerns; at issue is the contribution of *a particular way of making sense of the world*, of a certain way of relating to the past, which can be regarded as a specific characteristic of professional history exercised by historians. Accordingly, the question is not merely one of how historical writing can be of public relevance, but how history *qua* history and historians *qua* historians, as practitioners of a specific way of making sense of the world, could contribute to public life and public agendas – if such a thing is possible at all.

In the most general terms, it is the relevance of historical sensibility for our contemporary life and the question of the form this historical sensibility is supposed to take today that is at stake in the abundance of the proposed conceptual revisions we have witnessed lately. This is the main concern of Hayden White's recent embrace of the notion of the practical past (White 2014), of efforts to reconceptualize notions of time and temporality, either somewhat sharply (Ermarth 2011) or more modestly (Bevernage and Lorenz 2012), of calls to re-examine our relations to the past in the broadest terms (Paul 2015), or of *The History Manifesto*, co-authored by historians Jo Guldi and David Armitage (2014), a short book offering a lengthy scholarly proposal that is manifesto-like only in its title. The curious thing about all these proposals is that the urge for the deep conceptual change they attest to seems unappeasable by them. The reason for this is that the logic of proposals is a rather self-preserving practice in which any proposal is just an invitation for another to 'go beyond' it tomorrow. The result is a situation best described by the Rolling Stones hit (*I Can't Get No) Satisfaction*, where the permanent desire for satisfaction is accompanied by knowledge of the impossibility of getting it (as is conceded in the parentheses that, tellingly, precede the main theme). This impossibility, I believe, lies at the very heart of the logic of proposals. In their efforts to trump each other, proposals defy the very possibility of fulfilling their objective, namely, the achievement of a 'radical' conceptual shift concerning not only yesterday's proposals but the subject of all proposals: a change that cannot be superseded the next day.

Such desired changes are changes in conditions of possibility, which, by definition, are not well-formulated and deliberate proposals but hidden dispositions that make deliberate proposals possible and establish their confines. They can be unveiled by deliberate acts of academic critique (a practice that proposals build upon), but cannot be replaced by these very same acts. Hence most of the proposals concerning the reconceptualization of history (or of anything else practically) are brilliant in unveiling and analyzing that which they wish to supersede or exchange, but helpless and clumsy in offering new configurations – simply because, to repeat my point, *a spectacular conceptual shift is not something that can be offered as a proposal.*

If proposals are nevertheless able to unveil what they consider to be wrong conceptualizations, it is precisely because those conceptualizations are not regarded as being theirs anymore. But if something is properly left behind, as they all seem to think, if something does not apply anymore, then it simply makes no sense to suppose that it left a vacuum of thought and was not already exchanged for something else, even if this new something still remains to be properly articulated. Therefore, in an intellectual atmosphere with a shared sense that certain conceptual dispositions no longer apply, the task is not to devise something that could fill a supposed vacuum of thought, but to look around within our own cultural practices and come to terms with what is already going on instead of what no longer applies. The sensible thing to do in this situation is, I think, to get out of the circuit of proposals, to halt, to stop for a moment in the middle of the rush, to look around and attempt to understand something that we, at least to some extent, already have at our disposal.

To put it differently, I think that the challenge we face today in the theory and philosophy of history lies in making the implicit explicit. And it is precisely this task of understanding and of trying to articulate something already implicit that I wish to take on with regards to the question of how history *qua* history and historians *qua* historians shape public life today. The question itself, insofar as it demands universality and insofar as it concerns *the conditions* under which history as historical writing might be able to live up to its own apparent expectations, is a rather theoretical one. It means that no answer to this question will enable answering the question about *how*, in what particular way, historians could *make* history instrumental for public life in the first decades of the twenty-first century. What answering the question about the conditions brings to light instead is the mode in which history *inevitably* is of public relevance today, regardless of particular proposals concerning the *how*. Practically speaking, what such an answer could suggest is, at best, a way to distinguish between viable and less viable proposals: between proposals that work with new conceptualizations and those that eventually fall prey to that which they wish to supersede.

As for sketching the mode in which history *qua* history inevitably is of public relevance today, my point of departure will be the dual meaning of the word history, understood both as the course of events and as historical writing. The reason for this is that professional historical writing and the philosophy of history that offered an overall interpretation of the course of human events accompanied by an overall meaning to a postulated movement of history were joint products of a time when the concept of history as such became thinkable in the period that Koselleck (2004) calls *Sattelzeit*.[2] Due to their interdependence (of which I will talk more about later), they exhibit a shared set of conceptual tools. Yet the theoretical work of the last decades has revolved around the agenda that we should drop any philosophical and theoretical talk of history in the former sense and reserve the word exclusively for theorizing historical writing.[3]

Now, my basic contention runs counter to this and goes as follows: examining the sense in which it is possible to talk about the movement of history *today*, that is, tracking a conceptual shift concerning the enterprise of philosophy of history as a philosophy of the course of events, reveals a great deal about the outlines of a conceptual shift concerning history as historical writing. In other words, the reconceptualization of the latter does not come in the shape of proposals but as a necessary entailment of the way we already think differently about the movement of history, about how change takes place in human affairs. Traces that we already do so – and that it is possible again to talk about the movement of history in the first place – are, I think, clearly detectable in the work of philosophers like Alain Badiou or Jean-Luc Nancy. It is equally apparent in the more specific aim of Eelco Runia to devise an up-to-date philosophy of history, and, however unintentionally, it is implied in Frank Ankersmit's recent work on historical experience. Separately, none of these efforts break away (and some of them do not even try to break away) from the conceptual framework of the philosophies of history of the Enlightenment and German Idealism. However, they all indicate aspects in which they do, and seeing those aspects together might result in a quasi-substantive philosophy of history that conceptualizes the movement of history in a new framework (a situation that I outlined in more detail in Simon 2015b).

That being said, on the coming pages I will run the following argument to answer the question of how history *qua* history *inevitably* shapes public life. As a first step, I will begin by sketching the notion of history that a quasi-substantive philosophy of history might offer today. In doing so, I will outline the sense in which this quasi-substantive view of history as the course of events differs from the developmental view of classical philosophies of history and attempt to explore the temporal configuration that underlies this new movement of history. The notion of history that emerges from these investigations is what I will call *history as a disrupted singular*. What this means is that whereas the notion of history harbored by classical philosophies of history accounted for change as the development of a single ontological subject – humankind, reason or freedom – within a flow of time, the concept of history that I think we already have at our disposal accounts for change by considering disruptions in time that bring about ever new ontological subjects – new human communities – in terms of identity shifts.

In the next step of the argument I will try to unpack the conceptual consequences that the notion history as a disrupted singular has for the questions of how we relate to the past and how we think about the task of historical writing. What I will try to show is that historical writing – by providing *essentially contested knowledge of the past* – is the best tool we have for negatively indicating the contours of the future community that is presently taking place. Although we cannot have knowledge about what we are to be (about what community is coming to existence), historical writing functions as the indicator of what we will *not* be by revealing what we no longer can be. Eventually, all this will enable me to argue that historical writing is not as much a contribution to public agendas as the very arena in which public life is at stake. It is the very arena because history as the course of events is our public endeavor per se, within which historical writing acquires the aforementioned function and which renders historical writing possible in the first place.

The movement of history

Thinking about history as the course of events begins not in the past but in the idea that the past should be seen together with the present and the future. The substantive philosophies of history of the Enlightenment and German Idealism did exactly this when they postulated an ultimate meaning of an entire historical process in the future, which retrospectively explains past events as directed toward a future fulfillment. Later, in the postwar period, it was exactly this operation that became the primary target of criticism: the supposed knowledge of the future from which knowledge of the past could be derived was the main ground for ridiculing and for refuting the entire substantive enterprise as illegitimate (cf. Danto 1985, 13).

This specific constellation that could not withstand postwar criticism is, of course, not the one that could or should be reinstated. The unity of past, present and future in the shape of a continuous temporal plane as a matter of knowledge in its entirety, the flow of time as the background against which the unfolding of *a single ontological subject* as the substance of the historical process – humanity, freedom or reason – could take place *within* and *as* the whole of history, the view that Maurice Mandelbaum (1971) called the developmental view, is not a temporal configuration that could underlie the movement of history *today*.[4] The philosophy of history of our times, if it intends to take critiques seriously, cannot be other than *quasi-substantive*.[5] It can still be a philosophy of history inasmuch as it postulates a movement and a mechanism (or a pattern) *to account for change* in the course of events just like substantive philosophies of history did; but it can be only quasi-substantive inasmuch as due to an abandonment of temporal unity, it lacks a proper substance as the development of a single unfolding subject as history.

Be that as it may, for historians and philosophers alike, the seduction of developmental and substantive thinking is still hard to withstand. The authors of *The History Manifesto*, for instance, still assume temporal unity in arguing for 'thinking about the past in order to see the future' (Guldi and Armitage 2014, 4), while Alain Badiou somewhat habitually associates what he sees as 'the rebirth of History' with the 'rebirth of the Idea' – which, for him, is still the 'idea of Communism' (Badiou 2012, 6). Badiou's insistence on something like the Idea that cannot but retain the function of a substance in a historical process is all the more unfortunate because it overshadows Badiou's more important and less essentialist thoughts on a future other than the fulfillment of something that is already and always was there, unfulfilled. In his more important and less essentialist moments Badiou rather talks about a future we have to think today exactly in order to avoid substantive thinking, namely, *the future coming-to-existence of an ontological subject that had no prior existence*. This, I believe, is what Badiou sees in recent riots as the birth of 'people, who are present in the world but absent from its meaning and decisions about its future, the *inexistent* of the world' (Badiou 2012, 56). As potential subjects of a historical process, the previously 'inexistent' and the Idea are, I think, irreconcilable. They are different in kind, just as the way they respectively come about. The Idea that is yet to be fulfilled as an ultimate meaning comes about in a development of becoming, while the previously 'inexistent' is just being born without a previous stage out of which it could develop in order to eventually reach a point of becoming.

To avoid Badiou's mistake of taking recourse in a substance in the course of events, the first task of a quasi-substantive philosophy for our times is to think a future as the 'coming' of a new subject that does not 'become,' a subject that is about to be born *without* originating in and unfolding from the past. And this precisely is the leitmotif of Jean-Luc Nancy's idea of a community in its happening, the prospect of the announcement of a future 'we,' which, I think, is what a quasi-substantive philosophy of history has to take as its point of departure. Only as its point of departure, however, because even if Nancy (1993) does equate the coming-to-existence or coming-to-presence of a future 'we' with history in order to escape substantive thinking, his notion of history is anything but historical by virtue of lacking the dimension of change in a crucial respect. As to the efforts to escape substantive thought, Nancy tries to think the 'taking place' of a subject in its very act of happening. Thinking the subject of a human community it in its very act of happening means that 'rather than an unfolding, rather than a process or procession, the happening or the coming – or, more to the point, 'to happen,' 'to come,' 'to take place' – would be a nonsubstantive verb and one that is nonsubstantifiable' (Nancy 2000, 162). That such 'coming' or 'taking place' of a subject entails the abandonment of the entire idea of development is especially clear when Nancy assures readers that the subject in question 'does not come from the homogeneity of a temporal process or from the homogeneous production of this process out of an origin,' and 'that the origin is not and was never present' (Nancy 1993, 162).

As for the lack of the dimension of change in a very crucial respect, that is coded into what I see as the perpetual stream of Nancy's notion of 'coming' and 'taking place.' Unlike a process of becoming that implies a motion directed towards an altered condition, the motion implied by a perpetual 'coming' keeps its subject in the very same condition. Whereas the 'becoming' of the substance in substantive philosophies of history entailed a concept of change as stages of development leading to an ultimate fulfillment, Nancy's 'coming' does not lead to any ultimate altered condition nor to changes along the way, simply because there is no 'way' leading anywhere. Insofar as the future community (as the subject of history) is always in its happening, insofar as it is 'coming' without ever 'becoming,' it has forever to be unrealizable, forever to remain an unannounced 'we,' sentenced to infinite deferral. Thus, it seems that excluding the dimension of change is the price Nancy has to pay for equating history with the future, with a coming 'we,' which nevertheless enables him to cut ties with the past, to imagine a future ontological subject that has *no prior existence* and thus *no origin from which it could unfold.*[6]

Yet no philosophy of history (as the course of events) is possible without accounting for change, which, in turn, necessitates not only the future, but also the present and the past. Therefore, the task is to find a way to reconcile the idea of change and the idea of a perpetual coming-to-presence or coming-to-existence of a new ontological subject. Change, however, cannot have the same characteristics it had in substantive philosophies of history: it cannot mean stages of a development of a subject that nevertheless retains its self-identity. In the case of a future coming-to-presence or coming-to existence of a new ontological subject, change has to mean a change in that very identity, that is, a change of the subject of a postulated historical process. Change here has to mean *the perpetual alteration of ever new ontological subjects*, each of them being a coming 'we' without an origin, without a previous state from which they could develop. Just because the coming-to-existence of a new ontological subject has to be of no origin in order to avoid substantive thought, it does not have to mean that it cannot be superseded by another one, and then another one, again and again.

Now, having a look at current philosophies of history, what brings together the recent efforts of Runia (2014) and Ankersmit (2005) is precisely their shared interest in the most momentous changes in human affairs: changes that are deeply traumatic; changes that are the result of events they both label 'sublime;' changes that destroy 'the stories we live by,' (Runia 2014, 124) and changes through which 'one has become what one is no longer' (Ankersmit 2005, 333). These disruptive changes – of which the French Revolution is the paradigmatic example for both of them – appear as discontinuities in identity constitution, as dissociations from the past. If the stories that a certain 'we' lives by are destroyed in these disruptive changes, then what is born in the midst of such traumatic events is a new 'we' that is discontinuous with and dissociated from the 'we' whose stories have been destroyed. Or, to put it differently, in such momentous changes a new subject is being born, from whose viewpoint the destroyed stories must have belonged to a 'them' which, as a 'them,' once was also born in the midst of a momentous change and as a previous 'we' it also had to have its 'them' to dissociate from, a 'them' that once was also a 'we,' and so on – all this making up a movement or mechanism based on discontinuous change.

Within such a movement (a movement that I outline in more detail in Simon 2015b) the identity of a certain 'we' cannot be established by invoking its past simply because that is only *its* past, *not its* history. Runia, very much in line with Nancy, associates the latter with the future in claiming that 'our history really is before us' (Runia 2014, 8). Aside from this remark, however, Runia does not have much to say about the future. His more interesting claims concern the past – particularly the claim that it is due to the aforementioned momentous changes that the past can be known, that it is due to them that 'we come to see what is lost forever: what we are no longer' (Runia 2014, 16). As a result, with this claim, the most important aspect of introducing the dimension of change in the shape of ruptures becomes apparent. It is the recognition that the past and the future are subjects of activities of a different kind, that they satisfy different kinds of desires. *In a quasi-substantive philosophy of history the past is a matter of knowledge and the future is a matter of existence, while the movement of history is the perpetual transformation of the matters of existence into the matters of knowledge.*

To sum up, there are two points to keep in mind when thinking about history as the course of events today. First, in order to be only quasi-substantive, the future in which a quasi-substantive philosophy of history begins must be the coming-to-existence of a new ontological subject. Second, in order to qualify as a philosophy of history that explains change, a quasi-substantive philosophy of history has to posit a series of comings-to-existence of new-born subjects, separated from each other by disruptive, momentous events, instead of speaking of one single subject that could play the role of a substance in a historical process. Neither Nancy's philosophy nor recent philosophies of history interested in change fulfil both conditions. But the ideas they entertain separately – that of 'coming' and that of momentous change – can nevertheless be put to work to confine and inform each other.[7] The concept of history that emerges from this operation *is history as a disrupted singular*, a concept that I would like to introduce in the following section in order both to review and elaborate on what I have said so far.

History as a disrupted singular

A philosophy of history that wishes to avoid substantive thought can employ the word history in three distinct senses: in a prospective sense, in a retrospective one, and, most importantly, in a sense that encompasses both as a movement. The *prospective sense* is the one that had a prominent role in the previous section: it is history as equated with the future, our history ahead of us – our 'coming' community. It means neither the course of events concerning things done nor historical writing, but things about to be done. It concerns a future existence of which we cannot have knowledge, for it is not a matter of epistemology but of ontology, if anything. Finally, as a 'coming' without ever 'becoming,' it indicates a clear break with the developmental view that characterized substantive philosophies of history as well as historical writing as it became institutionalized in the early nineteenth century.

The *retrospective* is the familiar sense of historical writing. The different understanding of the prospective, however, requires a modification to the retrospective sense too, which concerns the function of historical writing in identity constitution. For if the future is not the final stage of a 'becoming,' then our retrospective stance cannot be based on the view that understanding something means inquiring into *its* past (from which it unfolds and proceeds to its future state). In the retrospective stance of a quasi-substantive philosophy of history there is nothing like a different past state of the otherwise same present identity; there is only another identity. One might nevertheless object by noting that there is nothing new here, given that the past has been the 'other' ever since the institutionalization of the discipline. And the objection would be partly right, but only partly. It is true that even in the developmental view the past was the 'other.' Yet that 'other' was always an earlier version of a present 'we,' much like in the *Terminator* movies, where the T-800 (the living tissue over a metal endoskeleton) is an earlier version of the 'advanced prototype' T-1000 (the mimetic poly-alloy), as the T-800 actually refers to its successor. In other words, the past 'other' in the developmental view is who the present 'we,' notwithstanding and despite its altered past states, *always* was. In distinction, in a quasi-substantive philosophy of history the 'other' is who the coming 'we' *never* was.

To rephrase things more emphatically, the 'other' is *another* ontological subject, meaning that historical writing cannot answer 'our' identity questions by turning to the past anymore. It cannot answer the question of who 'we' are, because 'who we are' now means 'who we are about to be' prospectively, in the happening of 'our' history, which, by definition, cannot be known. Thus, in a quasi-substantive philosophy of history, the retrospective stance associated with historical writing shifts from an approach that positively connects to an approach that disrupts. Similarly to negative (*apophatic*) theology, according to which God cannot be described in positive terms, history in this sense can answer our identity questions only by negation. Nevertheless, the negative answers inform us about who we are not, and by virtue of their exclusion, they can still be indicative of what the coming 'we' is about to be. This negative definition gains significance in the light of the irony of the story, namely, that if prospectively 'we' never become, and if retrospectively we can know only what 'we' are not, then we can never know who 'we' actually are. *What we can know, what historical writing can tell us, is who we no longer are and hence what the coming 'we' cannot be.*

Finally, and most importantly, it is necessary to consider these two senses of history as they meet at a present point of disruption, from which the former sense of history applies prospectively and the latter retrospectively. Seen together, the past, the present and the future make up what I would call *history as a disrupted singular*. On the long run, consisting several disruptive moments and transformations, this is the mechanism of a perpetual transformation of unknowable 'coming' histories into dissociated, apophatic pasts. From points of disruption, the retrospective and the prospective stances satisfy two different kinds of desires. Yet, as odd as it may sound, points of disruption also function as points of connection, given that it is seen from these points that both sides of history as a disrupted singular play the same endless game: identity formation.

This history as a disrupted singular departs both from the late-eighteenth-century invention of history as a collective singular, as it was dubbed by Koselleck (2004, 33–37), and from the Koselleckian interpretative scheme. There is a dual departure because Koselleck's analytical framework is based on the very same temporal configuration as its subject of analysis, the concept of history as a collective singular. To sketch the framework very briefly, in its core there are two anthropological constants, the categories of a 'space of experience' and a 'horizon of expectation,' whose inner relations structure the experience of time. The kind of change that can happen in the Koselleckian framework is a change in the internal relation of these categories, like the change Koselleck associates with *Neuzeit*, when expectations moved away from previous experiences in an accelerating fashion, giving way to the temporal configuration in which history as a collective singular became thinkable. But however far expectations may move from experiences, Koselleck's categories work on the premise of continuous succession, as they themselves are products of the notion of history whose birth and characteristics Koselleck investigates. However thin that continuity between experiences and expectations might become in *Neuzeit*, both experiences and expectations concern one single ontological subject whose past and future is at stake in a present moment. The one single subject, whose association with both the past and the future takes place in a present moment, necessarily creates temporal unity and continuity.

Contrary to this, the temporal configuration that underlies the concept of history as a disrupted singular is based on discontinuity and disruption. The past cannot be a space of experience simply because it no longer concerns the experiences of the same ontological subject that comes-to-existence on the prospective side, but the experiences of a 'them' that is anything but the 'we' in its formation. In a similar vein, the future cannot form a horizon of expectation as it simply does not concern the prospective projection of a past subject, but the birth of another subject that did not exist previously. To put this in a somewhat thesis-like way: the temporal configuration that underlies the notion of history as a disrupted singular is not a relation between a space of experience and a horizon of expectation within a flow of time, but a *space of dissociated knowledge* and a *horizon of existence* against the background of a disruption of time.[8]

Our apophatic past

The movement of history as a disrupted singular sketched above sets the conditions under which history as historical writing operates as knowledge about our past. Insofar as historical writing is about past events and occurrences, the role attributed to the retrospective stance in the overall picture is instructive of the function and role of historical writing. To run a brief review, in the previous section it became clear that the past can only be a negative contribution to a coming identity; its instrumentality lies in our attempts at defining who a coming 'we' is about to be by indicating what the 'we' in question can no longer be. According to the analogy to apophatic theology also mentioned in the previous section, I would like to call this past our *apophatic past*. This may sound somewhat outlandish or clumsy, but is at least indicative of the function of our backward stance in identity constitution. Besides, sounding outlandish may not be a bad thing after all, taking into consideration what the phrase stands for.

But what exactly does the phrase stand for? What exactly do I mean by an apophatic past? To begin with, I mean a dissociated past. Yet, I mean much more than a simple present dissociation from a past condition or state of affairs. The apophatic past can only be understood in relation to the future, which is not the result but the source of a backward stance. This is so because it can only be a postulated future viewpoint, the viewpoint that one has in a coming community, from where the past looks apophatic, from where the past appears as a matter of dissociated knowledge about what the coming community is not and what it cannot be. The importance of this operation cannot be overstated. For if the coming 'we' cannot know its identity, it has no other choice than to attempt a self-definition – a self-definition which can never fully succeed – by negation, by making use of the only usable thing at hand in that matter, the apophatic past, and hence by the practice that studies and creates (creates by studying/studies by creating) such a past: historical writing.

The first thing I have to concede about this notion of an apophatic past is that it seems to be at odds with the two most fashionable recent proposals about how we should relate to the past: the practical past as advocated recently by

Hayden White, and the notion of a present past. To start with the former, when White (2014) turns to Michael Oakeshott's distinction between the practical and the historical past (introduced in *Experience and Its Modes* in 1933), what he is concerned with is not the conceptual redefinition of the distinction, but a re-evaluation of its respective sides. On Oakeshott's account, the distinction looks like this: the historical past is a 'dead past' and its distinctness lies in 'its very disparity from what is contemporary' (Oakeshott 1966, 106), while the practical past comes to the fore 'wherever the significance of the past lies in the fact that it has been influential in deciding the present and future fortunes of man, wherever the present is sought in the past' (Oakeshott 1966, 103). Whereas the historical past describes the relationship of professional historians to the past, the practical past describes our everyday attitude towards it. As it stands, White seems to be perfectly content with this conceptual framing. But unlike Oakeshott, who passed a positive judgment on the historical past in order to grant the autonomy of historical knowledge by showing that it is a distinct mode of experience in its own right, White – having very different objectives – calls for an embracement of the practical past.[9]

His embracement, however, suffers from the same deficiency that *The History Manifesto* does: the advice to tell stories about the past that might guide our future actions exhibits the notion of temporality entailed in the developmental view.[10] As I have dealt with this issue more extensively on another occasion (Simon 2015a), I would here like to mention only the core of the problem with the concept of history that White has lately advocated. It is that the notion of the practical past – and, actually, the entire distinction between the historical and the practical past – makes sense only on the premise of a historical process within which an unfolding subject retains its self-identity in the midst of all changes in appearance. Accordingly, it does not come as a surprise that 'continuity in change' is a recurring theme in the argument of White (2014, 68, 100–103), describing the temporal structure within which the practical past makes sense. White's insistence on this temporality and on the idea that 'we need the illusion of substance' (White 2014, 103) insofar as we want to act upon stories based on the practical past, clearly exhibits the very same temporal order upon which classical philosophies of history were erected. What is more, White (2014, 14–16) explicitly associates these philosophies of history with the pursuit of the practical past (White 2014, 14–16), which, needless to say, is indeed in sharp contradiction with a quasi-substantive philosophy of history, with the notion of history as a disrupted singular and with a past that is apophatic.

As for the notion of the present past, the intellectual environment in which White raised the issue of the practical past was already sparkling, thanks to the freshly emerging notion of 'presence'. It seems to entail a timelier – or, as Ghosh and Kleinberg (2013) indicate, maybe even the timeliest – offer to account for our relations to the past. Besides the literary and cultural theorist Hans Ulrich Gumbrecht (2004), the two names that pop up most often in discussions of the notion are the ones whose ideas were already instructive in the previous sections: Runia (2014, 49–83) and Nancy (1993). There is, however, a crucial difference that usually goes unmentioned. It is only Runia for whom presence means the presence of the past and for whom the past (that is, by definition, a non-present) can break its way into the present. In contrast to this, presence for Nancy always concerns the future as a coming-to-presence; instead of talking about something (the past) breaking into the present, Nancy's ideas rather leave the present void of presence. Due to this all-important difference – on which I will elaborate later – it is not on Nancy's but on Runia's premise that the notion of presence pervaded the post-millennial theory and philosophy of history.

In Runia's theory the past seems to be able to make its way into the present on two levels. The first level concerns historical writing, regarding which Runia endows the linguistic trope of metonymy with the capability to transfer presence and claims that 'historical reality travels with historiography not as a paying passenger, but as a *stowaway*' (Runia 2014, 81). The second level concerns existence, and Runia's claim is that 'the past may have a presence that is so powerful that it can use *us*, humans, as its *material*' (Runia 2014, 88). His primary example for this is the case of the Dutch historians of the Srebrenica commission, who, according to Runia (2014, 17–48), reproduced or 'acted out' the defense and argumentation of Dutch soldiers whose acts (the killing of 8000 Bosnians under their 'guidance') they were supposed to be studying. Discussions of these two levels blend in Runia's work, often resulting in unnecessary confusion about the notion of 'presence.' Thus, for the sake of clarity it seems important to note that it is one thing to state that texts can, due to present human intervention, be crafted to convey presence (what literary theory calls experientiality),[11] and another to claim that a past existence invades and takes over the present without present human intervention, as Runia appears to think in the passage quoted above.

Even though I find this idea of human passivity considerably troublesome, I have to admit that it is nevertheless on this second, ontological level that the notion of the present past might be useful for efforts that seek to reconceptualize time and temporality in a way different from the developmental view. That being the case, the question to ask is: Can this notion be linked in any way to history as a disrupted singular? At first glance, the answer seems to be a rather obvious 'No, it cannot.' Indeed, how could anyone imagine that the past that breaks into and takes over the present, a past with which the present necessarily becomes *associated*, has anything to do with the apophatic past, *dissociated* from the present?

The answer I wish to suggest is that the notion of 'presence' in historical theory and thus the idea of the present past can be regarded as the counterpart of what I call the apophatic past. Not in the sense of their being each other's evil twins, and not as if one could be favoured and set up as a standard to follow against the other. Moreover, neither are they counterparts in the sense that one of them could be recommended for historical practice at the expense of the other, nor complements in the sense that one could apply to historical practice while the other could describe a relation to the past beyond the concerns of professional historical writing. This constellation may perfectly describe the relationship between the historical past and the practical past in Oakeshott's and White's thinking. But in the case of the concept of history as a disrupted singular, the link between the present and our apophatic past concerns a more primordial and elementary relation in which they are counterparts insofar as they are *existentially bound together*.

This existential binding stems from the characteristics of the prospective side of history as a disrupted singular. Only together do the present past and our apophatic past attest to the fact that the coming 'we' is never an achievement but only the *prospect* of a 'we,' of the history we have ahead of us. Because the 'we' in its happening and coming-to-presence is never realized, *our* apophatic past also cannot be fully 'realized' as the past as such (the entirety of the past). If the future coming-to-presence and coming-to-existence provides the basis for retrospective dissociation, and if this future coming-to-existence is never achieved, full dissociation from the past can never take place. Consequently, there has to be another past that is not apophatic and not dissociated. And insofar as the backward stance of historical writing is a backward stance, then its territory is the past as such, and this territory cannot be merely our apophatic past about which we can have dissociated knowledge, but also a past that breaks through, a present past.

Thus whenever we say 'past,' and whenever we say that historical writing is about the past, this past is an inseparable blend of the present and the apophatic past, a blend of our associative and dissociative measures. The past that historical writing is about, is neither purely present and associated, nor purely dissociated and apophatic, that is, neither purely *ours*, nor purely *not ours*. As odd and counterintuitive as it may sound, because the point of orientation is always the coming 'we,' in a quasi-substantive philosophy of history *the past is ours by virtue of our never having had it, and the past is not ours by virtue of our still having it.*

Whenever and in whatever respect we still have the past in the present – whenever and in whatever respect the past has 'presence' in the present – the past fills the present with existence. It would be hard, or even impossible, to imagine that the present is devoid of existence, and if the coming 'we' is, by definition, non-presence, then the present has to be filled with existence provided by the past. And in this sense the past is even more extremely present than Runia thinks, and the 'we' in its happening is even more extremely only coming-to-presence (that is, even more extremely non-presence at every present moment) as Nancy thinks. Nevertheless, the more distinct and the more extreme they look, the more the present and the apophatic past demand and complement each other. To encapsulate the essence of all this, I would like to offer the following thesis: *The notion of the past as such necessitates the interdependence and intertwinement of a past that is ours by virtue of being dissociated and non-present (the apophatic past) and a past that is not ours by virtue of being associated and made present (the present past).*

Essentially contested historical knowledge

That being said, there is a question that introduces further complexity: if the retrospective side of history as a disrupted singular is historical writing as knowledge about our apophatic past, and if *the past as such* is not only apophatic but also present (that is, not entirely dissociated and therefore not entirely a matter of knowledge), then how could historical writing live up to its implied task? Can historical writing be knowledge about the past, notwithstanding the extent to which the past is not dissociated but present?

The answer, I think, is a rather rewarding one. To unpack it, I would like to contrast once again the distinction between the practical and the historical past with the distinction between the apophatic and the present past. As to the former, the practical past/historical past divide implies a not-so-hidden distinction between matters of existence and ethics on the 'practical' side and matters of knowledge on the 'historical' (which is also the bulk of the criticism White receives in Lorenz 2014, 45–46). The historical past, the dead past, may be the equivalent of the apophatic past in my apophatic past/present past division in the most crucial sense that both are defined by dissociation. The same equivalence may concern the practical past and the present past insofar as both are defined by an associative relation between past and present. Yet the historical past in White's and Oakeshott's account is not only a dissociated but also a *disinterested* and *detached* past, studied for its own sake. It is precisely on the basis of this attributed disinterest and detachment that the notion of the historical past is deprived of ethical and existential concerns and consequently becomes a matter of historical knowledge. Correspondingly, it is due to the attributed interest and engagement on the side of the practical past that ethics takes over knowledge.

Now, contrary to this, the apophatic past/present past distinction is anything but a clear division between disinterest and detachment about the past on the one side and interest and continuing present engagement on the other. The apophatic past is just as much a presently engaged past as its counterpart, the present past. What distinguishes and also makes them counterparts is that the apophatic past engages by negation, while the present past engages by affirmation. This dual engagement, and, more importantly, the intertwinement and contemporaneity of the apophatic and the present past as the very same past, collapses matters of knowledge and ethics into each other. Consequentially, due to the inescapability of matters of existence and ethics when it comes to studying the past, historical writing cannot be other than *essentially contested historical knowledge* about the past.

I believe that this perfectly accounts for the question of why all we have are contested histories in the sense of historical writing and why the case is necessarily so. That the past cannot be anything but the terrain of contested knowledge can best be explained by a counterfactual argument highlighting the circumstances under which the past could be uncontested knowledge. The past could be the plane of pure, uncontested and fully dissociated knowledge only if the future 'we' would 'become' – that is, if history as the course of events would eventually end in the ontological becoming of an all-encompassing subject, if the vision of substantive philosophies of history of the Enlightenment and German Idealism came true, if the ultimate fulfillment of the historical process had already happened. Though it usually goes unnoticed, the practical success of those philosophies of history would have petrified the past and hence would have erased the practice of historical writing. For if an ontological subject – humankind, reason, or freedom – would achieve its ultimate truth as history, then historical writing could not be responsible for anything else than for the backward extension of that truth unfolding in history: for writing the ultimate, one and only story of the achievement.

Ironically enough, this backward extension was the founding principle of historical writing in the shape of a search for the ultimate meaning of the past, even though the actual practice of historical writing never lived up to this principle. In light of all this, it can be said that, since its institutionalization, historical writing has had to face one single ominous threat that came in two interrelated forms. The threat of turning itself into uncontested knowledge approached historical writing either as a potential coming true of the future ultimate meaning of substantive philosophy of history, or as potential self-annihilation through living up to its own founding principle and establishing an ultimate meaning of the past. That such a thing cannot reasonably happen is, I think, wonderfully exhibited in the inescapable feature of the prospective side of history as a disrupted singular. As long as there is no 'becoming' prospectively, as long as there is no ultimate fulfillment of a historical process, historical writing is on the safe side as essentially contested knowledge of the past (that is, of the inseparable blending of the present past and *our* apophatic past).

We are history

Arriving at this point, and in place of a conclusion, I cannot escape attempting a more or less clear answer to the initial question about how history *qua* history inevitably shapes public life. Yet the previous section about the function of historical writing entailed by a quasi-substantive philosophy of history was already, in fact, an implied answer to that question. Thus the best I can do here is to summarize the implied answer: historical writing as essentially contested historical knowledge – where contestation is due to the inseparability of matters of knowledge and matters of ethics – 'contributes' to identity formation by revealing what a coming 'we' cannot be, thereby negatively indicating the contours of that very coming 'we' that must remain unknown. In other words, the inevitable public relevance of history as historical writing lies in its constitutive engagement in history as the course of events. Moreover, if history as the course of events is a concept we deploy to make sense of the project of working out senses of togetherness (in terms of 'coming' communities), it can reasonably be viewed as a public endeavor per se – and this is what history as historical writing is ultimately engaged in.

Given all this, the question that demands an answer is not whether this 'contribution' shapes public life, but whether it is best described in terms of a 'contribution.' The point I would like to make is that in a quasi-substantive philosophy of history the question of a contribution may not even be asked. The reason for this is what I hope to condense in a formula that already features in the title: 'We are history.' Although, I have to concede, the phrase 'we are history' might mean many things, I certainly do not wish to allude to the British miniseries of the same name, in which the comedian Marcus Brigstocke made fun of historical documentaries, however hilarious its episodes might be for viewers. What I primarily mean by 'we are history' is that *historical writing is not so much a contribution to public agendas as the very arena in which public life is at stake.* It is the arena itself because of history's dual meaning: because historical writing, its very possibility and the particular shape it takes, is preconditioned by how we *conceptualize* history as the course of events. Insofar as we have a notion of history regarding the course of events, and insofar as this notion concerns a public endeavor, historical writing cannot but share in the stakes of the endeavor by which it is preconditioned.

There is, however, a logical alternative to this constellation: no concept of history as the course of events, no historical writing. But again, insofar as we are engaged in public endeavors to bring about change in human affairs, we need a concept of history as the course of events that launches that very endeavor, which, in turn, renders historical writing possible. It is not just an accident that the postwar criticism of substantive philosophies of history occurred simultaneously with the most famous essay decrying the public irrelevance of history from White (1966). This simultaneity, I believe, very well supports my ultimate point, namely, that professional historical studies lost touch with the non-academic world less because historical writing failed to keep up with contemporary ways of literary and artistic meaning attribution, as White suggests, and more because history as historical writing lost touch with a concept of history as the course of events. Lacking ties to such a concept is nothing less than lacking ties to our best effort to launch and make sense of the public endeavor of bringing about change in human affairs. To regain its public relevance, historical writing needs badly to re-connect to a philosophy of history: because insofar as we have a concept of history as the course of events – be it either substantive or quasi-substantive – we are history.

Notes

1. The above picture, which characterizes the history of historical writing as a series of crises and in which current crisis-talk centers around the public weightlessness of the discipline, can, of course, be challenged. Nevertheless, what can hardly be denied is that talking about the public weightlessness of the discipline has been quite a common theme for some time. To be more accurate, it has been quite a common theme since White (1966), regarding which I can offer the following story. Whereas analytical philosophy of history was interested in 'the special conceptual problems which arise out of the practice of history as well as out of substantive philosophy of history' (Danto 1985, 1), and consequently, it remained indifferent to the question of the public relevance of historical writing, the Whitean narrativist approach aimed at the transformation of the discipline precisely on the grounds that it detected a public disinterest in, or even a disdain for, academic history. In order to restore the status of historical studies, White advised historians to keep up with ways of meaning constitution deployed by contemporary art and literary writing. As Whitean narrativism quickly superseded analytical philosophy of history in the 1970s (or at least in the 1980s) and came to dominance, its transformative spirit spread over the discipline while fusing with other lines of thought. At its most extreme, fused with postmodern theories, this transformative spirit took the shape of the suggestion that if historical writing cannot be transformed into something better, then we would do better to forget about it (Jenkins 1999). The transformative intentions, however, survived the demise of postmodern theories. Today, when there is a sense of a necessity to take stock of the theories of the last decades on the one hand (Partner 2009; Spiegel 2009), on the other hand the transformative intentions remain but take a very different shape, as is most tangible in the overwhelming debates around *The History Manifesto* co-written by Guldi and Armitage (2014). For my intervention see Simon (2015a).
2. *Sattelzeit* is the period between 1750 and 1850, when – according to Koselleck – the transition from early modern to modern took place. Although in discussions of Koselleck it often features as a firm periodization effort, Koselleck (1996, 69) rather regarded the concept pragmatically (as a means to manage the enterprise of conceptual history), and also complained about the utility of the concept (suggesting that *Schwellenzeit* would be a better name).
3. For different but equally classic arguments about the illegitimacy of philosophizing about history as the course of events within the analytic tradition, see Popper ([1957] 2002) and Danto (1985). For a less known but nonetheless instructive critique from the same tradition, see Mandelbaum (1948). For an 'end of history' argument (with an overview and additional arguments about the consequence regarding historical writing as well), within the context of postmodernism, see Jenkins (1999, 26–66). For an argument against the ban, see Runia (2014, 49–53), who also points to a qualification I would like to add. Outside departments of history and philosophy – among political scientists and evolutionary biologists (and practically everyone else) – philosophizing about the course of events continued to be practiced in the postwar period. The point is that *philosophy of history understood as the course of events was deemed to be illegitimate, dangerous, and impossible precisely by those who, in one way or another, otherwise claimed expertise in the disciplines related to the enterprise (philosophy and history).*

4. To be clear, I do not wish to conduct an inquiry into the *nature* of time or the temporality of history. Instead, I look for a specific way of conceiving time that we may call 'historical,' which might enable us to talk about history as the course of events again without falling prey to substantive thinking. Also, by talking about history as the course of events, I do not wish to talk about the *nature* of a historical process. What I think (and what has to become clear at the end of this essay) is that *conceptualizing* history as the course of events is our best effort to initiate, render possible, and make sense of the endeavor of bringing about change in human affairs.

5. In a recent article (Simon 2015a), I dealt more extensively with the unfeasibility of the developmental view on the occasion of discussing White (2014) and Guldi and Armitage (2014). In another article (Simon 2015a) and a talk I gave at The Institute of Historical Research in London under the title 'A Quasi-Substantive Philosophy of History,' I also dealt more extensively with the movement of history and with the features of a quasi-substantive philosophy of history. Here, I do not wish to recite everything I said on those occasions, and even though in this and the next section – for the sake of better understanding – I have to touch upon issues I dealt with in the aforementioned articles and talk, my main objective is to elaborate the issue further by drawing the consequences of it for history as historical writing.

6. Nancy's efforts to think the 'coming' or 'taking place' of a community without appealing to substantive ideas may have a resemblance to the Derridean messianic project and Derrida's notion of a 'future-to-come.' What nevertheless clearly separates them is that the 'emancipatory promise' Derrida (1994) wishes to retain, even in its most contradictory form, cannot be made sense of without getting rid of the developmental structure that houses it. Emancipation is gradual empowerment and it is actually the paradigmatic political action of the industrial era, perfectly suited to the developmental view of history. Giving a messianic edge to the emancipatory project is less a useful tool and more an obstacle to think a notion of history different from the one we inherited from the Enlightenment and German Idealism, which is what I am after in this essay.

7. They can be put to work despite the rather huge differences of the theories in which these ideas are embedded. To mention a few, Nancy's coming 'we' has nothing to do with Ankersmit's focus on Western civilization as a definite subject of change; Ankersmit's trauma is the loss of an old world, while Runia's trauma is rather connected to the events that lead to such loss. Whereas Runia's 'presence' is the past taking over the present, Nancy's 'presence' concerns not the past but the future, the presently non-presence of existence. Furthermore, Nancy does not attribute a mechanism to history in any sense, Ankersmit does not do so deliberately and Runia often exceeds the framework to which I have restricted him. Runia even gives in to substantive thinking eventually by means of a cultural evolutionary vocabulary (Runia 2014, 179–202), overshadowing his focus on discontinuities with postulating a deeper, *all-encompassing* continuity. But the point I want to make has not so much to do with the rational reconstruction of their ideas; my point is only that by putting these thinkers to work in a certain way permits conceiving of the movement of history as a quasi-substantive philosophy.

8. I do not wish to claim here that we have new anthropological constants whose internal relations structure historical time in general. I use these expressions

in a restricted sense, only to explain the temporality of the notion of history as a disrupted singular.

9. As Harlan (2009) argues, a couple of decades later Oakeshott underwent a re-evaluation of his own, growing more sympathetic towards the practical past.

10. If White's turn to the notion of the practical past were a movie, its Wikipedia page would discuss it in terms of earning 'mixed to average' reviews. For a positive one, see Domanska (2014), for a less positive one, see Lorenz (2014).

11. On experientiality, the classic is Fludernik (1996), who defines narrativity as mediated human experientiality. For her updated view on the question of whether historical accounts can qualify as narratives in terms of experientiality, see Fludernik (2010).

Disclosure statement

No potential conflict of interest was reported by the author.

References

Ankersmit, Frank. 2005. *Sublime Historical Experience*. Stanford: Stanford University Press.

Badiou, Alain. 2012. *The Rebirth of History*. Translated by Gregory Elliott. London: Verso.

Bevernage, Berber, and Chris Lorenz. 2012. "Breaking up Time: Negotiating the Borders between Present, Past and Future." *Storia della Storiografia* 61: 31–50.

Danto, Arthur C. 1985. *Narration and Knowledge: Including the Integral Text of Analytical Philosophy of History*. New York: Columbia University Press.

Derrida, Jacques. 1994. *Specters of Marx: The State of the Debt, the Work of Mourning and the New International*. London: Routledge.

Domanska, Ewa. 2014. "Hayden White and Liberation Historiography." *Rethinking History* 19 (4): 640–650.

Ermarth, Elizabeth Deeds. 2011. *History in the Discursive Condition: Reconsidering the Tools of Thought*. London: Routledge.

Fludernik, Monika. 1996. *Towards a 'Natural' Narratology*. London: Routledge.

Fludernik, Monika. 2010. "Experience, Experientiality, and Historical Narrative: A View from Narratology." In *Erfahrung und Geschichte: Historische Sinnbildung im Pränarrativen*, edited by Thiemo Breyer and Creutz Daniel, 40–72. Berlin: De Gruyter.

Ghosh, Ranjan, and Ethan Kleinberg, eds. 2013. *Presence: Philosophy, History, and Cultural Theory for the Twenty-First Century*. Ithaca, NY: Cornell University Press.

Guldi, Jo, and David Armitage. 2014. *The History Manifesto*. Cambridge: Cambridge University Press.

Gumbrecht, Hans Ulrich. 2004. *The Production of Presence: What Meaning Cannot Convey*. Stanford: Stanford University Press.

Harlan, David. 2009. "'The Burden of History' Forty Years Later." In *Re-figuring Hayden White*, edited by Frank Ankersmit, Ewa Domanska, and Hans Kellner, 169–189. Stanford: Stanford University Press.

Jenkins, Keith. 1999. *Why History? Ethics and Postmodernity*. London: Routledge.

Koselleck, Reinhart. 1996. "A Response to the Comments on the *Geschichtliche Grundbegriffe*." In *The Meaning of Historical Terms and Concepts: New Studies on Begriffsgeschichte*, edited by Hartmut Lehmann and Melvin Richter, 59–70. Washington, DC: German Historical Insitute.

Koselleck, Reinhart. 2004. *Futures Past: On the Semantics of Historical Time*. New York: Columbia University Press.

Lorenz, Chris. 2014. "It Takes Three to Tango. History between the 'Practical' and the 'Historical' Past." *Storia della Storiografia* 65: 29–46.

Mandelbaum, Maurice. 1948. "A Critique of Philosophies of History." *The Journal of Philosophy* 45 (14): 365–378.

Mandelbaum, Maurice. 1971. *History, Man & Reason: A Study in Nineteenth-century Thought*. Baltimore, MD: The Johns Hopkins University Press.

Nancy, Jean-Luc. 1993. "Finite History." *The Birth to Presence*. Translated by Brian Holmes and others, 143–166. Stanford: Stanford University Press.

Nancy, Jean-Luc. 2000. *Being Singular Plural*. Stanford: Stanford University Press.

Oakeshott, Michael. 1966. *Experience and Its Modes*. Cambridge: Cambridge University Press.

Partner, Nancy. 2009. "Narrative Persistence: The Post-postmodern Life of Narrative Theory." In *Re-figuring Hayden White*, edited by Frank Ankersmit, Ewa Domanska, and Hans Kellner, 81–104. Stanford: Stanford University Press.

Paul, Herman. 2015. "Relations to the Past: A Research Agenda for Historical Theorists." *Rethinking History* 19 (3): 450–458.

Popper, Karl. [1957] 2002. *The Poverty of Historicism*. New York: Routledge.

Runia, Eelco. 2014. *Moved by the Past: Discontinuity and Historical Mutation*. New York: Columbia University Press.

Simon, Zoltán Boldizsár. 2015a. "History Manifested: Making Sense of Unprecedented Change." *European Review of History* 22 (5): 819–834.

Simon, Zoltán Boldizsár. 2015b. "History Set into Motion Again." *Rethinking History* 19 (4): 651–667.

Spiegel, Gabrielle. 2009. "The Task of the Historian." *The American Historical Review* 114 (1): 1–15.

White, Hayden V. 1966. "The Burden of History." *History and Theory* 5 (2): 111–134.

White, Hayden. 2014. *The Practical Past*. Evanston: Northwestern University Press.

History, power and visual communication artefacts

Katherine Hepworth

The Reynolds School of Journalism, University of Nevada, Mail Stop 310, Reno, NV 89557, USA

ABSTRACT

The role visual communication plays in disciplining and governing our thoughts, identities and behaviours has seldom been given the attention it deserves in historical investigation. This article argues that visual communication artefacts are a valuable source of historical evidence, particularly for historians who are interested in the interplay of ideology and power. Artefacts are approached from the epistemological position that they cannot be value neutral. The countless artefacts we see and use in daily life constantly reinforce or contradict our beliefs, values and self-identities. It is in reaction to this constant push and pull with the artefacts around us that we form, maintain and re-form our understandings of the world and of ourselves. This article presents a theory of how visual communication artefacts are imbued with the governance ideologies of the time and place in which they were created. It argues that visual communication artefacts disseminate governance ideologies through time and space, in ever lessening degrees of discipline and control. For the historian interested in power, ideological shifts or changing popular attitudes, visual communication artefacts are therefore a rich, largely untapped resource. In order to frame the argument, this article begins by outlining my deconstructionist perspective on the role of historians and histories. This is followed by an argument for the Foucauldian understanding of governmental power and discourse technologies as robust theoretical foundations for a theory of how discourses become embodied in artefacts. It concludes by suggesting the opportunities for using discourse technologies (embodied governance) as a framework for investigating the role of artefacts in power exchanges.

Introduction

Material culture plays a significant role in governing the behaviours, identities and thoughts of individuals in most societies. Despite the infrequent use of material culture by historians as remnants of old disciplinary networks, artefacts from the past can give historians valuable insights into how power has been wielded in the past (Borish and Phillips 2012, 465). This assertion is based on relativist investigations into the role of the historian, the nature of history writing and the interrelationship of power networks and visual communication artefacts. Artefacts acquire disciplinary and governing properties similarly to the way they acquire meaning, through association and practice (Hodder 2003, 161). Visual communication artefacts contain additional governing properties because they are inherently communicative, and communication is inextricably bound together with power, knowledge and governance. I argue that artefacts govern through power exchange phenomena I have called 'embodied discourse technologies'. Embodied discourse technologies are proposed as the means through which artefacts can persuade argue and absorb ideological biases (Hepworth 2012, 148). The theoretical foundations of embodied discourse technologies are discussed, and some examples of how their identification can benefit the study and writing of history are provided.

What is a visual communication artefact?

For the purposes of this article, any artefacts that have a significant visual communication function are grouped together as 'visual communication artefacts'. This includes a large portion of the things commonly grouped together in the humanities as 'material culture'. Some of the individual artefacts referred to under the umbrella term visual communication artefacts include: advertisements, logos, media artefacts in all their forms, moving images, computer and smartphone operating systems, photographs, regalia, software, signs, uniforms and websites. The only artefacts not included in the catch-all term are those without a significant visual communicative function; for example, certain musical instruments, recording devices, computer hardware and other such non-descript items.

The term 'visual communication artefacts' is intentionally used in this article instead of 'material culture' for two reasons. First, the emphasis on the visual in the first term has more relevance to my academic interests and expertise. Second, in the twenty-first century an increasing proportion of visual communication artefacts are immaterial, such as logos, websites, software and other digitally stored media. These immaterial communication artefacts are part of the artefact pool I seek to describe, and the term 'material culture' seems an unlikely term to use when arguing for their importance. Nevertheless, the interdisciplinary field of material culture research has contributed much to the study of artefacts generally, and these contributions are acknowledged where relevant throughout this article.

Visual communication artefacts are singled out as the objects of interest in this article because they, more than other artefacts, act to change attitudes, behaviour and intentions through persuasive, rhetorical presentation of information. Whether the communication of these artefacts purports to be objective, as in the case of directional signage, consciously persuasive as in the case of a public education campaign (to encourage recycling, for example), or fantastical, as in the advertising for a luxury brand, the visual communication artefact depends on rhetorical devices to persuade their users and viewers to change their attitudes and behaviours (Kostelnick 2004, 218). As will be elaborated upon further in this article, the rhetorical devices contained within visual communication artefacts are tools in the service of greater social and political forces (Cruikshank 1996, 234).

Historian as context

This article takes its premise from the thought of a select group of relativist philosophers and historians. Specifically, principles of the ancient Greek philosophical school of the Pyrrhonic sceptics, Annales historian March Bloch and political philosopher Michel Foucault are heavily drawn on. While Foucault needs no introduction, the Pyrrhonic sceptics and Bloch are perhaps less well known. A short introduction to the lesser known of these influences is provided here to give some context to the following arguments.

In ancient Greece, there were two schools of Sceptics: the academic, after the famous learning institution the Academy; and the Pyrrhonic, followers of Pyrrho (Bosley and Tweedale 2006, 406; Kuzminski 2010, 5; Perin 2010, 2). Of the two schools, the academic sceptics generally asserted that no-one can know anything; one of the more extreme philosophic positions in ancient Greece. The Pyrrhonic Sceptics have a similar, but more moderate view, suggesting that 'we cannot know anything, *including the fact that we cannot know anything*' (Kendall and Wickham 1999, 10, their emphasis). The second part of this statement moderates the first by further extending the commitment to relativism, and thereby acknowledging the possibility that the sceptical position may be wrong. This Pyrrhonic scepticism about the certainty of one's own knowledge heavily influences my perspective on the value of the historian. Honouring this relativist perspective on knowledge, I give the historians assertions, beliefs and findings far less value than they are commonly given.

Another influence on my views of historians and histories is Bloch, who co-founded, with Lucien Febvre, the Annales school. This is a disparate group of historians, originating in France in the 1920s, but working globally today (Bentley 1999, 110–112). Bloch was a deconstructionist ahead of his time. Historian Alun Munslow could have been summarising Bloch's attitude to history when he wrote, in 2006, that '[p]erhaps the most valuable things we can write about the past are those that emerge from recognition of its representational frailties and epistemological uncertainties' (Munslow 2006, 76). Reacting against the so-called scientific method of Leopolde von Ranke and his proponents, Bloch advocated turning history on its head. He rejected the search for origins that preoccupies so many historians (then and now) and instead argues that the most recent historical evidence has the most value. His reasoning for this approach is that the older and less tangible a source is, the less reliable the evidence it provides will be. He also emphasises the importance of the historian's context, and explores the relationship between the past and the present throughout his work (Burke 1990, 15; Green and Troup 1999, 302). Bloch acknowledges that the historian and his present-day context, irrespective of his personal views, inevitably influence all histories (Bloch 1953, 45). The discovery of the importance of historians' present-day context to all their history writing leads Bloch to determine that the present, and remnants of the past which have endured to the present day, are the most revealing starting point for history writing.

While Foucault needs no introduction, it is helpful to detail the particular aspects of his work that affect my perspective of historians and histories. One of the key parts of Foucault's work that has shaped my view on the role of historians is his career spanning interest in what he variously refers to as archaeological shifts, epistemic breaks and knowledge ruptures (Foucault 1969, 178, 181, 1971, 371 and 372, 1976, 10). These are the points at which common widespread societal or professional understandings are usurped by others. As commonly understood beliefs about the world shift dramatically on occasion, he argues, so too do historians' interpretations of past events. For Foucault, historical research is significant because of its capacity to reveal these shifts, and to reveal the unconscious biases of the historian (Foucault 1969, 11 and 12). He argues that historians' attempts at explanation of the past can only ever be descriptions of their own prejudices. Therefore, they are only interesting to the extent that the historian himself is an object of study (White 1973, 29).

While I do not share the extremity of Foucault's perspective on the personal nature of history writing, I do view that personal context is the most valuable aspect of the historian's contribution to history writing. This position acknowledges the historian's creative contributions, but takes into account its limits. The sometimes seemingly unique creative output of individuals is inevitably allowed, guided and, in a sense, regulated by our internal and external limits. The following pages elaborate on the internal and external limits to individual authorship and creativity imposed by the historian's cognitive and environmental biases.

If historians are most valuable for their context, then ascertaining which activities most effectively communicate that context becomes important for historical rigour. While all the historian's behaviours, communications and thoughts are guided by his context, some are more demonstrative of that context than others. At every moment, all people, including historians, are subject to a myriad of both conscious and unconscious influences on a daily, let alone moment by moment, basis. Whether or not we are aware of them, these influences affect our behaviour, observations and thoughts, allowing relative statements to appear absolutely true to any one person within their specific circumstances. Relativist philosopher R. J. Hankinson, for example, acknowledges that there is a whole realm of judgements we make constantly that we are not aware of, either because they appear to us to be objective truths, or because we do not notice we are making them (Hankinson 1999, 42 and 43).

First order judgements

Hankinson elaborates on this by separating all kinds of thought into two groups, first order judgements, and second order judgements (Hankinson 1999, 42 and 43). First order judgements are not judgements in the strict sense, as they do not relate to belief as such. Rather, the term 'first order judgement' is a way of referring to 'implicit judgements made within cognitive systems', or judgements people make when they intend to state a fact (Chalmers 2004, 233). First order judgements could also be described as the 'content-bearing cognitive state' associated with every conscious experience (Chalmers 2004, 177). A first order judgement is therefore what the historian's brain does in immediate response to the external stimulus of an experience.

This cognitive state, or first order judgement, is subjective in the sense that it is influenced by conditions that the person making the judgement is unaware of conditions of the present and the past. It is a pure encapsulation of the historian's context without the addition of authorial or creative layers. The relative truth of first order judgements – in spite of their apparent solidity to the person making them at the time they are made – is evident in the case of hallucinations and dreams. These experiences give us first-hand demonstrations that it is possible to have a content-bearing cognitive state without an associated external experience (Chalmers 2004, 220). First order judgements are influenced by several conditions of the culture, time and place in which the person making them is situated. The historian's first order judgements are the most significant, since they carry the most detail of context, what is seen and what is omitted at a particular juncture. Hankinson's other category of thought, second order judgement, is the mode of thought traditionally valued by historians.

Figure 1 lists some of the conditions that contribute to the inherent, but usually unnoticed, subjectivity of first order statements. The table in Figure 1

Factors	Conditions of the past	Conditions of the present
Internal	Attitudes Observations Memories Stress	Attitude Emotion Mental resources Stress
External	Previous exposure to the situation, and similar situations	Environment Physical resources

Figure 1. Conditions affecting first order judgements.

is divided into two kinds of conditions (past and present), and two kinds of factors (internal and external), which overlap. The term 'internal factors' refers to conditions within each person's mind and body, and the term 'external factors' refers to conditions existing outside of the individual. 'Conditions of the past' that affect observation include previous exposure to the present situation; accumulated past attitudes, memories and observations; as well as previously experienced stress. 'Conditions of the present' that affect observation in the present include environment and physical resources (external factors), present attitude or state of mind, present emotional state, available mental resources or skills, and current stress levels (internal factors). No matter how objective or true a statement appears to the historian making it, the conditions listed in Figure 1 ensure that the statement will not appear true to others who view the same material.

Although he did not use the term first order judgement, Foucault elaborated upon how first order judgements affect the historian. In *The Archaeology of Knowledge*, he refers to the simultaneity of that which is 'already-said' and 'never-said', emphasising how some things appear obvious to the historian, while others do not appear at all (Foucault 1969, 27). Philosopher John Rajchman elaborates on this aspect of Foucault's work, commenting that Foucault's 'idea is that not all ways of visualising or rendering visible are possible at once. A period only lets some things be seen and not others. It "illuminates" some things and so casts others in the shade' (Rajchman 1988, 92). Every statement, and every artefact, found in the historical record is therefore significant both for what it states, and for what it omits. It is for this reason that Foucault posits the discovery of what is presented as true and false at a particular historical juncture is one of the most valuable services history writing provides to society (Foucault 1977, 79).

The statements that are acceptable at a particular juncture, as well as the things left unsaid, provide valuable information about the context in which the historical document was created. Context, particularly the historian's context, is important to my view of history. Context amounts to the discourses that shape and control the various aspects of the historian's thoughts and life: his identity, professional life, home life, recreational pursuits and communicative capacity. This emphasis on context in my approach to history writing is yet another influence from Bloch and Foucault. Their efforts at making the past accessible inevitably involved extensive contextualisation of their findings. Bloch described the historian's context as 'like a knot in which are intertwined a host of divergent characteristics of the structure and mentality of a society' and he sought to capture these various strands in his own historical work (Bloch 1953, 32). He describes the importance of acknowledging how all historical events and artefacts are the result of multiple factors; historical authorship is just one among many. They are accidents in the sense that each event is one outcome from a range of infinite possibilities.

Foucault also emphasised context and the range of historical potentialities, or 'conditions of possibility' as he referred to them, throughout his career (Foucault 1970, 57). He argues that any artefact, event or text can, and should be, viewed as an accumulation of chance historical decisions (Foucault 1977, 76). He goes on to say, 'there is nothing to be gained from describing [past events and thought] … unless one can relate [them] to … practices, institutions, social relations, political relations, and so on' (Foucault 1967, 284). Much of Foucault's work was therefore devoted to describing how previously used logic contributed to the formation of public attitudes and institutional biases that were previously hidden or considered 'natural'.

Second order judgements

Second order judgements are those the historian makes when he is aware of expressing his own biases, opinions or preferences. In this sense they can also be considered reflective judgements, because they include evidence of reflection on the part of the person making them (Chalmers 2004, 176; Mölder 2010, 248). Second order judgements are influenced by all of the same factors as first order judgements, with the addition of the observer's intended contribution of a particular judgement or stance. This is the realm of the historian's creative output: the sum of the historian's first order judgements, with their reflection on historical investigation and consequent creative interpretation overlaid. The items in Figure 1 suggest that while observations are subjective, some are more subjective than others; specifically, that second order judgements are more subjective than first order judgements (see Figure 1).

This particularly relativist view of the historian's role is somewhat anti-historical and against the grain of the conventional view. As Munslow observes, although

> most historians would not argue that historical method is scientific, there remains this strong sense of being rationally and objectively in touch with a potentially understandable, causally analysable and truthful past. Those who argue otherwise simply cease to be a historian. (Munslow 2006, 63)

Historian Hayden White conveniently coined a term for this kind of position. The 'anti-historical historian', he writes, 'writes "history" in order to destroy it' (White 1973, 26). While I am not intending to destroy history as such, I am motivated to examine its functioning as a discipline.

Histories as vehicles

Given that the historian is most important in terms of his context, the histories he writes become important as vehicles to communicate that context. Histories are *vehicles* in the sense that they pass on the individual historian's interpretations of the past; they are summaries of the methods, values and knowledge applied by historians from their respective cultures, places and times. From this perspective, the ambiguities, interpretations and uncertainties involved in history writing, once derided at worst or ignored at best, become valuable, and inextricable from the historical subject matter.

This is a middle road, lying somewhere between the scientific perspective that history writing is objective fact telling, and the claims of certain post-structuralists that history is entirely the creative imaginings of the individual historian. I suggest each written history is a combination of the historian's creativity and reasoning (second order judgements) as well as the inevitable remnants of his context (as illustrated by his first order judgements). The history is valuable for its presentation of the interplay between the historian's context, and the relationship of that context with the historical subject(s).

Power as capacity

One way to understand the significance of the historian's context is to view context through the lens of Foucauldian power. Specifically, Foucault's work on discourses, and a type of power he refers to as government. To illuminate the relationship between history, historians, discourses and governmental power, a short contextualisation of the Foucauldian view of power is provided below.

Before Foucault's work in the 1970s, power was conceived in terms that cast history, artefacts, and communication in a very different light than they are commonly thought of today. Throughout the history of Western thought, power has been understood to be one of two things: 'a kind of generalised capacity to act' or the capacity, as well as the right, to act (Hindess 1996, 1). This understanding of power stemmed from a general assumption that it was possible for a ruler to have absolute power over his subjects.

These views were greatly influenced by the English philosopher Hobbes' book *The Leviathan*, in which he explains sovereignty in practice. This work outlines what eighteenth-century philosopher Rousseau later terms 'the social contract'. According to this social contract, all people are born with certain freedoms and abilities to provide for themselves. However, in a 'state of nature' – a theoretical place where there are no allegiances between men, and therefore no support structures – people face constant mortal threats that lead them to group together for safety. Hobbes' understanding of the theoretical basis of sovereignty to a state involves an exchange: in order to receive the advantages of citizenship, individuals give up their freedoms to a ruler (Hobbes 1985, 237). This view of power has influenced humanities research generally and is still current in some fields.

The state of nature reasoning explained above rests on a conceptualisation of power as a measurable, tradable commodity that can accumulate in objects, institutions, people and positions. Following this idea, it would theoretically be possible for particular histories and artefacts to accumulate power through association and use. For example, a king's crown would be seen as a receptacle of power. The power of the crown is innate, due to its possession and use by the king, and this power is felt by all who see it, let alone those few people who will wear it. Until the 1970s, it was similarly assumed that historians could have absolute authority over their subjects, as rulers had over their subjects.

However, as political theorist Barry Hindess observes, 'Hobbes' argument here involves a confusion between the idea of power as a capacity and the idea of power as a right' (Hindess 1996, 15). Foucault's work on power (1980–1988) challenges this traditional Hobbesian perspective. He understood power to be inherently dispersed in nature, temporarily accumulating in processes, relationships and actions. As a process, power is unquantifiable, potentially infinite and encompassing all 'attempts to influence the actions of those who are free' (Hindess 1996, 18). In this definition, political theorist Hindess uses the term 'free' loosely, to refer to all individuals who have some level of capacity to make decisions about their own lives. Foucault elaborates that power 'is everywhere, not because it embraces everything, but because it comes from everywhere' (Foucault 1980, 93). His understanding of power is much like a scientific description of energy, in the sense that it can neither be created nor be destroyed, but it can be transformed into different states.

If power is a process rather than a quantifiable commodity, then the power vested in the king's crown must be contextual rather than innate, as suggested in the previous example. From a Foucauldian perspective, neither artefacts nor histories can accumulate power. The crown is only awe inspiring to people who are both aware of its importance in a given tradition, and have a meaningful connection with that tradition. The appearance of an artefact having and holding power is contingent upon the values and prior knowledge of the users and viewers of the artefact, as well as the space it inhabits. Histories and artefacts are therefore only as powerful as the relationships in which they are enmeshed at particular places and times. This understanding of power and artefacts has dramatically influenced the field of anthropology and shaped the formation of the field of material culture studies. This innovation has the potential to have a similar influence in the field of history.

One of the main ways Foucault talks about power transforming into different capacities is through various knowledge forms. He asserts that power is, in essence, knowledge. Anthropologist Juris Milestone elaborates that human endeavour necessarily organises and systematises knowledge, resulting in the formation of knowledge disciplines (for example, science, art and history). These disciplines are then used to understand and manipulate people as groups (for example, as a citizenry, or as delinquents). It is in this defining of subjects to be dominated or managed that power capacities manifest (Milestone 2007, 179). History writing plays a role in the defining of groups of peoples, and therefore directly affects power relationships in which their historical subjects are involved.

Foucault also describes capacities of power as 'a question of government …. To govern, in this sense, is to structure the possible field of action [or capacities] of others' (Foucault 1982, 789 and 790). This definition of power as capacity introduces Foucault's understanding of 'government' as a specific kind of attempt to harness power. This definition of government is central to understanding how artefacts control or 'govern' their users and surroundings. Dean and Hindess provide the established definition of Foucault's government, stating that 'government is the conduct of the conduct, where the latter refers to the manner in which individuals, groups and organisations manage their own behaviour' (Dean and Hindess 1998, 3). Governmental power works at the level of individuals, as well as in small and large group situations. It is bound up with the concept of economy, the idea that there is a 'rational and legitimate' order of things and people that good governance aims to achieve (Foucault 1978, 208).

As well as involving power capacities, the acts of defining subjects and systematising knowledge necessarily involve communication. Attempts to harness power therefore always incorporate some level of communication, and communication necessarily involves power exchanges (Foucault 1982, 786 and 787). The extent to which artefacts communicate then is the extent to which they have a capacity of power. Although Foucault identifies power and communication as separate phenomena that are linked, visual communication design practice can be seen as a disciplinary effort to combine them as much as possible.

Visual communication artefacts are necessarily more concerted efforts to govern than artefacts without significant visual communication properties because of their communicative capacity, and how this quality is tied up with power and knowledge (Tunstall 2007, 4). As well as being part of Foucault's definition of government, the idea of 'conducting the conduct' could also be used as an extremely concise description of the role of visual communication artefacts. Despite their many forms, shapes and sizes, visual communication artefacts share the common purpose of changing activities, attitudes or emotional states of viewers indirectly, through communication intended to somehow alter their knowledge (Kostelnick 2004, 218).

Artefacts as truth effects

Government involves the promotion of 'rationalities', or ways of thinking that render some people, institutions and objects truthful or common sense while rendering others false (Gordon 1991, 8). Governmental rationalities can therefore be seen as varying worldviews or ways of producing truth. At all levels of human organisation, governmental rationalities give rise to what Foucault refers to as 'truth effects', or the views about historical events, ourselves and others that we come to perceive as truths (Munslow 2006, 65; Noonan 2004, 30).

Material culture plays a governing role in establishing individual and community-wide truth effects. On an individual level, material culture artefacts contribute to self-government, the internalising of societal discourses. On community and societal levels, material culture artefacts contribute to social production of attitudes, behaviours and intentions (Gordon 1993, 76; Hegmon 1992, 519; Prown 1993, 1). Artefacts govern in the sense that they are imbued with governmental rationalities that contribute to production of truth effects by their viewers and users (Gagliardi 1990, vi).

When it comes to promoting governmental rationalities, visual artefacts are particularly potent aspects of material culture. Political scientist Mitchell Dean describes how peoples, territories and even individual identities must be visualized in order to be governed. He describes how 'a map, a pie chart, a set of graphs and tables, and so on ... all make it possible to "capture" who and what is to be governed' (Dean 2010, 41). Dean highlights what several other political scientists have observed: visual devices are essential to governmental rationality (Anderson 2006, 173; Kostelnick 2004, 215; Rose 2008, 36).

Sociologist Nicholas Rose argues that visual communication artefacts are used to give knowledge a sense of stability or durability. He refers to visual communication artefacts as 'little machine[s] for producing conviction in others ... [they are] material techniques of thought that make possible the extension of authority over that which they seem to depict' (Rose 2008, 36 and 37). The visual communication artefacts in Rose's examples all depend on a prior visual literacy for their capacity to govern. Without the requisite frame of reference to understand a chart or a map, we cannot be subject to it. Therefore, in the process of acquiring visual literacies, we are all complicit in the process of being governed by such artefacts (Anderson 2006, 173; Hill and Helmers 2004, 1; Hindess 1996, 106).

Because of these governmental rationalities, visual communication artefacts are never neutral; they are always either reinforcing or challenging the established rationalities of the people surrounding them and the environments in which they are placed. For example, in an office environment the furniture and decor 'play an important part in calling out "appropriate" attitudes and responses' in workers (Witkin 1990, 328). Conversely, controversial art pieces are usually shocking, at least in part, because they challenge the dominant governmental rationalities of the societies in which they are exhibited.

Although material culture artefacts (beyond the text) are seldom considered as serious historical sources, they have much to offer historians. Specifically, visual communication artefacts can help historians understand the culture of the time and place where the artefact was produced and used, because, as discussed earlier, artefacts document the governmental rationalities and ideologies of past times (Borish and Philips 2012, 466; Riello 2009, 25). In the vein of Bloch's ideas, I argue that there are two significant advantages for the historian in treating artefacts as primary historical sources. The first is providing extra information that was not recorded in textual sources. The second is giving the historian access to visual arguments presented on or in artefacts that could not be documented textually by even the most talented commentator (Blair 2004, 49; Gordon 1993, 91).

Artefacts as rhetoric

Historians of technology Steven Lubar and W. David Kingery highlight the important evidentiary contribution artefacts make to the historical record, emphasising their rhetorical capacity and the value of this rhetorical nature to historians (Lubar and Kingery 1993, ix). Visual communication artefacts, in particular, are rhetorical in the sense that they have a persuasive capacity (Blair 2004, 43). The acts of viewing and interacting with an artefact inevitably affect our thought at both the levels of first order and second order judgements.

This is a compelling way of thinking about the rhetorical nature of artefacts, because it suggests that the ideological biases embodied in artefacts are some-how both fluid and active. The rhetorical force and the nature of the argument among artefacts change according to their context (Dilnot 2010, 14). Who views an artefact, and the nature of their connection with the artefact's sites of consumption and production considerably affects the artefact's rhetorical force. The communication of rhetoric depends upon four conditions: the arte-fact itself, the viewer's first order judgements about it (prior experience and knowledge, beliefs and values), the viewer's second order judgements about it (conscious judgement, reasoning and thought) and the context in which the communication between artefact and the viewer occurs.

Interactions with artefacts as arguments

Other historians go further than Lubar and Kingery's position, accrediting artefacts with a limited degree of agency (Bush 1994, 228; Harvey 2009, 6; Rosenstone 2001, 256). Because each artefact is a product of the social and technological practices from which it emerged and in which it is used, it carries truth effects of those practices with it. These truth effects include governmental rationalities, as well as the dominant discourses of the time. When artefacts are all of the same society, time and place, their rhetorical capacities are in accord, and one truth effect dominates the scene. The whole environment has a rhetorical unity. For example, in a le Corbusier designed house, carefully maintained and fitted out with sympathetically selected furniture and art from the Modernist movement.

However, in our everyday lives, the objects and images that surround most of us seldom have such rhetorical unity. Globalised distribution and production ensure that we are surrounded by things designed and produced in communi-ties that are vastly different from our own in terms of attitudes, environment and resources. These things are influenced by discourses, and governmen-tal rationalities that produce a wide array of rhetorical effects are seldom in harmony when placed together. The overall rhetorical effect of settings full of such discordant things is the antithesis to the lovingly preserved le Corbusier house, and is often akin to an argument.

Design historian Anne Bush sees collections of artefacts as arguments, while socio-political historian Karen Harvey emphasises the argumentative relationship between artefacts and their users. Although arguments are logic structures typically associated with language, Blair argues that artefacts can be considered argumentative to the extent that they persuade their viewers or users to their attitudes, behaviours or intentions. He elaborates on this by identifying the argumentative style of artefacts as that referred to by Aristotle as the 'enthymeme'. This is an argument where 'the arguer deliberately leaves unstated a premise that is essential to its reasoning' (Blair 2004, 41). In the case of an artefact, the unstated premise is its function, as well as its visual message. By using an artefact, or trying to deduce its former use, the historian is drawn 'to participate in its [his own] persuasion by filling in that unexpressed premise' (Blair 2004, 41). This description of the functioning of artefacts as enthymemes has parallels to the description of visual communication artefacts framing territories and people to be governed, as well as making us complicit in being governed.

The difference between verbal argument and argument between artefacts is that the argument waged among artefacts is silent and usually static, relying on immersive and visual communication for its rhetorical effect. Hodder asserts that 'people both experience and "read" material culture', differentiating between two ways of relating to an artefact, one immersive, the other literate (Hodder 2003, 164). Reading in this sense includes language-based literacy, but also encompasses cultural and visual literacy.

Cultural and visual literacy can be thought of as ways experiencing artefacts that rely on a pattern-recognition approach, wherein the artefacts' individual attributes are recognised among previously seen or felt artefacts retained in the mind's eye. Immersive and literate experiences of artefacts can happen concurrently. However, to read an artefact, one necessarily must have an immersive experience of reading it, while an immersive experience does not require literacy. The process of artefacts governing individuals and communities can occur from afar, in the sense that artefacts are frequently used and viewed at a cultural, spatial and temporal distance from when and where they were created. Philosopher Anthony Blair argues that the potency of communication by visual communication artefacts reduces with increasing distance from their sources (Blair 2004, 52). Artefacts acquire other governmental rationalities through the interplay of factors relating to point of origin: time, place, space and production technologies. When artefacts are used at a distance from the sites of their design and production, the potency of the governmental rationalities in which they were enmeshed at their site of production is therefore also reduced.

Figure 2. Reenactor holds a replica of the Roman military standard, Aquila or eagle. Source: Hans Splinter, https://www.flickr.com/photos/archeon/4882187679/

While artefacts participate in some governmental rationalities at their sites of production, they are enmeshed in others through association and use. For example, architecture, images and symbols from grand, ancient cultures, particularly Rome, are frequently used to shape popular perceptions and legitimise rule (see Figure 2) (Geertz 1999, 15; Mattingly 2010, 11). Nations are established, legitimised and maintained using artefacts and rituals that have a compelling connection to the past but current cultural quiddity. Historian Eric Hobsbawm describes this process as 'the invention of tradition' (Hobsbawm 1992, 4). He argues that the more arcane a symbol is, the more potent its power. For example, the symbol of an eagle with wings outspread once served the practical purpose of identifying the armies of the Roman Empire. Now that practical purpose has long since faded, he argues, the symbol gains potency as a representation of legitimate rule.

Visual communication artefacts, in particular, are extensively used by nation states 'as a visual shorthand to represent shared ideals' promoting an officially sanctioned and mediated version of national values (Hill and Helmers 2004, 4). This mediation of Empire or national ideals through artefacts is vital for maintaining the legitimacy of rule.

However, as postprocessual anthropologist Ian Hodder states, with changing cultural context, the same symbol that is used to maintain governmental legitimacy can take on different functions (Hodder 2003, 165). For example, when a motorcycle associated with infamous biker gangs features an eagle on

Figure 3a. Great seal of the USA.
Source: El Coleccionista de Instantes

Figure 3b. A Harley Davidson petrol tank.
Source: Tomás Fano, https://www.flickr.com/photos/tomasfano/7149301763/

its petrol tank, a symbol more commonly used to represent empires or nations (most notably in the present day by the USA), it acquires a different, more subversive meaning. In the instance of the eagle representing empire or nation state, the symbol is used to reinforce the legitimacy and establishment traditions of the state (Hobsbawm 1992, 4). When the eagle becomes associated with biker gangs, it becomes an anti-establishment symbol, part of what sociologist Dick Hebdige calls a style of revolt (see Figure 3) (Hebdige 2002, 2).

Governance through embodied discourse

As has been shown, scholars from various disciplines have identified artefacts as governing and rhetorical by nature, and the relationships in which they are enmeshed as frequently argumentative. For these statements to be accurate, there must be some mechanism through which artefacts retain the biases of their associations, origins and uses, at least for a limited amount of time and in a limited socio-cultural context. Although these meanings are dependent on users and context for their governmental effect, and despite the fact that meanings in artefacts change even with the same audience, artefacts must nevertheless be able to retain meaning in some way. While scholars have shown interest in this area, none have yet to delve into theorising the mechanics of governmental power as it relates to artefacts. This article offers the concept of embodiment as a means to understand how artefacts temporarily retain meaning.

Specifically, this article asserts that artefacts embody discourses. Discourses are specific kinds of communication patterns Foucault identifies in historical archives. These are governmental rationalities of sorts, bound up in the systematisation of knowledge and production of truth (Rose 2007, 143). While the term 'discourse' is not extensively used by historians, 'inferential evidence of invisible structures and patterns', or discourses, are commonly identified by historians (Munslow 2006, 50).

In his discussion of discourses and discourse technologies, Foucault's objective was partly to demonstrate the artificiality of notions of progress and partly to question the apparent inevitability of current modes of thought (Kendall and Wickham 1999, 4). Similarly, by using discourse technologies as a framework for investigating artefacts, I seek to demonstrate the artificiality of notions of the objective artefact. By looking at how each individual device (each unique quality or element) of an artefact relates to a technique, which in turn relates to a force, it is possible to demonstrate the rhetorical nature of even the most seemingly innocuous artefacts.

Foucault suggested that discourses were fuelled by 'a disparate set of tools and methods' that he called 'technologies', using the word in its widest sense (Foucault 1977, 26). He identified many individual technologies, such as the technology of sexuality. This was a shorthand way of referring to the tools and methods that people use to construct our own and each other's understandings of sexuality (Stoler 1995, 17). The concept of technologies is influential, and scholars working in a range of disciplines have identified technologies pertinent to their own fields of research. Sociologists Judy Motion and Shirley Leitch refer to these technologies as 'discourse technologies', in reference to the capacity of technologies to convey discourses (Motion and Leitch 2002, 45). Throughout the rest of this article, Motion and Leitch's term is used both for the sake of clearly identifying their relationship to discourses, and for differentiating them from other meanings of the word 'technology'.

Sociologist Nicholas Rose has provided an anatomy of discourse technologies. He argues that technologies are constituted of three kinds of attributes: forces, techniques and devices (Rose 1996, 42). Forces are the part of discourse technologies made up of 'an assembly of forms of knowledge' (Rose 2006, 52). In the case of artefacts that include text, an easily identifiable force would be the language words are written in. In the example of the coin below, the language is English (see Figure 4).

Techniques are the collected assortment of effects, tricks and strategies found in an artefact that 'produce certain practical outcomes' (Rose 2006, 52). They are the tools used to express a technology within the limits of forces. So, using the example of words on a coin, there are three techniques used within the force of language (English): the currency amount, the nation name and a faith message. Each has a practical communication outcome. While forces are descriptions of broad influences that affect many artefacts, techniques are strategies used to more precisely direct meaning in a specific artefact. Devices are the mechanical forms generated by forces and tailored by techniques within discourse technologies (Rose 2006, 53). They are dependent on both forces and techniques.

Figure 4. Silver dollar, 1924.

Force	Techniques	Devices
English	"one dollar"	one
		dollar
	"United States of America"	United
		States
		of
		America
	"In God we trust"	In
		God
		We
		Trust

Figure 5. Anatomy of the discourse technology of language in the silver dollar.

Referring back to the example of the coin in Figure 4, each individual word on the coin is a device (see Figure 5).

As a starting point for investigating discourses embodied in artefacts, two discourse technologies that are common to all artefacts have been identified: discourse technologies of content and discourse technologies of form. Discourse technologies of content relate to what is most easily identified as the substance of the artefact. In the example of the coin in Figure 4, the content is the symbols present on the coin, as well as the meaning of the words on the coin. The explanations of devices, forces and techniques relating to words on the coins were examples of discourse technologies of content.

Discourse technologies of form relate to the outer form of the artefact, the shape it has and the materials it is constructed from, as well as to the form of individual attributes within, or on the artefact. In the coin example, the outer form includes its circular shape, and the metal silver, from which it is made. Each of three groups of words linguistic messages on the coin: the currency amount, the nation name and a faith message also have a form. Continuing the example of an artefact containing text, the form of that text would include the typeface, type size, type colour, type case and type weight. These two kinds of discourse technology, of form and content, can be used as a framework for investigating discourses within artefacts. Looking at the production processes used to make an artefact, in combination with the date it was made, can reveal governmental rationalities inherent in the production of that artefact. The non-textual visual content of the coin can also be broken down into devices, forces and techniques.

As the coin example above shows, Rose's anatomical breakdown of discourse technologies into forces, techniques and devices provides a practical starting

Production technology	Production date	Production value	Typical distribution	Typical use
Letterpress printing	1901	Economical	Mass consumption	Advertising posters
	2014	Expensive	Niche markets	Wedding invitations

Figure 6. Shifting cultural value of a production technology over time.

point from which to investigate how artefacts embody discourse. This process of identification of individual elements is highly subjective, and will therefore produce different results when different historians study the same artefacts. This is a virtue of using discourse technologies to study historical artefacts, as it removes all pretences at historical objectivity. This identification of devices, forces and techniques is not a creative or analytical act. It is important that the historian uses his first order judgements to collect the information, in order for this process to reflect his discursive context as much as possible.

Once the elements of the embodied discourse technologies are identified, their relationship with the spatial, temporal and user contexts surrounding the artefact can be considered. This too is a subject process, however, this stage relies on second order judgements. By comparing the discourse technologies embodied in artefacts to their societal context, it is possible to build up a picture of how the embodied discourses relate to broader discourses within that society. This process allows the historian to gather a lot of non-textual information about the historical subject (Hepworth 2012, 145). This information can in turn be used to piece together a vision of the historical discourses at play in a given time and place. Each individual historian's piecing together of past discourses is inevitably an amalgamation of his own context and the historical subject (Figure 6).

Use of a production technology can give very different discursive signals depending on the temporal and environmental circumstances surrounding that use. The power relationships in which artefacts are enmeshed change over time, even when their production technologies do not. For example, printing methods are one variety of production technologies. The cultural and ideological associations of various printing processes have changed over time (see Figure 3). Letterpress printing, once an inexpensive mass communication technology with low cultural status, has in recent times become a niche, high-end production process. The fact that a poster was printed using letterpress printing in 1901 suggests it was an item for mass consumption, as letterpress was a common and economical printing process. In contrast, a poster printed using letterpress in 2014 suggests it is an exclusive item, as letterpress is now a niche production process used primarily for bespoke artisan work. It is therefore essential to document as much contextual information as it is possible to glean from the historical artefact and its immediate environment.

Conclusion

This article has argued that visual communication artefacts provide a potent source of evidence for relativist historical investigation. Histories are vital vehicles for communicating the historian's unique contextual understanding of his object of study. Artefacts generally, and visual communication artefacts in particular, have been shown to govern in the sense that they rhetorically act on one another, the spaces they occupy and on the people who view and use them. The further away in culture, time and space an artefact gets from its root source, the less likely it will be to maintain its original potency, and the more likely it will be to take on new meanings, and with them, new rhetorical force. The enduring presence of the Roman Standard, an eagle with spread wings, is just one of countless examples of the enduring cultural relevance of particular symbols, through vastly different cultures, times and regimes. It has also been asserted that, by definition, the more visual communication an artefact conveys, the more enmeshed in power relations it becomes.

This 'arguing' between artefacts through the means of embodied discourse technologies provides exciting opportunities for historians. Artefacts have the potential to be just as revealing of communication patterns, past modes of thought and discourses as the textual archives that are typically the domain of historical investigation. Using the theoretical tools Foucauldian scholars have provided, it is possible for us to 'read' the power dynamics between artefacts, spaces and users of the past with the kind of rigorous investigation previously restricted to textual sources.

References

Anderson, B. 2006. Imagined Communities: Reflections on the Origin and Spread of Nationalism, *New Edition*. London: Verso.

Bentley, Michael. 1999. Modern Historiography: An Introduction. London: Routledge.

Blair, J. A. 2004. "The Rhetoric of Visual Arguments." In Defining Visual Rhetorics, edited by Charles A. Hill and Marguerite H. Helmers, 41–62. London: Routledge.

Bloch, Marc. 1953. The Historian's Craft: Reflections on the Nature and Uses of History and the Techniques and Methods of Those Who Write It. New York: Vintage Books.

Borish, L. J., and Murray G. Phillips. 2012. "Sport History As Modes of Expression: Material Culture and Cultural Spaces in Sport and History." Rethinking History 16 (4): 465–477.

Bosley, Richard, and Martin M. Tweedale. 2006. Basic Issues in Medieval Philosophy: Selected Readings Presenting the Interactive Discourses Among the Major Figures. Peterborough: Broadview Press.

Burke, Peter. 1990. The French Historical Revolution: The Annales School, 1929–1989. Stanford: Stanford University Press.

Bush, A. 1994. "Through the Looking Glass: Territories of Historiographic Gaze." Visible Language 28 (3): 219–231.

Chalmers, David J. 2004. The Conscious Mind in Search of a Fundamental Theory. New York: Oxford University Press.

Cruikshank, Barbara. 1996. "Revolutions Within: Self-Government and Self-Esteem." In Foucault and Political Reason: Liberalism, Neo-Liberalism and Rationalities of Government, edited by Andrew Barry, Thomas Osborne, and Nikolas S. Rose, 231–252. London: Routledge.

Dean, Mitchell. 2010. Governmentality: Power and Rule in Modern Society. Los Angeles, CA: Sage.

Dean, M., and B. Hindess. 1998. Governing Australia: Studies in Contemporary Rationalities of Government. Cambridge: Cambridge University Press.

Dilnot, C. 2010. "Being Prescient Concerning Obama, or Notes on the Politics of Configuration." The Poster 1 (1): 7–29.

Foucault, Michel. 1967. "On the Ways of Writing History." In Essential Works of Foucault 1954–1984 Volume 2: Aesthetics, edited by James Faubion, 279–295. London: Penguin.

Foucault, Michel. 1969. The Archaeology of Knowledge. London: Routledge.

Foucault, Michel. 1970. The Order of Things: An Archaeology of the Human Sciences. London: Routledge.

Foucault, Michel. 1971. "Nietzsche, Genealogy, History." In Essential Works of Foucault 1954–1984 Volume 2: Aesthetics, edited by James Faubion, 369–389. London: Penguin.

Foucault, Michel. 1976. The History of Sexuality. London: Penguin.

Foucault, Michel. 1977. Discipline and Punish: The Birth of the Prison. London: Allen Lane.

Foucault, M. 1978. "Governmentality." In Essential Works of Foucault 1954–1984 Volume 3: Power, edited by Paul Rabinow, 201–222. London: Penguin.

Foucault, Michel. 1980. The History of Sexuality, Volume I: An Introduction. New York: Vintage Books.

Foucault, Michel. 1982. "The Subject and Power." Critical Inquiry 8 (4): 777–795.

Foucault, Michel. 1978. "Security, Territory and Population." In Essential Works of Foucault 1954–1984 Volume 1: Ethics, edited by Paul Rabinow, 67–71. London: Penguin.

Gagliardi, P, ed. 1990. Symbols and Artifacts: Views of the Corporate Landscape. New York: Aldine de Gruyter.

Geertz, C. 1999. "Centers, Kings and Charisma: Reflections on the Symbolics of Power." Chap. 1 In Rites of Power: Symbolism, Ritual and Politics Since the Middle Ages, edited by Sean Willentz, 13–38. Philadelphia: University of Pennsylvania Press.

Gordon, C. 1991. "Governmental Rationality: An Introduction." Chap. 1 In The Foucault Effect: Studies in Governmentality, edited by Graham Burchell, Colin Gordon, and Peter Miller, 1–52. London: Harvester Wheatsheaf.

Gordon, Robert. 1993. "The Interpretation of Artifacts in the History of Technology." In History From Things: Essays on Material Culture, edited by Steven Lubar and David Kingery, 74–93. Washington: Smithsonian.

Green, Anna, and Kathleen Troup. 1999. The Houses of History: A Critical Reader in Twentieth-Century History and Theory. Manchester: Manchester University Press.

Hankinson, R. J. 1999. The Sceptics. London: Taylor & Francis.

Harvey, K. 2009. History and Material Culture: A Student's Guide to Approaching Alternative Sources. London: Routledge.

Hebdige, D. 2002. Subculture: The Meaning of Style. London: Routledge.

Hegmon, Michelle. 1992. "Archaeological Research on Style." Annual Review of Anthropology 22: 517–536.

Hepworth, K. 2012. "Government Emblems, Embodied Discourse and Ideology: An Artefact-Led History of Governance in Victoria, Australia." PhD thesis, Swinburne University of Technology.

Hill, C. A., and M. H. Helmers. 2004. Defining Visual Rhetorics. London: Routledge.

Hindess, B. 1996. Discourses of Power: From Hobbes to Foucault. Oxford: Blackwell.

Hobbes, T. 1985. Leviathan. London: Penguin.

Hobsbawm, E. 1992. The Invention of Tradition. Cambridge: Cambridge University Press.

Hodder, I. 2003. "The Interpretation of Documents and Material Culture." In Collecting and Interpreting Qualitative Materials, edited by N. K. Denzin and Y. S. Lincoln, 155–175. London: Sage.

Kendall, G., and G. Wickham. 1999. Using Foucault's Methods. London: Sage.

Kostelnick, C. 2004. "Melting-Pot Ideology, Modernist Aesthetics, and the Emergence of Graphical Conventions: The Statistical Atlases of the United States, 1874–1925." In Defining Visual Rhetorics, edited by C. A. Hill and Marguerite Helmers, 215–242. London: Routledge.

Kuzminski, Adrian. 2010. Pyrrhonism: How the Ancient Greeks Reinvented Buddhism. New York: Lexington Books.

Lubar, Steven, and W. David Kingery, eds. 1993. History From Things: Essays on Material Culture. Washington, DC: Smithsonian Institution Press.

Mattingly, D. J. 2010. Imperialism, Power, and Identity Experiencing the Roman Empire. Princeton, NJ: Princeton University Press.

Mölder, Bruno. 2010. Mind Ascribed: An Elaboration and Defence of Interpretivism. Philadelphia: John Benjamins.

Motion, J., and S. Leitch. 2002. "The Technologies of Corporate Identity." International Studies of Management and Organisation 32 (3): 45–64.

Milestone, Juris. 2007. "Design as Power: Paul Virilio and the governmentality of design expertise." Culture, Theory and Critique 48 (2): 175–198.

Munslow, A. 2006. Deconstructing History. Routledge: London.

Noonan, Jeff. 2004. Critical Humanism and the Politics of Difference. Montreal: McGill-Queen's Press.

Perin, Casey. 2010. The Demands of Reason: An Essay on Pyrrhonian Scepticism. Oxford: Oxford University Press.

Prown, Jules David. 1993. "The Truth of Material Culture: History or Fiction?" In History From Things: Essays on Material Culture, edited by Steven Lubar and W. David Kingery, 1–19. Washington, DC: Smithsonian Institution Press.

Rajchman, John. 1988. "Foucault's Art of Seeing." October 44: 88–117.

Riello, Giorgio. 2009. "Things That Shape History: Material Culture and Historical Narratives." In History and Material Culture: A Student's Guide to Approaching Alternative Sources, edited by Karen Harvey, 24–46. London: Routledge.

Rose, N. 1996. "Governing 'Advanced' Liberal Democracies." In Foucault and Political Reason: Liberalism, Neo-Liberalism and Rationalities of Government, edited by A. Barry, T. Osborne, and N. Rose, 37–64. London: Routledge.

Rose, Nicholas. 2006. "Governing 'Advanced' Liberal Democracies." In The Anthropology of the State: A Reader, edited by Aradhana Sharma, and Akhil Gupta, 144–162. Hoboken: Wiley-Blackwell.

Rose, G. 2007. Visual Methodologies. London: Sage.

Rose, N. 2008. Powers of Freedom: Reframing Political Thought. Cambridge: Cambridge University Press.

Rosenstone, Robert A. 2001. "October as History." Rethinking History 5 (2): 255–274.

Stoler, A. L. 1995. Race and the Education of Desire: Foucault's History of Sexuality and the Colonial Order of Things. Durham: Duke University Press.

Tunstall, Dori. 2007. "In Design We Trust: Design, governmentality and the tangibility of governance." IASDR07. Hong Kong, China: The Hong Kong Polytechnic University.

White, H. 1973. "Foucault Decoded: Notes From Underground." History and Theory 12 (1): 23–54.

Witkin, R. 1990. "The Aesthetic Imperative of a Rational-Technical Machinery: A Study in Organizational Control Through the Design of Artifacts." In Symbols and Artifacts: Views of the Corporate Landscape, edited by Gagliardi, 169–184. New York: Walter de Gruyter.

Index

Aboriginals' place in Australian history 82–4
absolute preconceptions 110
abuse of memory 40
acceleration of history 31–5, 38, 45–6
Accoyer commission 41–2
activism *see* political activism
Adiv, Udi 54
age of commemoration 4, 30–49; *see also* France
agonistic pluralism 67
Alexandroni Brigade 53, 55
Althusser, Louis 54–5
anachronism 44
analysis of *Historikerstreit* and History Wars 84–8; *Historikerstreit* II 85–6; History Wars II 86–8
Analytical Philosophy of History 98
Ankersmit, Frank 36, 77, 98, 107–110, 120, 123–4
Annales School 140
antagonism 67
anti-history 144
anti-Semitism 86
Antick, Paul 61–3
apophatic past 6, 127–32
Appleby, Joyce 76, 97
Arab American Action Network 64
Archaeology of Knowledge 143
Aristotle 100, 150
Armitage, David 7, 118
Aronson, Ronald 3
artefacts 147–53; as arguments 149–53; as truth effects 147–9; *see also* visual communication artefacts
artificiality 153
assimilation 42–3
Assman, Aledia 31
'atto in atto' 97
attribution 133

Austin, J. L. 99
Australian History Wars 75–92; analysis of controversies 84–8; conclusion 88–90; description of controversies 79–84; introduction 75–9
autonomy 60

Badiou, Alain 120, 122
Bar-Tal, Daniel 58
Barbie, Klaus 40
Beard, Charles 97
Becker, Carl 97
Bédarida, François 77
Ben-Artzi, Yossi 57
Berger, Stefan 23
'Bhopal to Bridgehampton' 62–3
'big data' 7
'Black Armband History' 82–3
Blainey, Geoffrey 82–3, 88
Blair, Anthony 150
Bloch, March 140–41, 143, 148–9
Blom, Tannelie 107
Bracher, Karl Dietrich 81
brèches 38
bridging narratives 67
Brigstocke, Marcus 133
Broszat, Martin 80–81
Bruckner, Pascal 41
bulimia of commemoration 40
Bush, Anne 150

Calliope's ascent 93–116
Candau, Joel 39–40, 43
capacity 145–7; *see also* power
cartographic erasure 64
case of Rasmea Odeh 63–5
changing history? 88–90
Churchill, Winston 111
'cinema of advocacy' 66
Clark, Anna 83–4

Clark, Manning 82–3
Classical Antiquity 75–6
Cohen, Sande 59
Cold War 23
collaboration 40
Collective Memory Reader 45
Collingwood, R. G. 96, 100–103, 106, 109–110
coming-to-existence 122–3, 125–7, 130, 132–3
Comment on écrit l'histoire 98
communautarisme 32, 42–4
communication: about complex events 105–7; about simple events 103–4; language in 102–3; visual communication artefacts 138–60
Communism 34–5, 122
competition of memory 41–2
conditions of the past 143
conditions of possibility 144
conditions of the present 143
conducting the conduct 147
Confino, Alon 55–7, 61
consciousness 100–103
consequences of Proustian project 22–4
conspiracy theories 80, 83
constatives 99, 105–6
contemporary crisis of memory 30–49; *see also* France
content-bearing cognitive state 142
contested knowledge 121, 131–2
context 143–4
contextualizing memory 34, 45–6
continuity in change 128
'court of history' 66–7
crimes against humanity 18, 51
'crisis' of history 31, 36–9, 117–21
crisis of identity 34–5, 37
crisis of memory 30–49
crisis of time 38–9
critique of discourse 30–49
Croire en l'histoire 39
crystallization of difference 42
cultural politics of historicization 57–60
current situation 1–11
cynicism 8, 45

Danto, Arthur 98, 105, 107–110
Davies, Martin 52, 58–60
Davison, Graeme 83
de Ruggiero, Guido 111
de-annexation from Soviet Union 12–13
dead past 128
Dean, Mitchell 147–8
decolonization 31

defining visual communication artefact 139–40
defragmentation of theory of history 111–13
defragmenting philosophy of history 93–116; *see also* rhetoric
degrees of agency 149–50
demarxization 34
democraticized history 61
deportations 17–19
déracinement 33
description of *Historikerstreit* and History Wars 79–84; *Historikerstreit* 79–82; History Wars 82–4
developmentalism 121
devices 154–6
Dewey, John 97
discrimination 87
discursive condition 9
discussing complex events 105–7
disembodied discourse 153–6
disrupted singular 120–21, 124–7, 130–31
dissent 7, 9, 12–13
dissidence 18–20, 23–4
dissociation 109–110, 127–30, 132
Donnelly, Kevin 83
Dosse, François 41
Droysen, Johann Gustav 96–7
DuBois, Ellen 7–8
durability 148
duty of memory 40, 43

Edasi 15
Electronic Intifida 63
Elstrok, Helmut 14
elucidation 37
emancipation of memories 45–6; *see also* Nora, Pierre
embodied discourse technologies 138–9, 153–5
embracement 128
emotions in communication 102–3
emplotment 33, 35–7, 45–6
engagement 3–4, 63–5, 94, 131–2
Enlightenment 120–21, 132
enthymeme 100, 150
epistemic breaks 141
eppur si muove 93–6
era of awakening 13–16
Estonia 12–29; conclusion 22–4; historians in power 20–22; introduction 12–13; 'new era of awakening' 13–16; restoration of independence 18–20; 'return of the repressed' 16–18
Estonian Heritage Society 14–17, 21–2

Estonian National Independence Party 19
ethics 131–2
ethics-talk 59
ethnic cleansing 51, 53, 55–7, 62
Ethnic Cleansing of Palestine 57
ethos 99
Euchner, Walter 81
European Union 23
Evans, Richard 77
evocation of awareness 104
exactitude 43
exile 17
existential bonding 130
Experience and Its Modes 128
experience in rhetoric 100–102
experiential turn 94–5, 100
'explaining' the Holocaust 85–6
explosion of memory 36, 39–40
externalization of meaning 10

Fabrication of Aboriginal History 83
falsification of history 41–2
fascism 111
fault lines in time 38
Febvre, Lucien 140
Ferenczi, Thomas 39
Fest, Joachim 80–81
figuration 10
'filling in the blank spots' 22–4
first order judgements 142–4
Fish, Stanley 2
folklore 16, 57
followability 98
Footnotes in Gaza 61
forced migration *see* ethnic cleansing
Foucault, Michel 57–8, 65, 140–47, 153
foundational myths 54–5
foundations of history 96–9
France 30–49; age of commemoration as
    narrative construct 33–6; conclusion
    45–6; memory malady 39–45;
    'presentism' 36–9
Frankfurter Allgemeine 79
Freedom for History 40–41
French Republic 32, 42–4
French Revolution 106–7, 123–4
Friedländer, Saul 80
function of history 132–3; *see also*
    quasi-substantive philosophy of history;
    we are history

Gallie, W. B. 98
Gaullism 34
Geiss, Imanuel 81
Geldof, Bob 5

generalized memory 41
genocide 42, 44, 57, 79, 85–8
Gensburger, Sarah 40
German Idealism 120–21, 132
Ghosh, Ranjan 128
Ginzberg, Carlo 56, 98–9
Giscard-D'Estaing, Valéry 34
given reality 37–8
global oil shock 34
globalization 149–50
'goings-on' 103–4
governance through discourse 153–6
governmental rationalities 147, 149–50
Grönholm, Pertti 20
guerrilla warfare 17
Guicciardini, Francesco 109–110
guilt 55, 79, 82–3
Gulag Archipelago 34
Guldi, Jo 7, 118
Gumbrecht, Hans Ulrich 128–9

Habermas, Jürgen 79–81, 85–8
Haifa 53–4
hallucinations 142
Hankinson, R. J. 142–3
Hansen, Ea 22–3
Hartog, François 37–9
Harvey, Karen 150
Haskell, Thomas 97
Hebdige, Dick 153
Hebraization 58
hegemony 30–31, 54–5, 59–60, 96–7
heritage protection 13–16
Hexter, J. H. 98
Hilal, Jamil 67
Hildebrand, Klaus 80–82
Hillgruber, Andreas 79–81, 86, 88
Hindess, Barry 146–7
Historia Magistra Vitae Est 76
historian as context 140–44; first order
    judgements 142–4; second order
    judgements 144
historians' behaviour 88–90
historians as nation-builders 12–29; *see
    also* Estonia
historical construction 37–8
historical encodation 32–3
historical methodology 7
historical narrative rhetoric 107–111
historical truth restoration 18–20
historicization 38–9, 57–60, 79–80
histories as vehicles 144–5
Historik 97
Historikerstreit 75–92; analysis of
    controversies 84–8; conclusion 88–90;

description of controversies 79–84;
  introduction 75–9
Historikerstreit II 85–6; *see also*
  Historikerstreit
history as disrupted singular 125–7
History Manifesto 7, 95, 111, 118, 122, 128
History and Policy website 95
history and power 138–60; *see also* visual
  communication artefacts
History, Rhetoric and Proof 98–9
History Wars II 86–8; *see also* Australian
  History Wars
history-as-discourse 66–7
Hitler, Adolf 18, 81
Hobbes, Thomas 145–6
Hobsbawn, Eric 151–3
Hodder, Ian 150–51
Hollinger, David 97
Holocaust 31, 42, 44, 79–82, 85–8;
  'explanation' for 85–6; *see also*
  Historikerstreit
horizon of expectation 38, 101–2, 104,
  106–7, 126–7
*How Peace Broke Out in the Middle
  East* 63
Howard, John 83, 87–8
Huizinga, Johan 108–110
human rights 24, 55
Human Rights Watch 65
Hunt, Lynn 76
Hurt, Jakob 15–16
Husserl, Edmund 100–104, 106, 108–9
Huyssen, Andreas 31
hypertrophy of memory 31

ideal of objectivity 75–92
ideological bias 139
illusion of substance 128
immigration fraud 64–5
impact of history 1–3
impossibility 118–19
In Defence of History 77
in media res 110–111
inclusion 41–2
incomplete syllogism 100
indigenous Australians *see* Aboriginals'
  place in Australian history
inexistent of the world 122
inferential evidence 153
information-management technology
  58–9
institutional history 53, 59
intentionality 100–103, 106
interactions with artefacts 149–53
interdependence 131

internalization of meaning 10
International Network for Theory of
  History 1–3, 93–6
interpretism 126
INTH *see* International Network for
  Theory of History
invention of tradition 151
Israel Studies 57
Israeli–Palestine peace process 51–3

Jackson Turner, Frederick 97
Jacob, Margaret 76
Jakobsen, Carl Robert 21
Jenkins, Keith 8, 59–60
Jews for Justice for Palestine 63
Journal of Palestinian Studies 57
Journal of the Philosophy of History 94
Judt, Tony 4, 6

kairos 110–111
kairotic experience 108
Kaspi, André 41–2
Katz, Teddy 53–5, 57
Keating, Paul 82–3, 87
keeping quiet 55
Kelam, Tunne 13, 19–20
Khmer Rouge 85
Kingery, W. David 149
Kleinberg, Ethan 128
Klug, Tony 63
knowledge ruptures 141
Kocka, Jürgen 80–81, 88
Koselleck, Reinhart 38, 106, 120, 126

Laar, Mart 13–17, 20–23
LaCapra, Dominick 8
Laclau, Ernesto 57–8, 67
Lagerspetz, Mikko 23
Lagrou, Pieter 44
Lalieu, Olivier 43
'Lamb of God' triptych 108–9
language: in communication 102–3; in
  rhetoric 100–102
Lavabre, Marie-Claire 40
Le Monde 41
legitimate order 147
Leitch, Shirley 153–4
lessons from *Historikerstreit* and History
  Wars 75–92
Leviathan 145
Liberté Pour L'Histoire 40
Lieux de mémoire 32–6, 39, 41
logic of proposals 117–21
lois mémoirelles 40–42
LPH *see* Freedom for History

Lubar, Steven 149
Luther King, Martin 106

McCloskey, Donald 98
McGuinness, Padraic 83
McIntyre, Ronald 101–2
MacIntyre, Stuart 83
macrocosmic malaise 45
Madisson, Tiit 18
mainstream narrativism 98
Mandelbaum, Maurice 121
mania 32–3
manipulated memory 40
Manne, Robert 83
march of civilization 82
Mason, Anthony 83
mass consumption 156
massacres 51, 53, 55, 79–80, 85–6
material culture 138–9, 147–9
May, Todd 51
meaningful contextualization 5
Megill, Allan 98
Memento Union 17–18
memory boom 31, 36
Memory, History Forgetting 40
memory malady 36, 39–45
'memory wars' 40
memory wave 31–2, 34, 37, 39–40
Meri, Lennart 13, 22
metonymy 129
Milestone, Juris 146
Mink, Louis O. 98, 107–8, 110
mnémotropisme 39–40
modernism 149
Molotov-Ribbentrop Pact 18–19
Mommsen, Hans 80–82
Morris, Benny 54, 57–8
Moses, Dirk 83–4
moshav 62
Motion, Judy 153–4
Mouffe, Chantal 57–8, 60, 67, 89
movement of history 121–4
Munslow, Alun 140, 144
myth-busting 77, 81

Nakba 52, 62–4
Nancy, Jean-Luc 120, 122–4, 129–30
narrative construct 30–49
Narrative Logic 98
narrative sentences 105
narrative substance 36–7
narrativism 5, 10, 93–4, 98, 134
nation building 13–16
national heritage movement 13–16
national trauma work 16–18

nationalist consciousness 80–81
NATO 23
Nazism 57, 85–6
neo-Zionist historiography 51
Neuzeit 126
'new civic religion' 43
'new era of awakening' 13–16
Nietzsche, Friedrich 31, 41
Nijhuis, Ton 107
+972 63
9/11 65
Nipperdey, Thomas 81
Nolte, Ernst 79–81, 85–8
Nora, Pierre 4, 31–40, 42–6
Novick, Peter 76

Oakeshott, Michael 2, 52, 96, 103–5, 112, 128, 130–31
Obama, Barack 110
objective analysis 32
objectivity *see* ideal of objectivity
obsession 39–41
occupation 53
Occupied Territories 54, 61–2, 64–5
Odeh, Rasmea 63–5
O'Gorman, Edmundo 96–8
Önnepalu, Tõnu 22
orations 98
Ortega y Gasset, José 96–8
Oslo peace process 51
outlines of quasi-substantive philosophy 117–37

Palestine 50–74; case of Rasmea Odeh 63–5; conclusion 66–7; cultural politics of historicisation 57–60; introduction 51–3; reflexive/political/vernacular pasts 60–63; Tantura massacre 53–7
Palestine Solidarity Campaign 63
pandemic fragmentation 93–6
Papon, Maurice 40
Pappé, Ilan 51–4, 57–8, 62, 67
'passion for social change' 7
'past-talk' 10, 51–3, 66–7
pathos 99
Päts, Konstantin 20
peace treaties 18–19
pedagogy and power 50–74; *see also* Palestine
Peled-Elhanen, Nurit 58
'pensiero e azione' 97
perestroika 21
performatives 99, 105–6
periodization 110
persuasion 99

phenomenology 100–102
philosophical foundations of history 96–9
philosophy of mind 100–103
Philosophy in the World 3
Phosphorite War 13
phronesis 112
Pihlainen, Kalle 51
place of Aboriginals in Australian history 82–4
Pol Pot 79, 81, 85
political activism 8, 63–5
political impartiality 51
political pasts 60–63
politics and silence 53–7
politics-talk 59
Popular Front 20–22
post-foundational intellectual culture 52, 66–7
post-millennial theory 129
post-Zionist history 51
postmodernism 77
potency of communication 150
power: as capacity 145–7; historians in 20–22; and pedagogy 50–74; and visual communication artefacts 138–60
power dynamics 157
practical history 96–9
'practical past' 2–3, 52, 118
Practical Past, The 99
pragmatism 97–8
Présent, nation, mémoire 35
presentism 36–9
progressive politics 3
project verbs 105
propaganda 57, 112
proper history 8
proto-argument 100
Proust, Marcel 22–4
Proustian projects 22–4
prudence 112–13
pseudo-politics 43
public discussions on history *see* Australian History Wars; *Historikerstreit*
public utility of history 75–92
Pyrrhonic Sceptics 140

Quadrant 83
quasi-substantive philosophy of history 117–37; apophatic past 127–31; essentially contested historical knowledge 131–2; history as disrupted singular 125–7; logic of proposals 117–21; movement of history 121–4; shaping public life 132–3

racism 46, 87–90
Rajchman, John 143
rational order 147
rational reconstruction 84
Realpolitik 21
Rebas, Hain 13
rebirth of history 122
Red Cross 56
Redfern Park Speech 82
reflexive pasts 60–63
Régimes d'historicité 38–9
regimes of historicity 37–8
relativist historical investigation 157
Rémond, René 40
repression 16–20
republic of historians 12–29; *see also* Estonia
res gestae 97
ressentiment 41
restoration of Estonian independence 13, 18–20
'restoration of true history' 22, 24
restorationism 20–23
restoring historical truth 18–20
restrained memory 41
reticence 55
retrospection 30–31, 94, 110
'return of the repressed' 16–18
Reynolds, Henry 83–4
rhetoric 75–6, 93–116
Rhetoric 100
rhetoric, artefacts as 149; Calliope's ascent 111–13; communicating complex events 105–7; communicating simple events 103–4; emotions/language in communication 102–3; *eppur si muove* 93–6; experience/language in rhetoric 100–102; of historical narratives 107–111; philosophical foundations of practical history 96–9
Rhetoric of the Human Sciences 98
Ricoeur, Paul 30–31, 40, 43, 94
Rose, Nicholas 148, 154–6
Rothberg, Michael 32, 45–6
Rousseau, Jean-Jacques 145
Rousso, Henri 39–40, 43
Rudd, Kevin 82
Runia, Eelco 120, 123–4, 129–30
Rüütel, Arnold 19

Sacco, Joe 61
Sarkozy, Nicolas 41–2
Sartre, Jean-Paul 3, 10
Sattelzeit 120
Save the World on Your Own Time 2

Savisaar, Edgar 12–13, 20–21
science of legitimation 23
Searle, John 99
second intifada 51
second order judgements 144, 149
seismography 39
self-comprehension 39
self-consciousness 15, 33
self-fulfilling prophecies 111
self-legitimization 58
sense of self 56
sense-making 106–7
Shakespeare, William 100
shifting cultural values 153–6
significance of historicity 2
silencing 53–8
simultaneity 143
Sir John Latham Memorial Lectures 82–3
slavery 40, 44
Smith, David Woodruff 101–2
'Smith in Palestine' 61–2
soberness 81–2
social cohesion 59–60
social contract 145
Solzhenitsyn, Aleksandr 34
sovereignty 145
Soviet annexation 12–13
space of experience 38, 101–2, 104, 106–7,
    126–7
specifics of *Historikerstreit* 79–82
specifics of History Wars 82–4
Srebrenica commission 129
Stalin, Josef 18, 31, 79, 81, 85
'state of nature' 145–6
statehood 18–20, 22
Stolen Generations 82, 87
Stora, Benjamin 44
Storia d'Italia 109
Storia del liberalismo europeo 111
story of age of commemoration 33–6
'Story of Home, The' 20
stowaways 129
Struever, Nancy 99
Stürmer, Michael 80
style of revolt 153
Sublime Historical Experience 108
subsuming history in rhetoric 111–13; *see
    also* Calliope's ascent
subversion 152–3
Suez Canal Crisis 61
symptoms 31–2, 36, 38–9, 41, 44–5

talking about simple events 103–4
Talking to the Enemy 67
Tallinn 13–14, 18–19

Tantura massacre 53–7
Tartu 12–16, 18–19
task of understanding 117–21
Telling the Truth About History 76–7
temporal acceleration 31–2, 36–9
temporary stabilizations 57–8
theory of experiential meaning 100–101
theory of history 2–6, 93–6, 111–13
thinking the past politically 50–74; *see also*
    Palestine
'Time of Horrors' 17
time-telling 112
Todorov, Tzvetan 40
toponomyc silences 58, 64
Torpey, John 44
torture 64–5
Touvier, Paul 40
transitional Estonia 12–13, 23; *see also*
    Estonia
trauma 16–18, 93–6, 124
triumph of restorationism 20–22
truth effects 147–9
truth effects *see* visual communication
    artefacts
Twofold Fall 86
Tyranny of Repentance 41

UN *see* United Nations
United Nations 53
universal equality 42–3
universally relevant periodization 33, 37
unlawful procurement of naturalization
    64–5
uprootedness 33, 38
usable past 58
utopia 38, 44

Vahtre, Sulev 14–15, 20
Valk, Heiki 20
valuable civil inquiries 99
Van Bouwel, J. 85
van Eyck, Jan 108–9
Van Fraassen, Bas 85
Veidemann, Rein 15
Velliste, Trivimi 13–14, 21
verbal fictions 36–7
vernacular pasts 60–63
Veyne, Paul 98
Vichy syndrome 39–40
'Vicissitudes of 1948 Historiography of
    Israel' 51–3
Vikerkaar 15–16
visual communication artefacts 138–60;
    artefacts as rhetoric 149; artefacts as
    truth effects 147–9; conclusion 157;

definition 139–40; governance through embodied discourse 153–6; historian as context 140–44; histories as vehicles 144–5; interactions with artefacts as arguments 149–53; introduction 138–9; power as capacity 145–7
von Ranke, Leopolde 140

Waning of the Middle Ages 108–9
war on terror 65
Watson, Don 83
we are history 117–37
Weber, E. 85
Weber, Max 37–8, 96

what use historians? 75–92
White, Hayden 2, 8, 10, 32–3, 36–7, 52–3, 56, 77, 98–9, 118, 128, 130–31, 133, 144
Windshuttle, Keith 83
Winkler, Heinrich August 81
working with trauma 16–18
World War II 17, 33, 79–80
Wulf, Meike 20

You're History 5

Zeitgeist 38
Zinn, Howard 6, 8
Zochrot 63

www.ingramcontent.com/pod-product-compliance
Ingram Content Group UK Ltd.
Pitfield, Milton Keynes, MK11 3LW, UK
UKHW020350010325
455677UK00021B/386